THE ULTIMATE BOOK OF PUB TRIVIA

BY THE SMARTEST GUY IN THE BAR

AUSTIN ROGERS

OVER **300** ROUNDS AND
MORE THAN **3,000** QUESTIONS

WORKMAN PUBLISHING • NEW YORK

Library of Congress Cataloging-in-Publication Data is available.

ISBN 978-1-5235-1052-8

Design by Galen Smith
Cover by Vaughn Andrews

Workman books are available at special discounts when purchased in bulk for premiums and sales promotions as well as for fundraising or educational use. Special editions or book excerpts can also be created to specification. For details, contact the Special Sales Director at specialmarkets@workman.com.

Workman Publishing Co., Inc.
225 Varick Street
New York, NY 10014-4381
workman.com

WORKMAN is a registered trademark of Workman Publishing Co., Inc.

Printed in the United States
First printing January 2022

10 9 8 7 6 5 4 3 2 1

CONTENTS

THE BEST DAMNED TRIVIA NIGHT:
An Introduction

reetings, reader! I'm Austin Rogers and I know stuff. Most famously, I proved my stuff-knowingness on a 12-game, $411,000 run on the acclaimed quiz show *Jeopardy!*. But long before my TV prowess, I hosted pub quiz nights.

When I started hosting 15 years ago, pub quiz, trivia night—whatever you might call it—existed but not anything like it does today. What started as a humble British hobby is now a multinational industry with dozens of businesses and thousands of individuals generating millions of dollars for bars, pubs, and special events. The near ubiquity of trivia nights is inescapable, and in cities like New York, my home, the wealth of choice in events to attend is staggering. But it wasn't always like this.

When I first got my feet wet as a pub trivia host, I didn't have much to go on: I was fresh off a winning appearance on the TV game show *Cash Cab* when a friend approached me. He was opening a new bar and thought a trivia night would be a good draw on an off night, and my expertise made me the perfect candidate to host.

Before the bar's grand opening, we spent several weeks traveling New York City, and attending as many pub quizzes as we could in search of a format that worked. In an era before the spate of prepackaged quiz nights such as Geeks Who Drink, Trivia Tryst, and NYC Trivia League, the pickings were slim and the quality of the product wanting. The meager offerings included monotone hosts, inanely simplistic questions, and incredibly specific topics that were solely the domain of specialists in niche categories (imagine an entire night's worth of questions on Pavement or *Golden Girls* quotes). It all pretty much sucked. I knew I could do better, so I cherry-picked positive facets of each quiz night I attended and ran with it to create the Best Damned Trivia Night I possibly could.

While researching the perfect trivia format, I found that a whole lot of quizzes I encountered were too specific, focusing on one subject (e.g., a *Back to the Future* quiz that tested patrons only on the minutiae of the movie's plot points). Why not include delightfully tangential trivia as well? Switch it up and get creative! Try this instead: "While *Back to the Future* was the top-grossing movie of 1985, this SNL alum comedy was the second-highest-grossing film of the year."*

Worse, so many attempted to be way too cutesy. ("In 1911, this famous painting was stolen . . . speaking of 'stealing,' he's the quarterback for the Pittsburgh *Steelers*!") Ugh. Just ugh. In a few odd cases, I discovered trivia nights that were also too specialized and obscure, bordering on the academic in their questioning ("It's bygone British railways trivia night!").

I observed the same outcome again and again in all these examples: One team got the lead right away and stayed there, making for a less dynamic competition where no one had any fun. Sure, the guy who memorized the names of 19th-century Scottish steam engines was having a great time, but everyone else was definitely bored out of their heads or just annoyed. Annoyed customers leave bars and never come back.

Armed with these newfound insights, I wrote every evening's quiz with three thoughts in mind: 1) Does any well-rounded team have a chance of winning? 2) Will there be different teams in the leader's spot throughout the night, giving hope to every participating team? 3) Can incentives like cash giveaways, free swag, gift cards, beverages, and meals scattered throughout the

*ANSWER: Beverly Hills Cop

evening keep it entertaining, even for those teams with no chance in hell of winning? The answer to all three questions is a resounding "yes."

The sheer amount of quiz books is innumerable. Bathroom readers and titles like *1,001 Questions about German Shepherds* populate the warehouse shelves of Amazon, and while they're all good and fun, none of them tell you how to monetize your overwhelming desire for minutiae. That all changes with this volume. Short of going on *Jeopardy!*, there are few ways to earn an income in the field of trivia. Tournaments, including Geek Bowl and SporcleCon, offer rare opportunities to profit from your inane knowledge, but otherwise, trivia is a pauper's game. Not so with hosting pub quiz and bar trivia. This book will help you set up a great quiz night for your friends and family at home or any gathering. It is also a primer on how to "go pro" and start your own trivia night at a local bar, restaurant, club, or special event.

The trivia rounds that follow contain the perfect formula for a diverse, entertaining, and engaging trivia night that keeps people playing and drinking, thus generating revenue. They are organized into 78 four-round quizzes, with each round rated by difficulty from 1 (you better get all of them right!) to 6 (PhD-level minutiae for only the true savant), and are sure to please any and all trivia fans.

And of course, if none of this works for you, put your own spin on it. Rip me off. You've already bought the book—I don't care if you follow my perfect instructions or not. I got paid!

JUST A
WHOLE LOT OF
PUB
TRIVIA

Chain Restaurants

1

1   Because of a preexisting copyright, Burger King franchises carry this name in Australia.

2

2   Entertainer Bob Hope suggested that founder Sandy Beall name his chain restaurant after this Rolling Stones song.

3

3   After a corporate realignment, both Carl's Jr. and Hardee's have a smiling one of these as a logo.

4

4   David Lynch probably hates the name of this Dallas-based breastaurant.

5

5   This restaurant chain is the number-one buyer of apples in the United States.

6

6   This chain is known as the St. Louis Bread Company in 100 stores in its original market.

7

7   Specializing in smoked and steamed fish dishes, Nordsee boasts 400 locations throughout Europe, North Africa, and the Middle East and is based in this European country.

DID YOU KNOW?

Unlike most other Jagger–Richards songs, the lyrics to Answer #2 were written entirely by Keith Richards, and much of the music was composed by Brian Jones. Even so, Mick Jagger says that it's "a wonderful song . . . I always enjoy singing it."

8

8   Because of lax image rights practices, China's Kungfu chain restaurant has as its logo a picture of this martial arts legend.

9

9   Popular in the UK, PERi PERi chicken is the signature dish of this South African–based fast-food chain.

10

10 Curiously or obviously, every location of this chain restaurant has closed down in Massachusetts and Maine.

ANSWERS - 1. Hungry Jack's - 2. "Ruby Tuesday" - 3. Star - 4. Twin Peaks - 5. McDonald's - 6. Panera Bread - 7. Germany - 8. Bruce Lee - 9. Nando's - 10. Red Lobster

ROUND 2 / DIFFICULTY LEVEL 1 2 **3** 4 5 6

Before and After

Here's how "Before and After" rounds work: I'll give you two clues separated by the word *AND* that form one compound answer. Think of one half, think of the other half, then find the word in the middle that joins them together. (No partial credit!) For example: This Billy Joel song will "get you high tonight" AND Lynchburg's famous whiskey. (Answer: Captain Jack Daniels.)

1 Australian singers of "All Out of Love" AND in the 14th century, Islamic scholar Ibn Taymiyyah was the first to codify this basic law of economics.

2 The location of the three rings of a three-ring circus AND the nickname of the US Navy Strike Fighter Tactics program.

3 In this song, "the pipes, the pipes are calling" AND the leader of Culture Club.

4 Kelly Ripa played a soap opera star whose character was killed off in this mid-2000s ABC sitcom AND the band behind 1989's top 10 hit "Epic."

5 The author of *Silent Spring* AND the former starting quarterback for the Arizona Cardinals and Cincinnati Bengals.

6 The leader of the Heartbreakers AND the generic name of the senior enlisted rank in the US Navy.

USEFUL FACTOID

The vaunted Superman debut in *Action Comics* #1 was only the first 13 pages. The rest featured decidedly less popular stories like Sticky-Mitt Stimson's vignette.

7 His group of Five had a number-one UK hit with 1964's "Glad All Over" AND civilian name of Kal-El.

8 Storied UK retailer of British-made home goods and clothing AND blacklight poster retailer for nineties mall kids.

9 Much of the choreography for this Beyoncé music video was inspired by a Bob Fosse routine AND the feeling's right in this Kool and the Gang song.

10 Three-word phrase indicating that someone is probably receiving bribes AND Robbie Williams rose to fame as a member of this boy band.

ANSWERS - 1. Air Supply and Demand - 2. Big Top Gun - 3. Oh, Danny Boy George - 4. Hope and Faith No More - 5. Rachel Carson Palmer - 6. Tom Petty Officer - 7. Dave Clark Kent - 8. Marks and Spencer Gifts - 9. Single Ladies Night - 10. On the Take That

Where They're Buried

1 Upon her entombment in the Pantheon along with her co–Nobel laureate husband, she became the first woman to be accorded the honor on her own merits.

2 He's interred at 122nd Street and Riverside Drive.

3 In 1840, nineteen years after his death on St. Helena, his remains were relocated to Paris's Dôme des Invalides.

4 From 1955 until 1971, her body's location was unknown; upon their discovery in Milan, her remains were initially displayed in her exiled husband's living room in Spain before being interred in Buenos Aires's La Recoleta Cemetery.

> **DID YOU KNOW?**
>
> Groucho Marx's early TV quiz show, *You Bet Your Life,* popularized the "Who's buried in [Answer #2's] Tomb?" question. The joke's true punch line, of course, is "no one"— he and his wife are entombed, not buried.

5 Her name and "1926–1962" are the only adornments to her spartan Westwood Memorial Park crypt.

6 Although Condé Nast, Tim and Wellington Mara, and fellow Yankee alumnus Billy Martin are buried in the Gate of Heaven Cemetery in Hawthorne, New York, no one there is more famous than this man, appropriately in graves number three and four.

7 On February 23, 1997, he was interred in Resurrection Cemetery in Madison, Wisconsin; David Spade was too grief-stricken to attend.

8 Every Russian czar except Peter II and Ivan VI is interred at Saints Peter and Paul Cathedral in this city.

9 As featured in an Oliver Stone movie, his grave is near those of Marcel Proust, Oscar Wilde, and Georges Bizet at Père Lachaise Cemetery.

10 Before her burial at Fairview Cemetery in Westfield, New Jersey, Stevie Wonder, Alicia Keys, and, unfortunately, R. Kelly sang at her service in nearby Newark.

ANSWERS - 1. Marie Curie - 2. Ulysses S. Grant - 3. Napoleon - 4. Eva Perón - 5. Marilyn Monroe - 6. Babe Ruth - 7. Chris Farley - 8. St. Petersburg - 9. Jim Morrison - 10. Whitney Houston

ROUND 4 / DIFFICULTY LEVEL 1 **2** 3 4 5 6

Random Stuff You Should Know

1 Nearly 50 years before the first organization met at La Rotisserie Française restaurant, a young Jack Kerouac invented and played his own version of this popular game.

2 Game Show Network's *Skin Wars* is a competition focused on this art.

3 Wade Winston Wilson is the name of this wisecracking, nearly invulnerable Marvel superhero.

4 Many legumes, including alfalfa and clover, have the ability to transfer this element from the atmosphere into their roots and, when the plant dies, the soil.

5 Jackie Chan's megahit *Police Story 3* went by this name in the United States.

6 Pointe du Hoc is a promontory that separates Utah Beach and this other code-named beach.

7 This automaker has traditionally manufactured standard roadsters, but since 1910, it has also been famous for its iconic three-wheeler sports cars.

8 The real name of this debonair star from the Golden Age of Hollywood was Archibald Leach.

9 This is the largest moon in the solar system.

10 One point each for the 12 franchise restaurants with the most locations in the world.

CHAN THE MAN

Jackie Chan's bit role in 1981's *The Cannonball Run* wasn't so memorable, but what the actor took from it became a Chan trademark: Jackie was so enamored by the film's post-credits outtakes that he insisted they be included in all his future action-comedy films.

ANSWERS - 1. Fantasy Baseball - 2. Body Painting - 3. Deadpool - 4. Nitrogen - 5. *Super Cop* - 6. Omaha - 7. Morgan - 8. Cary Grant - 9. Ganymede - 10. Tim Horton's, Arby's, Quiznos, Taco Bell, Wendy's, Domino's, Burger King, KFC, Pizza Hut, Starbucks, McDonald's, Subway

Flags

Name the country for each of the following flags!

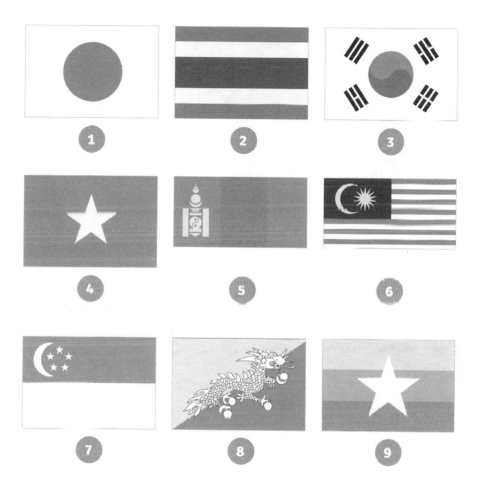

ANSWERS - 1. Japan - 2. Thailand - 3. South Korea - 4. Vietnam - 5. Mongolia - 6. Malaysia - 7. Singapore - 8. Bhutan - 9. Myanmar

5

Hudson Valley, New York

1 The Hudson River originates in these mountains, whose name is thought to originate from the indigenous Mohawk for "eaters of trees."

2 Vice President Teddy Roosevelt was at Lake Tear of the Clouds when he received a message that the health of this recently shot president had taken a turn for the worse.

TECHNICALITY ALERT

By the time it reaches Answer #5, the Hudson River no longer carries sediment, so it doesn't fit the criteria of "river." Thus, it's a tidal estuary. So is the East "River." Oh well.

3 This is the name for the area encompassing the cities of Troy, Schenectady, and Albany.

4 Dutch settlers' tale of sighting a white whale swimming the Hudson near Rensselaerswyck on March 29, 1647, inspired descendants, including this author.

5 This is the largest island on the Hudson River.

6 Designed by Frank Gehry, the Richard B. Fisher Center for the Performing Arts is the concert hall at this Annandale-on-Hudson liberal arts college.

7 His book *Kitchen Confidential* extensively documented this author's education at Hyde Park's Culinary Institute of America.

8 While the Dutch called the Hudson River *Noortrivier*, or "North River," they referred to this waterway as the "South River."

9 Depicting the king and queen of England's 1939 US visit, the 2012 film *Hyde Park on Hudson* starred this actor as FDR.

10 In 1962, to accommodate more traffic, this Hudson River crossing—and busiest motor bridge in the world—added a lower level.

Movie Math

"Movie Math" is a fun round. Like "Before and After," it challenges you to think of two different answers and put them together. If you're hosting, make the first question a freebie to explain the rules. You could say something like, "I'm about to read the names of two popular movies that would ordinarily have a number in the title, but I'm going to omit that number. Then I'll give you a basic math function to perform using those same numbers. Here's an example: '[Blank] Hour Photo PLUS [Blank] Flew over the Cuckoo's Nest' would be '1 + 1 = 2.'"

1 _____ *Years a Slave* MINUS _____ *Angry Men*

2 *Big Hero* _____ TIMES _____ *Legged Freaks*

3 _____ *Psychopaths* PLUS _____ *Days of Summer*

4 _____ *Feet from Stardom* DIVIDED BY _____ *Cloverfield Lane*

5 *Another* _____ *Hours* MINUS _____ *mm*

6 *Assault on Precinct* _____ PLUS *Gone in* _____ *Seconds*

7 *Death Race* _____ DIVIDED BY *Blues Brothers* _____

8 _____ *Easy Pieces* TIMES _____ *Degrees of Separation*

9 _____ *Shades of Grey* MINUS _____ *Ronin*

10 *Ocean's* _____ (1960) PLUS *Ocean's* _____ (2001) PLUS *Ocean's* _____ (2004) PLUS *Ocean's* _____ (2007) PLUS *Ocean's* _____ (2018)

LET'S ISSUE A RETRACTION

The *New York Times's* Janet Maslin savaged the original *Blues Brothers* in a 1980 review. And she even pointed out that the plot to save the orphanage by fundraising for its back taxes could've been avoided if the church-run institution had been tax-exempt in the first place. Which makes sense.

ANSWERS - 1. 0 (12 - 12 = 0) - **2. 48** (6 × 8 = 48) - **3. 507** (7 + 500 = 507) - **4. 2** (20 ÷ 10 = 2) - **5. 40** (48 - 8 = 40) - **6. 73** (13 + 60 = 73) - **7. 1** (2000 ÷ 2000 = 1) - **8. 30** (5 × 6 = 30) - **9. 3** (50 - 47 = 3) - **10. 55** (11 + 11 + 12 + 13 + 8 = 55)

Random Stuff You Might Know

1 New York City's detention center from 1838 to 1902, built in the Egyptian Revival style, had this relevant nickname.

2 This word describes the spacing between the inboard-facing edges of the rails on a railway track.

3 In classical music notation, *arco* instructs musicians to return to using the bow on their stringed instruments after previously receiving this instruction to pluck their instruments.

FUN FACT

Football player Terrell Owens and astronaut Chris Hadfield are both fans of Answer #6. The former because he hid it in his uniform for a flamboyant end zone celebration; the latter because holy cow, IT WORKS IN SPACE!

4 What's the capital of Malaysia?

5 The Collingwood Magpies, Richmond Tigers, and Western Bulldogs are all teams in this sport.

6 In 1964, Sanford Ink Company launched this iconic product, which spawned an entire brand.

7 Where in nature would you find a spinneret?

8 Created by *Marvelous Mrs. Maisel*'s Amy Sherman-Palladino, short-lived show *Bunheads* followed a showgirl who ended up teaching this art.

9 Kurt Cobain knew that this was element atomic number 3.

10 One point for each of the 12 artists whose paintings have sold at auction for the most money ever.

ANSWERS - 1. The Tombs - 2. Gauge - 3. Pizz. - 4. Kuala Lumpur - 5. Australian Rules Football - 6. Sharpie - 7. Spider or Insect Larva - 8. Ballet - 9. Lithium - 10. Bacon, Lichtenstein, Modigliani, Picasso, Rembrandt, Klimt, Rothko, Pollock, Gauguin, Cézanne, de Kooning, Da Vinci

8

Medicine

1 This ancient Greek physician is known as the father of medicine.

2 Studies find it is not massive concussions but many mild traumatic brain injuries that lead to this sports-related disease, abbreviated.

3 This is the name of the arm bone that runs from shoulder to elbow.

4 Anti-anxiety drug alprazolam is best known by this trade name.

5 Emptying into the right atrium, the superior and inferior of these veins return deoxygenated blood to the heart.

6 Killing between 50 and 100 million people, the influenza pandemic that began in this year caused 3 to 5 percent of the world's population to die.

7 In 1816, French physician René Laennec invented this heart and lung monitoring device.

8 This is the branch of medicine that deals with the treatment and prevention of cancer.

9 The human body, depending on the individual, has between 500 and 700 of these white-blood-cell-producing organs.

10 This organ removes old red blood cells and maintains a reserve of blood that can be used in case of hemorrhagic shock.

> **MORE THAN ANATOMY**
>
> We all know that song that goes "X bone connected to the Y bone," right? Well, it's not a skeletal study aid. It's a 1928 spiritual by NAACP leader James Weldon Johnson and his brother J. Rosamond Johnson, based on prophet Ezekiel's visions in the "Valley of Dry Bones."

ANSWERS - 1. Hippocrates - 2. CTE (Chronic Traumatic Encephalopathy) - 3. Humerus - 4. Xanax - 5. Vena Cava - 6. 1918 - 7. Stethoscope - 8. Oncology - 9. Lymph Nodes - 10. Spleen

Before and After

See page 2 if you need a refresher on the rules.

1 *Eat a Peach* was the first album by this band after its founder's death AND HBO miniseries about Easy Company's journey through World War II.

2 A snareless drum or a personal GPS device AND he has collaborated with Steven Spielberg on *Saving Private Ryan* and *Catch Me If You Can*.

3 The royal name of Canada's island province AND the subject of the documentary *Citizenfour*.

AROUND THE COUNTRY

The small town of Winslow, Arizona, of "Take It Easy" fame has a storefront with a fake reflection of a blonde in a Ford pickup truck. Don't know why anyone would travel to see something from an Eagles song, yet here we are.

4 The nickname of animated *Simpsons* villain Dr. Robert Terwilliger AND host famous for the sign-off "Help control the pet population—have your pets spayed or neutered."

5 His gravestone mentions his religious freedom statute and the founding of a university but not his presidency AND the capital of Missouri.

6 Sharon Stone had an early role in this sort-of-rhyming Carl Weathers cop movie AND the writer of "Running on Empty" and "Take It Easy."

7 The singer of "Nobody Does It Better" and "You're So Vain" AND polar opposites Rick and A. J. are San Diego private detectives in this eighties show.

8 Although the Vaaler and Fay versions exist, the Gem is the ubiquitous version of this office supply AND premade, license-free illustrations for use in personal publishing.

9 In 1853, David Smith of Vermont invented the spring-loaded version of this laundry device AND pictures of Betty Grable and Bettie Page.

10 Brandy joins Jennifer Love Hewitt and Freddie Prinze Jr. in this horror sequel AND Jessica Biel romances Cape Cod baseball player Freddie Prinze Jr. in this movie.

ANSWERS - 1. Allman Brothers Band of Brothers - 2. Tom Tom Hanks - 3. Prince Edward Snowden - 4. Sideshow Bob Barker - 5. Thomas Jefferson City - 6. Action Jackson Browne - 7. Carly Simon and Simon - 8. Paper Clip Art - 9. Clothes Pin Up - 10. I Still Know What You Did Last Summer Catch

Monty Python

1 Media outlets wryly commented that Trump's inauguration was accompanied by the theme song to *Monty Python's Flying Circus*, "The Liberty Bell" by this march composer.

2 What kind of parrot is the dead parrot?

3 Accompanied by a squishing noise, this famous Python symbol is a detail from Bronzino's Renaissance painting *An Allegory with Venus and Cupid.*

4 The 2012 London Olympics closing ceremony featured a performance by Eric Idle of this *Life of Brian* song.

5 This *Hitchhiker's Guide to the Galaxy* author is one of two non-Pythons to get writing credits on *Monty Python's Flying Circus.*

6 Nobody expects this.

7 Python alum Terry Gilliam's *Brazil* features this acclaimed actor as renegade air-conditioning technician Archibald "Harry" Tuttle.

8 This is the name of King Arthur's trusty squire.

9 The Crimson Permanent Assurance transform their corporate office into a pirate ship to open this 1983 Monty Python movie.

10 A famous Monty Python song is the inspiration for this term for unwanted email.

> **DID YOU KNOW?**
>
> Um, actually, everyone expected Answer #6. They literally gave you written warning of the accusation against you and ample time to prepare your defense.

Random Stuff You Might Know

1 In rugby, this player is positioned between two props and uses their feet to win possession of the ball for their team in a scrum.

2 Hits including "Heat Wave," "Where Did Our Love Go," "Baby I Need Your Loving," and many, many more were written by the two Holland brothers and this third songwriter.

3 The maker of Ritalin and Lamisil, pharmaceutical multinational Novartis is based in this country.

FUN FACT

Czar has the same origin as *kaiser* from Answer #4.

4 The German word for "king or emperor," *kaiser*, is directly derived from this ancient family name.

5 This three-letter unit is the international measurement of electrical resistance.

6 Valued at nearly $30,000, the ultra-rare Black Lotus is reportedly the most expensive card in this fantasy trading card game.

7 Billy Joel said this song was inspired by a night out with then-girlfriend Elle Macpherson, Whitney Houston, and future ex-wife Christie Brinkley.

8 "I am shocked—shocked—to find that gambling is going on in here" is a quote from this movie.

9 From 1966 until 1975, Bobby Orr played for this team.

10 One point for each of the 12 northernmost world capital cities.

Famous Families

1 Anderson Cooper is the great-great-great-grandson of this shipping and railroad tycoon.

2 The 15th century's Richard of York, the third Duke of York, adopted this as his last name, which came to refer to his family's dynasty as rulers of England.

3 Father Increase and son Cotton of this prominent Massachusetts family were divided over dissent and support, respectively, of the Salem witch trials.

4 Founded in 1600 by Ieyasu, this shogunate collapsed under his descendant of the same last name, Yoshinobu, in 1868.

5 According to the lore of Skull and Bones, a member of this prominent political family allegedly dug up the skull of Apache warrior Geronimo.

6 Beginning as a branch of the Capetian dynasty, members of this family have ruled France, Naples, Sicily, and Parma, and to this day are the monarchs of Spain and Luxembourg.

> **SEMANTICS, SCHEMANTICS**
>
> Willfully obtuse quizmasters may put their fingers to their glasses and say, "Well, actually, the Houses of Lancaster and York weren't their own Royal Houses; they were what's known as 'Cadet Houses.'" They're technically correct, but these people are Royal Pains.

7 *The Adventures of Ozzie and Harriet* starred all four members of this real-life family.

8 Who is Norah Jones's father?

9 Emigrating in the 1630s or 1640s, Dutch colonizer Claes Maartenszen bought a farm in what is now midtown Manhattan, beginning this famous family's three-century New York legacy.

10 Michael, an explorer, ethnographer, and son of this famously wealthy family, disappeared and is presumed to have drowned while on expedition in New Guinea in 1961.

ANSWERS: 1. Cornelius Vanderbilt - 2. Plantagenet - 3. Mather - 4. Tokugawa - 5. Bush - 6. Bourbon - 7. Nelson - 8. Ravi Shankar - 9. Roosevelt - 10. Rockefeller

4

Misconceptions

The following 10 clues are the canon, the old standbys, the tried-and-true trivia nuggets which everyone in their trivia career shall face.

1 The all-black garb of *Bunraku* theater puppeteers is credited with the modern-day depiction of these spies and assassins.

2 An 1876 staging of one of this composer's operas created the iconic—and ahistorical—image of the horned Viking helmet.

HISTORICAL INACCURACIES

Film and fiction have depicted the Battle of Thermopylae as being fought solely by 300 Spartans. That's wrong. They were the vanguard of the force defending the pass of Thermopylae alongside 700 Thespians and 900 Helots, 400 Thebans, and others.

3 This Roman word referred not to a place of emesis, but instead to the exit corridors of an amphitheater.

4 The word *ye*, as in "ye Olde Shoppe," is properly pronounced "the," as the lowercase *y* resembles this "th"-pronounced Old English letter, written thusly: þ.

5 Anywhere between 5,000 and 7,000 Peloponnesians and other Greeks joined in the Battle of Thermopylae, well more than the 300 Spartans led by this king.

6 "I never failed in mathematics. Before I was fifteen I had mastered differential and integral calculus," said this man.

7 Despite popular myth, dogs do not see in black and white; their vision instead resembles that of a human with this kind of color blindness.

8 Political opponents gave the purchase of Alaska this disparaging nickname.

9 The Moscow–Washington hotline was a teletype, then a fax machine, and now a secure email connection; it has never been this colorful device.

10 This company's Space Pen was not funded by NASA at the cost of millions of dollars; it was funded by the company's founder at a personal cost of $1 million.

ANSWERS - 1. Ninja - 2. Richard Wagner - 3. Vomitorium - 4. Thorn - 5. Leonidas - 6. Albert Einstein - 7. Red/Green Color Blindness - 8. Seward's Folly - 9. Red Telephone - 10. Fisher

Nineties Hip-Hop

1 Tupac's "Changes" extensively samples "The Way It Is" by this group.

2 Digable Planets' "Rebirth of Slick" is better known for this three-word parenthetical title.

3 Big Pun's "Still Not a Player" features vocals by this American R&B singer.

> **TOO SOON**
>
> "Changes" is the only song to date that has been posthumously nominated for the Best Rap Solo Performance Grammy.

4 Bone Thugs-N-Harmony's Grammy-winning hit "Tha Crossroads" was dedicated to the memory of their mentor and executive producer, this N.W.A. rapper.

5 What does the acronym *C.R.E.A.M.* stand for?

6 This Californian hip-hop group got their name from a street in Los Angeles County's South Gate.

7 Tony! Toni! Toné!, Bell Biv Devoe, and Boyz II Men, among many others, are popular groups from this subgenre of hip-hop and R&B that was pioneered by producers Jimmy Jam and Terry Lewis.

8 "Déjà Vu (Uptown Baby)" was the first single of the 1998 album *Make It Reign* by this duo.

9 In 2005, this 1990 Public Enemy album was selected for preservation by the Library of Congress as an important contribution to American culture.

10 Egyptian singer Abdel Halim Hafez's version of "Khosara Khosara" formed the main sample for this Timbaland-produced Jay-Z track.

ANSWERS - 1. Bruce Hornsby and the Range - 2. "(Cool Like Dat)" - 3. Joe - 4. Eazy E - 5. "Cash Rules Everything Around Me" - 6. Cypress Hill - 7. New Jack Swing - 8. Lord Tariq and Peter Gunz - 9. Fear of a Black Planet - 10. "Big Pimpin'"

Random Stuff You Might Know

1 In transportation, what are schraders and prestas?

2 What is the farthest-east territory in Asia on a Risk board?

3 There is evidence that the name of this Brazilian martial art finds its origin in Angola's Bantu language.

DID YOU KNOW?

After John Roebling died and Washington Roebling was stricken with the bends from working in pressurized caissons beneath the East River, Washington's wife, Emily, initially relayed her husband's directions from his bed and then took on the day-to-day supervision of the entire project in Answer #5. Many thought she was the actual project designer. She wasn't, but damn, she kicked its ass into shape. Best. Span. Ever.

4 This *Star Wars* actor's real last name is Hershlag.

5 John and his son Washington Roebling, respectively, designed and built this New York City landmark.

6 This soccer player has more international goals— among men or women—than anyone else in the world.

7 Because of a 1987 state supreme court ruling that full nudity and lap dances are protected speech, this US city has more strip clubs per capita than any other in the country.

8 With our modern sensibilities, it's ironic that Abraham Lincoln used this popular 19th-century song for his 1860 presidential campaign.

9 Who is Rebecca Romijn's husband?

10 One point for each of the 10 tracks from *Their Greatest Hits (1971–1975)* by the Eagles.

ANSWERS - 1. Bicycle Tire Valves - 2. Kamchatka - 3. Capoeira - 4. Natalie Portman - 5. Brooklyn Bridge - 6. Christine Sinclair - 7. Portland, Oregon - 8. "Dixie" - 9. Jerry O'Connell - 10. "Take It Easy," "Witchy Woman," "Lyin' Eyes," "Already Gone," "Desperado," "One of These Nights," "Tequila Sunrise," "Take it to the Limit," "Peaceful Easy Feeling," "Best of My Love"

Teen Dramas

1 Airing 10 episodes before being canceled, *Ravenswood* was a spin-off of this ABC family teen drama.

2 In *The O.C.*, Sandy Cohen often came into conflict with this father-in-law character.

3 In 1989, this teen drama aired *A New Start*, a two-part, special episode in which Erica gets pregnant and has an abortion.

> **FUN FACT**
>
> Drake was on Answer #3. He started from [that show]; now he's here.

4 Any surprise appearance by Georgina Sparks is a bad omen in this TV show.

5 Tyler Posey plays Scott McCall in this MTV show based on a 1985 high school comedy.

6 This English singer performed "Here with Me," the theme song to *Roswell*.

7 In which state does *One Tree Hill* take place?

8 Debuting against hits like *Mad about You*, *Friends*, and *Martin* doomed this Claire Danes teen drama to failure.

9 Will, Simon, Neil, and Jay attempt to score booze and get laid in this late-2000s British dramedy.

10 The spin-off *Time of Your Life* followed this *Party of Five* character as she moved to New York.

Before and After

See page 2 if you need a refresher on the rules.

1 The logo advertising products like the Snuggie and Pocket Fisherman AND hacktivist group Anonymous's Guy Fawkes mask is a Warner Bros. trademark from this movie.

2 R&B singer famous for "When a Man Loves a Woman" AND in 1987, this Peter Gabriel song won a record nine MTV Video Music Awards.

3 Bandmates Commerford, de la Rocha, Wilk, and Morello AND a term that describes how algorithms utilize knowledge gained from experience to automatically improve computer performance.

4 This *Friends* character's middle name was Muriel AND thought to be lost forever, a film copy of game seven of the 1960 World Series was found in this crooner's wine cellar.

PRO TIP

Anytime the Pittsburgh Pirates are mentioned in relation to a musical figure, the correct response is gonna be Answer #4. He owned 25 percent of the team. Yinz got that?

5 This cartoonist and fashion designer has made logos for bands like Radiohead and Bad Religion AND Will Ferrell's nickname in *Old School*.

6 He plays Reese Witherspoon's love interest in *Legally Blonde* AND band made up of daughters of a Beach Boy and a member of the Mamas and the Papas.

7 In various cultures, this animal is known as good luck, bad luck, and a witch's familiar AND a role for Hathaway, Berry, or Pfeiffer.

8 The first two names of Guess model and Playmate born Vicki Lynn Hogan AND born in Hawai'i, this Oscar winner claims both US and—more famously—Australian citizenship.

9 A 2006 animated movie about a tap-dancing penguin AND unit of velocity that is equivalent to .681 mile per hour.

10 On a compass, 315 degrees AND the location of the Cabinet, Situation, and Roosevelt Rooms.

ANSWERS - 1. As Seen on TV for Vendetta - 2. Percy Sledge Hammer - 3. Rage against the Machine Learning - 4. Chandler Bing Crosby - 5. Paul Frank the Tank - 6. Luke Wilson Phillips - 7. Black Cat Woman - 8. Anna Nicole Kidman - 9. Happy Feet Per Second - 10. North West Wing

New York Yankees

1 Finish this 6-4-3 double play: Koenig to Lazzeri to BLANK.

2 This famous Cubs first baseman finished his career as a player-manager of the 1913 and 1914 Yankees.

3 Former Yankee "El Duque" is the half brother of this retired journeyman pitcher.

4 In 2015, the Yankees organization surprised this former pitcher and longtime pitching coach with a plaque in Monument Park.

5 Who caught Don Larsen's perfect game in the World Series?

6 The Yankees built Yankee Stadium across the Harlem River from this stadium, the home of their former landlords.

FUN FACT

The Yankees are better than the Red Sox. Empirically. At the instantly dated time of this writing, 1,225 to 1,024. And 14 ties.

7 In 1990, pitcher Andy Hawkins became the first Yankee to ever lose one of these games.

8 This is the name of the global hospitality company running concessions at Yankee Stadium.

9 How many games did Joe DiMaggio's 1941 hitting streak last?

10 What is the most recent number to be retired by the Yankees?

Random Stuff You Might Know

1 According to Queen Mary University of London, goats from distinct regions develop these mannerisms differently.

2 What element is chemical symbol *At*?

3 The RC, IS, and GX are models by this automotive brand.

4 Nina Dobrev played this character on *Vampire Diaries*.

5 After the United States, this country is the world's second-largest producer of beef.

TOP OF THE CHARTS

The white oak tree prominently featured in IMDb top-rated film *The Shawshank Redemption* was split by lightning in 2011 and finally felled by high winds in 2016. So the tree, like the movie in which it appears, was incredibly overrated.

6 The Kyrie Eleison, Agnus Dei, and Dies Irae are segments of this musical Latin mass.

7 What is the capital of Nicaragua?

8 According to Principal Seymour Skinner, the phrase "Steamed Hams" comes from Albany, not Superintendent Chalmers's upstate New York hometown.

9 This food item is Taco Bell's best-selling individual item ever.

10 One point for each of the top 12 movies in the American Film Institute's "100 Years of 100 Movies" list.

Casablanca, The Godfather, Citizen Kane
Vertigo, Schindler's List, Lawrence of Arabia, Gone with the Wind, Singin' in the Rain, Raging Bull,
7. Managua - 8. Utica - 9. Doritos Locos Taco 10. The Searchers, City Lights, The Wizard of Oz,
ANSWERS - 1. Accents - 2. Astatine - 3. Lexus - 4. Elena Gilbert - 5. Brazil - 6. Requiem -

Musical Math

This round works just like "Movie Math." See the explanation on page 7 if you need a refresher on the rules.

1 Matchbox _____ MINUS Maroon _____

2 "_____ Luftballons" PLUS "_____ Light Years from Home"

3 "December _____ (Oh, What a Night)" MINUS "_____ Is a Joke"

4 _____ Live Crew TIMES _____ Dog Night PLUS _____ Non Blondes

5 "_____ Ways to Leave Your Lover" PLUS "Highway _____ Revisited"

6 Jurassic _____ TIMES Jackson _____

7 _____ Tree Hill TIMES "_____ Days a Week"

8 "Route _____" TIMES "Less Than _____"

9 _____ pence None the Richer TIMES _____ Inch Nails

10 UB _____ PLUS Eiffel _____

DID YOU KNOW?

The highway mentioned in Question #5 is nicknamed the Blues Highway. It runs from New Orleans, through Memphis and St. Louis, and ultimately through Minnesota to the Canadian border. Thus, it symbolically connected Duluth-born Robert Allen Zimmerman to the music he created as Bob Dylan. Or something like that.

Before and After

See page 2 if you need a refresher on the rules.

1 A prognosticating Pennsylvania rodent AND Paul McCartney, Michael Jackson, and this musician are the only people to sell more than 100 million albums as both a solo artist and member of a band.

2 The slogan of Nancy Reagan's war on drugs campaign AND this Anaheim-based band's breakout album *Tragic Kingdom* is diamond certified.

3 Molasses Swamp and Gumdrop Mountain board game AND this Minnesota-based dairy cooperative.

4 John Goodman stars as an American inheritor to the English throne in this 1991 box-office bomb AND this Jackie Gleason character is husband to Alice and a driver for the Gotham Bus Company.

5 Martin Sheen played President Jed Bartlet on this TV series AND this Microsoft font renders letters as a variety of symbols.

FUN FACT

President Bartlet was not supposed to be seen in the show's original drafts. Kinda like Wilson on *Home Improvement*, maybe?

6 This rapper, discovered by The Notorious B.I.G., finished fifth on 2009's *Dancing with the Stars* AND she did an infamous butt shoot for *Paper* magazine.

7 Apparently, nothing is real in this Beatles song AND Alphaville song, later reworked by Wayne Wonder (and used by Jay-Z).

8 This beer boasts that it is "cold certified" AND Alfred, Lord Tennyson's poem immortalized this military unit's 1855 Crimean War charge.

9 Founded in 1979, this Disney subsidiary's programs include *Outside the Lines*, *PTI*, and *Around the Horn* AND Justin, Chris, Joey, Lance, and JC.

10 Julia Roberts and Denzel Washington starred in this film version of a John Grisham novel AND this Stephen Hawking best-selling book attempts to explain physics and cosmology to the nonscientist.

ANSWERS - 1. Punxsutawney Phil Collins - 2. Just Say No Doubt - 3. Candy Land O' Lakes - 4. King Ralph Kramden - 5. The West Wing Dings - 6. Lil' Kim Kardashian - 7. Strawberry Fields Forever Young - 8. Coors Light Brigade - 9. ESPN Sync - 10. The Pelican Brief History of Time

Poetry

1 Thirteenth-century Sufi poet Rumi wrote in this language of Iran.

2 "Da DUM da DUM da DUM da DUM da DUM" is the best way to illustrate an unstressed and stressed line written in this rhythm.

3 Rhyming author Theodor Geisel is better known by this pen name.

4 What is the most common syllable pattern of haiku?

5 "There once was a man from Nantucket" is an opening to a famous version of this humorous poem style.

6 This word refers to a poem's final two rhyming lines, often used by Shakespeare in his sonnets.

7 Friedrich Schiller's "An die Freude" is best known as the choral lyrics to the final movement of this Beethoven symphony.

8 "Two roads diverged in a yellow wood" opens "The Road Not Taken" by this four-time Pulitzer Prize–winning poet.

9 The title of the play *A Raisin in the Sun* comes from the poem "Harlem" by this poet.

10 "Inferno," "Purgatorio," and "Paradiso" are the three parts of this epic poem by Dante.

WILD GUESS

Ninety percent of those answering Question #8 will say "The Road Less Traveled." There isn't a poem called that, yet everyone thinks there is. Total Mandela effect going on with this one.

6 Random Stuff You Might Know

1 In 2017, 92 percent of the 2.2 million voters of this Spanish autonomous community voted in favor of full independence.

2 Yale professors Ronald Rivest, Alan Perlis, and Michael O. Rabin have won the "Nobel Prize of Computing," an award named for this British mathematician.

3 This is the first and last name of the often violent husband to Stella in *A Streetcar Named Desire*.

4 Set in an optics factory, *The Most Beautiful* was a 1944 wartime propaganda film by this Japanese director of *Seven Samurai*.

5 What is the Spanish word for "in" or "inside"?

6 What item is the Kids Choice Awards trophy?

7 Utilizing heavy ropes, tractor tires, and other unorthodox apparatus, this training regimen was founded in 2000 by controversial figure Greg Glassman.

8 What was Dwight Eisenhower's middle name?

9 What is the capital of Belarus?

10 One point for each of the 10 Academy Award for Best Actress winners for the decade of the 2000s (2000 to 2009).

PRO TIP

Questions like #10 come up frequently throughout this volume; finite data sets are easily memorized. Best Picture, Actor, and Actress winners; US presidents; best-selling novels. The list of, well, lists goes on and on. Seek them out and enjoy them! Kings and queens; national capitals; state nicknames, flowers, and birds. Do it!

South America

1. Created by Pope Alexander VI, the 1494 Treaty of Tordesillas split up the New World, and South America specifically, between Spain and this European power.

2. Argentine footballer Lionel Messi plays for this European club.

3. This number-one hit single was the lead song of *Laundry Service*, the 2001 English-language debut by Colombian singer Shakira.

4. This icon of Incan civilizations means "The Old Peak" in the Quechua language.

5. Starring Ethan Hawke, this 1993 movie follows an Uruguayan rugby team's hardships while stranded in the Andes after a plane crash.

6. What is the capital of Colombia?

7. "El Libertador" Simón Bolívar was described as a falsifier, deserter, conspirator, liar, coward, and looter by this founder of modern communism.

8. Gaining independence from Great Britain in 1966, this is the only South American country whose official language is English.

9. Straddling Peru, Chile, Bolivia, and Argentina, this is the driest nonpolar desert in the world.

10. This South American country's name is derived from the Latin word for "silver."

> **WHEN IN DOUBT**
>
> If you're ever put on the spot, Answer #9 is one of those all-time great trivia guesses that'll make your friends say, "Whoa, you know what you're talking about," and even if you get the question wrong, they'll still be like, "We're just impressed . . . I've never even heard of that."

ANSWERS - 1. Portugal - 2. FC Barcelona - 3. "Whenever, Wherever" - 4. Machu Picchu - 5. Alive - 6. Bogotá - 7. Karl Marx - 8. Guyana - 9. Atacama Desert - 10. Argentina

Before and After

See page 2 if you need a refresher on the rules.

1 This "Make 'Em Say Uhh!" rapper had contracts to play for the Charlotte Hornets and Toronto Raptors AND with the head of a monkey and body of a fish, the Fiji mermaid was a hoax created by this famed circus founder.

2 A ukulele-playing musician or Dickensian child AND portrayed by comedian Allen, this was the main character of *Home Improvement*.

I ONLY FLY PRIVATE

The circus founder in Question #1 promoted singing sensation Jenny Lind. In order to ensure her privacy from the crowds that swarmed her, he purchased and constructed the world's first private railcar for her use.

3 Andrew Jackson rose to national fame because of his victory at the Battle of New Orleans after the official end of this conflict AND Amy Schumer parodied this Henry Fonda courtroom drama in a shot-for-shot remake.

4 The pen name of *Alice in Wonderland*'s author AND actor who portrayed Archie Bunker.

5 Jonathan, Jordan, Joey, Donnie, and Danny AND part of Rhode Island, this vacation spot is only 14 miles from Montauk, New York.

6 Loretto, Kentucky's red wax–sealed bourbon AND lead singer of Sugar Ray.

7 Hanna-Barbera's cat-and-mouse duo AND "Show me the money!" movie.

8 From 1974 to 1980, Bon Scott was the lead singer of this hard-rock band AND Green Lantern, Flash, and Aquaman's parent company.

9 The star of *Inside Man* and *Children of Men* AND the star of *Shanghai Noon* and *Marley and Me*.

10 His debut solo album was 1987's *Faith* AND the first openly gay player drafted by an NFL team.

ANSWERS - 1. Master P, T. Barnum - 2. Tiny Tim the Toolman Taylor - 3. War of 1812 Angry Men - 4. Lewis Carroll O'Connor - 5. New Kids on the Block Island - 6. Maker's Mark McGrath - 7. Tom and Jerry Maguire - 8. AC/DC Comics - 9. Clive Owen Wilson - 10. George Michael Sam

1999

1. Not only does this group with a number-three hit in 1999 like girls who wear Abercrombie & Fitch, but Chinese food makes them sick.

2. It took only 19 nominations, but in 1999 this soap actor finally won a Daytime Emmy.

3. In 1999, this Billy Blanks–invented workout-slash-martial-art reached peak popularity.

4. In 1999, this not-so-nice fellow who happened to be a ballplayer for the Atlanta Braves got in seriously hot water when he made racist, sexist, homophobic, and xenophobic comments about New York City.

5. What was Haley Joel Osment's character named in the 1999 film *The Sixth Sense*?

6. In a 1999 *Saturday Night Live* sketch, Darrell Hammond, who was playing presidential candidate Donald Trump, asked John Carpenter to be his running mate shortly after Carpenter became the first person to win the American iteration of this game show.

7. These four words were canine actor Gidget's popular 1999 commercial catchphrase.

8. Actor Ron Livingston has said, "That's kind of a heavy load to carry" when people tell him they quit their jobs after being inspired by his role in this 1999 comedy.

9. This third Harry Potter book was released in 1999.

10. Blame this 1999 movie for the prevalence of *Paranormal Activity*, *Cloverfield*, and other not-so-great found footage movies.

> **WHEELS WITHIN WHEELS**
>
> The trivia community tends to be pretty self-referential, so oftentimes clues on one notable show will come up on other shows. An example could be "John Carpenter's winning question featured this US president's appearance on the variety show *Laugh-In*." The answer, of course, was Richard Nixon.

Random Stuff You Might Know

1 Who was Henry VIII's second wife?

2 In 2012, Atlanta-based tea company Teavana was acquired by this corporate behemoth.

3 In 1984, despite a $5,000 per game fine imposed by David Stern, this basketball player refused to change his sneakers before games, creating a marketing juggernaut.

DID YOU KNOW?

A disturbing number of Americans know the country that is Answer #6 only from Chandler's address at 15 [Redacted] Road, [Redacted] in *Friends*.

4 Pristina is the capital of this newly independent, partially recognized state.

5 This word describes a nationalistic country run under the totalitarian rule of a militaristic single party led by a dictator embodied by a pseudo-religious cult of personality.

6 Most scientists agree that although coffee was cultivated in eastern Africa, this Arabian country was the first to roast, prepare, and consume the drink.

7 This loanword originally referred to a cloak and hood worn by residents of a region of France of the same name but later described a luxury motorcar with a top extending to cover both driver and passengers.

8 Also known as a millionfish or rainbow fish, this five-letter tropical fish is one of the most popular aquarium fish in the world.

9 One of Bollywood's highest-paid and most popular actors of all time, this entertainer went on to star in ABC's crime drama *Quantico*.

10 One point each for the 12 largest nongovernment for-profit employers in the United States.

ANSWERS - 1. Anne Boleyn - 2. Starbucks - 3. Michael Jordan - 4. Kosovo - 5. Fascist - 6. Yemen - 7. Limousine - 8. Guppy - 9. Priyanka Chopra - 10. FedEx, Hewlett Packard, Yum! Brands, GE, Berkshire Hathaway, UPS, Target, Home Depot, Kroger, IBM, McDonald's, Walmart

Antiques and Stuff

1 In addition to its spectacular art collection, this former Manhattan home of a robber baron features five centuries of furniture and clocks and is now a museum.

2 Fiona Bruce hosts the current iteration of this British TV show; Mark L. Walberg hosts its American counterpart.

3 The Antique Automobile Club of America stipulates that a car must be at least this many years of age for it to be called "antique."

4 This word refers to British antiques, designs, and architecture during the early Hanoverian dynasty of the 18th and 19th centuries.

5 In mechanical watches, this word describes a day/ night phase dial, stopwatch, date window, and other additional features.

6 A catalog of antique firearms reveals a potential fortune at the end of this 1998 British movie.

7 The highest-selling piece of antique furniture of all time, a cabinet nicknamed after this shuttlecock sport, sold for $36.7 million.

8 In addition to creating protectionist tariffs, the 1930 Smoot-Hawley Tariff Act defined an antique as anything made before this year.

9 Lasting from 1368 to 1644, this Chinese dynasty is synonymous with vases.

10 Selling for $30.8 million, a Leonardo da Vinci book described with this five-letter word is the most expensive book ever sold.

I'LL MEET YOU IN HELL

Just up the road from Answer #1 is the Cooper Hewitt, Smithsonian Design Museum. It is the former home of Answer #1's business-partner-cum-rival, Andrew Carnegie. "Tell him that I'll meet him in hell" were the final words of the former to the latter. Great guys, the robber barons.

ANSWERS - 1. Frick Collection - 2. *Antiques Roadshow* - 3. 25 - 4. Georgian - 5. Complication - 6. *Lock, Stock and Two Smoking Barrels* - 7. Badminton - 8. 1830 - 9. Ming - 10. Codex

Famous Feuds

1. In 1979, these two families appeared on the TV show *Family Feud*.

2. The founder of the Bank of New York was shot and killed by this founder of the company that would later become Chase Manhattan Bank.

3. This man was conveniently on vacation in Florida when six members of Bugs Moran's gang were machine-gunned in 1929's St. Valentine's Day Massacre.

IF YOU LIKE FAMILY FEUD . . .

. . . you'll love *Pointless*, a BBC game show that can best be described as "reverse *Family Feud*." You have to give an answer to a question that is both correct and answered by the *least* amount of people. It's a great study guide for a trivia buff. Think "London" is a terrible answer to "Name a European capital," as everyone will know it, but "Skopje" is a great one.

4. In 2005, a Mexican woman found she was in possession of the mountaineering ice ax used by Stalin's operatives to kill this Russian leader in 1940.

5. Diss tracks on the 2000 album *The Notorious K.I.M.* escalated the feud between Lil' Kim and this rapper, her erstwhile high school friend.

6. Years after the insult to his sister and the subsequent headbutt and red card, French soccer star Zinedine Zidane said he will never apologize to this Italian center back.

7. Mariah Carey said she hired extra security after feeling unsafe around this fellow *American Idol* judge.

8. Shakespeare's *Richard III* dramatizes the conclusion to the feud between these two families.

9. Metal band Avenged Sevenfold take their name from the biblical punishment rendered by God onto this son of Adam after his murder of his younger brother.

10. Described as descendants to the answer to Question #9, this monster and his mother famously feuded with Beowulf.

ANSWERS - 1. Hatfields and McCoys - 2. Aaron Burr - 3. Al Capone - 4. Leon Trotsky - 5. Foxy Brown - 6. Marco Materazzi - 7. Nicki Minaj - 8. Lancaster and York - 9. Cain - 10. Grendel

GOATs

1. Although this song was obviously deemed the greatest of all time by *Rolling Stone*, the album in which it appeared, *Highway 61 Revisited*, came in as only the fourth greatest of all time.

2. This Asian country is the world's largest producer of goat's milk.

3. BBC's 2002 list of 100 Greatest Britons placed this Irish-hating imperialist as number one.

> **PRO TIP**
>
> Ken Jennings is the GOAT. Fact.

4. Startling a myotonic goat causes this to happen, thus its more common name.

5. After losing to Jake LaMotta in 1943, this legendary fighter went on to win 91 straight bouts until 1951.

6. Persian for "made from wool," this word later came to describe a handmade mountain-goat-wool accessory garment.

7. An eponymous column reflects that the Roman Empire reached its greatest size during this emperor's reign.

8. Chattanooga, Tennessee, is one of the many municipalities to use goats in the clearing of this Japanese invasive species.

9. This slugger's Wins Above Replacement (WAR) is a staggering 182.4, well over pitcher Walter Johnson's 164.3, the second-greatest WAR of all time.

10. After finally being worn down, an unnamed children's book character would eat this dish with a goat or in a boat.

ANSWERS - 1. "Like a Rolling Stone" - **2.** India - **3.** Winston Churchill - **4.** Fainting - **5.** Sugar Ray Robinson - **6.** Pashmina - **7.** Trajan - **8.** Kudzu - **9.** Babe Ruth - **10.** Green Eggs and Ham

Random Stuff You Might Know

1 What is the capital of Paraguay?

2 A thermosetting phenol-formaldehyde resin, the early plastic polyoxybenzylmethylenglycolanhydride is known by this *B* word.

3 Keyboards, mice, webcams, and Bluetooth speakers are among the many peripherals that this Swiss computer accessory company makes.

4 Montana's many monikers include the Treasure State and this large nickname.

5 Although most of Peru speaks Spanish, approximately 13 percent of Peruvians speak this indigenous language.

COGNATE COGNITION

Great trivia geeks know that English excels at saying "yoink" to other languages' useful words. As a result, there are some really prevalent words that you should remember for quiz-bowl dominance, like *khaki* from Urdu; *pyjama* from Hindustani; and *condor*, *llama*, *jerky*, and *cocaine* from the answer to Question #5.

6 The keel-billed variety is the most depicted species of this famously billed bird.

7 This CW TV character was nicknamed the Bad Boy of the Upper East Side.

8 The highest possible NFL passer rating is 158.3; at 122.5 and 121.5, this player holds the top two regular season records.

9 Used in Christmas displays, this red-and-green plant is indigenous to Mexico.

10 One point for each of the second 13 states—that's 14 through 26—to join the union.

ANSWERS - 1. Asunción - **2.** Bakelite - **3.** Logitech - **4.** Big Sky Country - **5.** Quechua - **6.** Toucan - **7.** Chuck Bass - **8.** Aaron Rodgers - **9.** Poinsettia - **10.** Vermont, Kentucky, Tennessee, Ohio, Louisiana, Indiana, Mississippi, Illinois, Alabama, Maine, Missouri, Arkansas, Michigan

Map Time

Name each of the highlighted countries in Europe (1–6) and Africa (7–12).

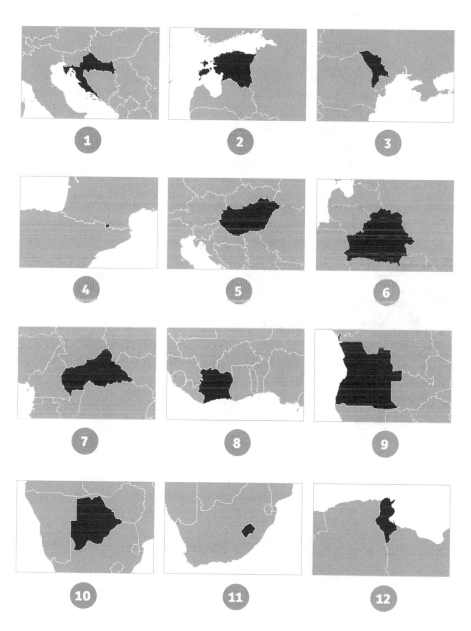

Information Technology

1 The four eras of information technology (IT) are designated as pre-mechanical, mechanical, electromechanical, and this current era.

2 This word is the *O* in CD-ROM.

3 Both the Bombe and Colossus electromechanical computers were made and used at this secret World War II British code-breaking headquarters estate.

4 Jack Kilby invented the world's first integrated circuit, or microchip, while working for this American electronics company.

5 A 1980 article in *Psychology Today* is most likely the first usage of this word describing a person who purposely finds and exploits weaknesses in computer systems.

THE VERY FIRST . . .

On August 11, 1994, for the price of $12.48 plus shipping, the first item ever securely bought via the internet was *Ten Summoner's Tales*, a compact disc by Sting.

6 This is the name for the observation that the number of transistors in a microchip doubles every two years.

7 What does the *C* in CRT stand for?

8 This computer information unit's name is a portmanteau of "binary digit."

9 This early computing device's name is derived from the Greek word for "something without base" or a "rectangular board."

10 In 1979, Swedish computer scientist Bjarne Stroustrup invented this alpha-symbolic computer programming language.

ANSWERS - 1. Electronic - 2. Only - 3. Bletchley Park - 4. Texas Instruments - 5. Hacker - 6. Moore's Law - 7. Cathode - 8. Bit - 9. Abacus - 10. C++

34

Netflix Shows

1. *Sense8* is a Netflix series created by these sibling *Matrix* writer-directors.

2. *Unbreakable Kimmy Schmidt*'s kidnapper character, Reverend Richard Wayne Gary Wayne, was played by this *Mad Men* actor.

3. Alison Brie, Will Arnett, and Aaron Paul provide voices for this animated Netflix program.

4. *Chasing Cameron* follows Internet personality Cameron Dallas, who gained fame on this now-defunct social media platform.

5. John Hodgman's Netflix special was named after this Norse word for "end of times."

6. Debuting March 2017, this Netflix and Marvel collaboration was criticized for Orientalism.

7. This talented young actor plays Eleven on *Stranger Things*.

8. This Netflix original series about a Venetian explorer is not set in a pool.

9. Uzo Aduba won the Primetime Emmy for Best Supporting Actress in a Drama for this Netflix role.

10. Set in the South Bronx, *The Get Down* was created by this *Romeo + Juliet* director.

> **APRIL FOOLS!**
>
> On April 1, 2016, every single description of every single Netflix program mentioned in some way *Full House* star John Stamos.

ANSWERS - 1. The Wachowskis - 2. Jon Hamm - 3. *Bojack Horseman* - 4. Vine - 5. Ragnarok - 6. *Iron Fist* - 7. Millie Bobby Brown - 8. *Marco Polo* - 9. "Crazy Eyes" - 10. Baz Luhrmann

ROUND 4 / DIFFICULTY LEVEL   1 2 3 4 5 **6**

Random Stuff You Might *Not* Know

1. Plus or minus 100, how many bridges are in New York City?

2. This is perhaps the world's most famous song named after a deodorant.

3. Consisting of 10 soldiers per legion and 500 altogether, this was the standard tactical unit of the Roman army.

4. "I would prefer not to" is the catchphrase of this Herman Melville character.

5. Although Hiragana and Katakana are native to Japan, these Japanese symbolic characters are Chinese derived.

FUN FACT
....
Answer #6 sucks. This is
the law of the land.

6. Brown School, Union Institute, Normal College, and Trinity College are former names of this tobacco-money-funded university.

7. Marine Corps Base Camp Pendleton is in this California county.

8. The name of a terrible South African mining plutocrat and politician lives on through this vaunted academic award.

9. Jazz musician Olu Dara is the father of this rap artist.

10. One point for each of the 10 plagues of Egypt.

ANSWERS - 1. 1,444 (1,344 to 1,544) - 2. "Smells Like Teen Spirit" - 3. Cohort - 4. Bartleby, the Scrivener - 5. Kanji - 6. Duke - 7. San Diego - 8. Rhodes Scholarship - 9. Nas - 10. Blood, Frogs, Lice/Gnats, Flies/Animals, Pestilence of Livestock, Boils, Thunderstorm of Hail and Fire, Locusts, Darkness, Death of Firstborn

Famous Sayings and Idioms

1 Now meaning "improperly rushed through a legal process," getting THIS originally referred to having lands seized by eminent domain to build a transportation system.

2 Scholars argue over whether this phrase, meaning "it's now up to you," originated with tennis or with basketball.

3 Before 1928, your great idea could not have been the best thing since this.

> **THINGS THAT ARE OLDER THAN ANSWER #3**
>
> Liquid-fueled rockets. Quartz clocks. The Big Bang theory (the theory, not the show). Paper towels. Cheeseburgers. Garage door openers. Water-skiing. Toasters.

4 This dairy saying meaning "there's nothing you can do about it now," dates back to 1659.

5 This idiom, meaning someone is "unhinged," was first recorded in 1897 and most likely referred to the unstable bottom of a leisure chair.

6 Often paired with "piece of," this word became synonymous with "easy."

7 Meaning "the subject occurred or arrived mid-conversation about said subject," this vaguely evil phrase has been in English since 1666.

8 The length of machine gun ammunition belts, commonly sold fabric bolts, the volume of dirt in a grave, a ship's sails, and a football game have all been discredited as the origin of this measurement term.

9 October 31, 2020, saw the semirare astronomical occurrence that this saying refers to.

10 Despite popular legend, this saying meaning "to reveal everything" has no basis in sailors being scammed into purchasing the wrong domestic animal.

ANSWERS - 1. Railroaded - 2. Ball in Your Court - 3. Sliced Bread - 4. It's no use crying over spilled milk. - 5. Off Your Rocker - 6. Cake - 7. Speak of the Devil - 8. The Whole Nine Yards - 9. Once in a Blue Moon - 10. Let the Cat Out of the Bag

Before and After

See page 2 if you need a refresher on the rules.

1 In 2014, Google launched an underwater "street view" of this decaying Australian natural wonder AND right over left then left over right makes this maritime rope process tidy and tight.

2 After retiring from baseball and joining Chock full o'Nuts, he became the first Black vice president of an American corporation AND this fictional character nicknames a cannibal's captive Friday.

3 Perhaps about a riverboat, this was rock band Mountain's biggest hit AND this fictional character's catchphrase is "Off with their heads."

4 "I spent a lot of money on booze, birds, and fast cars—and the rest I just squandered," said this Manchester United soccer legend AND Christopher Guest's 2000 canine mockumentary.

5 The Yankees retired his jersey number 1 AND the director of 1978's rock concert film *The Last Waltz*.

6 Talib Kweli's bandmate in Black Star AND Rick Rubin and Russell Simmons's record label.

7 A reptilian idiom for "superficial sympathy" AND the performers of "Everybody Wants to Rule the World."

8 Semisonic's iconic "last call" song AND dwarves invade Kevin's bedroom leading him on an adventure across the centuries in this 1981 film.

9 The English Royal Observatory maintains this solar standard AND owned by a London publishing company, this local city guide features cultural happenings.

10 Swedish Eurodance group Rednex's 1995 novelty hit AND the 46th POTUS.

LEAVE IT TO THE FRENCH

From the International Meridian Conference in 1884 until the establishment of the UTC in 1978, France refused to adopt the world's standard time.

ANSWERS - 1. Great Barrier Reef Knot - 2. Jackie Robinson Crusoe - 3. Mississippi Queen of Hearts - 4. George Best in Show - 5. Billy Martin Scorsese - 6. Mos Def Jam - 7. Crocodile Tears for Fears - 8. Closing Time Bandits - 9. Greenwich Mean Time Out - 10. Cotton Eye Joe Biden

Baseball

1 From 1902 to 1914, the Cleveland Indians were nicknamed the Naps after this player-manager during that time span.

2 Between 1974 and 1976 there were four occasions of a team "forfeiting" this position.

3 With 285 occurrences throughout his career, Craig Biggio is second only to Hughie Jennings' all-time number for this stat.

4 In 1910, he was the first president to throw out a ceremonial first pitch.

5 What team was the beneficiary of "Merkle's Boner" in 1908?

6 Contrary to popular rumors, Harry Frazee did not sell Babe Ruth to fund this kind of endeavor.

7 Lou Gehrig's death, Ted Williams's last .400-plus season, and Joe DiMaggio's 56-game hitting streak all happened in this year.

8 Universally derided as the worst of all time, the 1976 White Sox uniform included this nontraditional garment.

9 This Orioles and Giants great is widely regarded as the best player-manager combination of all time.

10 What is Bo Jackson's real first name?

Random Stuff You Might Know

1 Richmond, Baltimore, Philadelphia, Boston, and the Bronx all have houses or monuments dedicated to the memory of this American poet and short-story writer.

2 *In the Land without Feelings, Battle the Freeze Machine,* and *Adventure in Wonderland* are all subtitles to eighties TV specials and movies featuring these American Greetings characters.

3 A 1953 airspace encounter between Eisenhower's presidential aircraft *Columbine II* and an Eastern Airlines airplane led to the creation of this famous call sign.

4 This hit song was the 2015 debut single by then-teenage rapper Silentó.

5 What does the *FM* of FM radio stand for?

6 Maseru is the capital of this enclaved, landlocked African nation.

7 This company is the world's largest manufacturer of race cars.

8 This culinary category is literally French for "outside the work."

9 With a venomous spur on its hind foot, this monotreme is one of the world's few venomous mammals.

10 One point for each of the top 12 casual dining restaurants with the most locations worldwide.

HERE'S THE DEAL

There is no airplane called the answer to Question #3. Whichever or whatever plane the president is on assumes this as a call sign. When the president is not on board, the planes go by *Special Air Mission* plus a number.

ANSWERS - 1. Edgar Allan Poe - 2. Care Bears - 3. Air Force One - 4. "Watch Me (Whip/Nae Nae)" - 5. Frequency Modulation - 6. Lesotho - 7. Porsche - 8. Hors d'Oeuvre - 9. Platypus - 10. Kelsey's Original Roadhouse, Olive Garden, Ruby Tuesday, Nando's, Outback Steakhouse, TGI Fridays, Buffalo Wild Wings, IHOP, Denny's, Chili's, Applebee's, Waffle House

40

Generics

1 This name for solid carbon dioxide was first copyrighted in 1925.

2 This now generic word for a potentially dangerous athletic apparatus was originally a trademark of the Griswold-Nissen [Answer] & Tumbling Company.

3 BF Goodrich first trademarked this word for their device originally meant to easily close rubber boots.

4 Made famous for its usage in Houston, the Monsanto Company still owns the trademark for this surface.

5 Inflated cushioning is the generic for this trademarked name for a packing product.

6 Sunbeam Products owns this trademark for an electric slow cooker.

7 Despite common usage, this word for a large waste container was once a trademark.

8 Describing a single-piece garment, Onesie is a trademark of this baby food company.

9 Meaning "a semiconvertible topped car," the word *Targa* is a trademark of this automaker.

10 Most hockey fans know that this vehicle is a trademarked name.

> **FUN FACT**
>
> Answer #8 has one of the oldest trademarked logos in American history. It consists of a 1928 baby picture of retired teacher, Ann Turner Cook. As of 2021, she was residing in South Florida and writing crime novels.

ANSWERS - 1. Dry Ice - 2. Trampoline - 3. Zipper - 4. AstroTurf - 5. Bubble Wrap - 6. Crockpot - 7. Dumpster - 8. Gerber - 9. Porsche - 10. Zamboni

Dodge, Duck, Dip, Dive, and Dodge

1 *Nam phrik* is a fish or shrimp paste–based spicy chili dipping sauce from this country.

2 In 2011, the Dodge Viper was spun off into the new SRT brand while Dodge's entire truck line was rebranded as this.

3 The 1953 film *Duck Dodgers in the 24½th Century* sees Daffy Duck and his sidekick Porky Pig vie with the yet unnamed Marvin the Martian for control of this planet.

ESPN8: THE OCHO

Inspired by the joke network ESPN8 in *Dodgeball: A True Underdog Story*, the real ESPN network in 2017 turned ESPNU into The Ocho for one day, showing actual dodgeball, roller derby, and other niche sports.

4 Scientists recently discovered Cuvier's beaked whales capable of diving up to a mile deep for an hour at a time off the coast of Cape Hatteras in this US state.

5 "Da' Dip" is a hip-dipping 1997 hit by this hip-hop artist.

6 Gunfighters and deputies Wyatt Earp and Bat Masterson made their name in this Kansas frontier city.

7 The Mighty Ducks of Anaheim were a 1993 expansion team alongside this other NHL franchise.

8 This four-time Olympic gold medalist and LGBTQ+ and HIV/AIDS activist has been called "probably the greatest diver in history."

9 Dip is an evil hairy dog that drinks people's blood in the myths of this easternmost autonomous community of Spain.

10 In 1895, the Dodgers were so named because Brooklyn residents were known for "dodging" this kind of public transit.

ANSWERS - 1. Thailand - 2. Ram - 3. Planet X - 4. North Carolina - 5. Freak Nasty - 6. Dodge City - 7. Florida Panthers - 8. Greg Louganis - 9. Catalonia - 10. Trolleys

Geography

1. This river, Europe's largest by watershed and discharge, flows solely through Russia.

2. The centermost of the Seven Hills of Rome, this hill has been called "the nucleus of the Roman Empire."

3. This city was known as Saigon until 1976.

4. Named after a Polish hero of the American Revolution, Mount Kosciuszko is the tallest mountain in this country.

5. This body of water bears the name of a famous explorer and separates Tierra del Fuego from mainland South America.

6. Also known as Signal Peak, the 8,751-foot-tall Guadalupe Peak is the tallest mountain in this US state.

7. Bishkek is the capital of this vowel-deficient nation.

8. This is the largest island in the Mediterranean Sea.

9. In what state is the city of Ypsilanti?

10. Furka, Grimsel, Gotthard, and Susten are all passes in this country.

TRIVIA INSIDER

In the trivia world, Answer #7 is something of a running joke. If, as quiz master, you wish to elicit a groan from your audience of seasoned trivia dorks, incorporate a question wherein this difficult-to-spell country is your answer.

ANSWERS - 1. Volga - 2. Palatine Hill - 3. Ho Chi Minh City - 4. Australia - 5. Straits of Magellan - 6. Texas - 7. Kyrgyzstan - 8. Sicily - 9. Michigan - 10. Switzerland

43

Random Stuff You Might Know

1 The Belfast Good Friday Agreement of 1998 effectively ended this period of Irish sectarian violence.

2 According to urban legend, this Chevrolet model did not sell well in Latin America because its name translates (sort of) to "doesn't go" in Spanish.

3 A Harry Potter scar, an R2-D2 paint scheme, and Sauron's One Ring have all adorned the great dome of this university as pranks.

4 A. J. Baime tells the true story of 1960s Le Mans races in his book *Go Like Hell*, which became this movie.

5 What food did FDR famously serve King George VI and the Queen of England on their 1939 visit to his Hyde Park, New York, estate?

6 This Canadian actor plays multiple clones in BBC America's *Orphan Black*.

7 Cofounded by a famous rapper and music exec Jimmy Iovine, this accessory maker is a wholly owned subsidiary of Apple.

8 After *Phantom of the Opera*, this is Broadway's second-longest-running show and longest-running revival.

9 The Dassler Brothers founded these two sportswear brands.

10 One point each for the top 11 wool-producing countries on Earth.

CRAZINESS

The rivalry between the Dasslers' two brands in Question #9 goes deep. The town of Herzogenaurach became known as "the town of bent necks," as everyone assessed their neighbors' allegiances by inspecting their footwear. Elderly residents say one brother even slept with the other's wife. Adi and Rudi Dassler are buried in the same cemetery but as far from each other as possible.

ANSWERS - 1. The Troubles - 2. Nova - 3. MIT - 4. *Ford v Ferrari* - 5. Hot Dogs - 6. Tatiana Maslany - 7. Beats - 8. *Chicago* - 9. Adidas and Puma - 10. South Africa, Sudan, India, UK, Iran, Turkey, Argentina, New Zealand, US, China, Australia

44

US History

1. He is known as the father of the Constitution.

2. This general led the Savannah Campaign, better known as his March to the Sea.

3. She founded the American Red Cross.

DID YOU KNOW?

Leonwood's first product was his Maine Hunting Shoe—now known under a different, answer-ruining name—which remains virtually unchanged in design since 1911.

4. He was the only US president born outside the lower 48 states.

5. In 1912, a man named Leon Leonwood founded this famed outdoors retailer.

6. In 1837, he invented the first commercially successful steel plow, creating a business giant that to this day bears his name.

7. The Teapot Dome scandal plagued this president's tenure.

8. The so-called First Lady of Civil Rights, Rosa Parks, sued this rap group for using her name in a song.

9. He was the longest-serving and arguably most important chief justice of the Supreme Court.

10. In 1947, he became the first pilot to break the sound barrier.

ANSWERS - 1. James Madison - 2. William Tecumseh Sherman - 3. Clara Barton - 4. Barack Obama - 5. L.L.Bean - 6. John Deere - 7. Warren G. Harding - 8. Outkast - 9. John Marshall - 10. Chuck Yeager

Before and After

See page 2 if you need a refresher on the rules.

1 Selling 21,529,464 worldwide, this car make and model was known as the "ladybird" in France AND this lazy US Army comic character constantly pesters Sergeant First Class Snorkel.

2 In 1871, Queen Victoria opened this South Kensington concert venue AND "Maneater" and "Private Eyes" duo.

3 Despite being a senator for more than a decade, this Kentucky Tea Party personality still calls himself an "outsider" AND the songwriter of "Blackbird" and "Lady Madonna."

4 The antihero of *Goodfellas* AND the fictional town setting of *Back to the Future*.

5 They're laboratory mice whose genes have been spliced AND former HUD secretary Ben Carson's previous career.

6 TV's Blossom, Bubbles, and Buttercup AND Cyndi Lauper song about having a blast.

7 The oil boom from the Bakken Formation has greatly lowered this midwestern state's unemployment rate AND she played Jane Volturi in the *Twilight* series.

8 This is the oldest home venue of any National Hockey League team AND Mormons believe that this biblical landmark is in Missouri.

9 Name for a popular custom ice cream creamery AND band behind the hit "Interstate Love Song."

10 *Guys and Dolls* song made popular by Sinatra AND she rode through Coventry naked in protest of her husband taxing his tenants at a high rate.

PRO TIP

The term *peeping Tom* refers to the man who looked at the naked rider in Question #10, despite orders to the contrary. Although the rider is based on an actual woman named Godgyfu who was mentioned in the Domesday Book (an 11th-century survey of England's citizens), the voyeur was added to the legend around the 17th century.

ANSWERS - 1. Volkswagen Beetle Bailey - 2. Royal Albert Hall and Oates - 3. Rand Paul McCartney - 4. Henry Hill Valley - 5. Pinky and the Brain Surgeon - 6. Powerpuff Girls Just Want to Have Fun - 7. North Dakota Fanning - 8. Madison Square Garden of Eden - 9. Cold Stone Temple Pilots - 10. Luck Be a Lady Godiva

Bad Movie Descriptions

It's not the movies that are bad; it's the descriptions that suck. Name that flick!

1 1939: A young girl travels to a new place, kills the first person she meets, and joins up with three strangers to kill again.

2 1998: A casual alcoholic becomes increasingly frustrated with his veteran friend's manifestation of PTSD.

3 2016: A man accidentally slaughters a group of *Branta canadensis*, becoming an American hero on an estuary.

4 1984: A heroic EPA official shuts down an illegal nuclear reactor made by unemployed college professors.

5 1980: A novelist suffers increasingly bad writer's block over the course of a winter.

6 1942: A bar owner's ex-girlfriend has serious baggage.

7 2003: Two friends finally return a family heirloom to its place of manufacture.

8 1977: A military strike radicalizes an orphan into following a foreign religion, leading to future terrorist attacks.

9 2013: Sandra Bullock has a really bad day at work.

10 1991: An amateur chef gives advice to a young woman starting her professional career.

DEEP DIVE

A keen Redditor pointed out the nuanced meaning of this quote from Answer #10: "I ate his liver with some fava beans and a nice Chianti." It's quite likely the character, a psychiatrist himself, is being treated with drugs called monoamine oxidase inhibitors (MAOIs). The three things you can't consume with MAOIs are liver, beans, and wine.

ANSWERS - 1. *The Wizard of Oz* - 2. *The Big Lebowski* - 3. *Sully* - 4. *Ghostbusters* - 5. *The Shining* - 6. *Casablanca* - 7. *Return of the King* - 8. *Star Wars* - 9. *Gravity* - 10. *The Silence of the Lambs*

Random Stuff You Might Know

1 This legendary Homeric character designed the Trojan Horse.

2 Jade Thirlwall, Perrie Edwards, Jesy Nelson, and Leigh-Anne Pinnock are the original members of this British girl group.

WHOA

....

The giant Easter Island heads are called Moai. Underneath those giant heads are little bodies partially buried in the ground. For real!

3 Famous for its giant heads carved from stone, Easter Island belongs to this nation.

4 A 2002 BBC poll selected this Bette Midler song as the UK's most popular song played at funerals.

5 The award for the player who best exemplifies sportsmanship and community involvement in baseball has been named after this athlete since 1973.

6 Despite striking visual similarities to the rapper's work, installation artist James Turrell has repeatedly denied that he had anything to do with the direction of this Drake music video.

7 This is the term for the geo-cultural region that spans central Iran through northern Iraq to eastern Syria and eastern Turkey.

8 Despite its name, this famous piece of headwear holds only three quarts.

9 The name for a pack of cyclists, *peloton* is archaic French for this military unit.

10 One point for each of the top-10-grossing retailers by product sales in the US (as of 2020).

ANSWERS - 1. Odysseus - 2. Little Mix - 3. Chile - 4. "Wind beneath My Wings" - 5. Roberto Clemente - 6. "Hotline Bling" - 7. Kurdistan - 8. 10-Gallon Hat - 9. Platoon - 10. Walmart, Amazon, Kroger, Costco, Walgreens, Home Depot, CVS, Target, Lowe's, Albertsons

Nineties Sitcoms

1 This never-seen sitcom neighbor wrote a book called *The Psychophysiological Indices of Amorous Connections among Termites of the Southwest*.

2 This Ukrainian-born *Resident Evil* star had a guest appearance as a French foreign exchange student in a 1989 episode of *Married with Children*.

3 Actors Patrick Duffy and Sasha Mitchell played uncle and nephew on both *Dallas* and this nineties sitcom.

4 The Hackett brothers' Sandpiper Air from the sitcom *Wings* was based here.

5 What were the names of *either* of Sabrina the Teenage Witch's aunts?

6 In a 1992 debate, Vice President Dan Quayle cited this sitcom's star's single motherhood as an indication of a breakdown in American values.

7 Falling in just behind "Here's Johnny!" and "D'oh!," *TV Guide* ranked this *Seinfeld* catchphrase as the third best TV catchphrase of all time.

8 Who sang "Tossed Salad and Scrambled Eggs," the theme song to *Frasier*?

9 Before *The Big Bang Theory*, Sara Gilbert and Johnny Galecki were both stars of this sitcom.

10 What was the name of the Tanners' dog in *Full House*?

FUN FACT

Whenever you watch an old rerun of *Full House*, remember that the dog has been dead for two decades. Look, that's just the truth.

13 Before and After

See page 2 if you need a refresher on the rules.

1 The third of the British TV trio including Jeremy Clarkson and Richard Hammond AND an ancient spring festival, International Workers' Day, or aviation distress call.

2 "If it don't fit, don't force it, you can grease it, make it easy" were the original (dirtier) lyrics to his song "Tutti Frutti" AND there's no evidence that this epithet-known English king spoke English.

3 The US Forest Service mascot AND a legendary Alabama football coach.

4 The founder of the Mormonism AND TGI Fridays founder Alan Stillman named this steakhouse by picking two random names from the New York phone book.

5 This manufactured pop group's only hit in the US was 2000's "Never Had a Dream Come True" AND this stupidly expensive denim company's pocket stitching is a script *A*, often in Swarovski crystals.

6 Julia Roberts plays Tess playing Julia Roberts in this sequel AND Brad Pitt won a 1996 Golden Globe for his supporting actor role in this sci-fi movie.

7 She stars alongside Vanessa Hudgens in the 2012 film *Spring Breakers* AND John Astin on TV, Raul Julia on film, and Nathan Lane on stage have all portrayed this family patriarch.

8 This July 21, 1861, engagement was known to the Confederates as First Manassas AND Jenny, Bubba, and Lieutenant Dan say this a lot.

FUN FACT

Confederates are losers. Both literally and figuratively. With a loser flag, flown by losers.

9 Mellencamp's "Hurts So Good" was released under this stage name AND Jules, Ellie, and Laurie mock one another over red wine in this sitcom.

10 2007 Simon Pegg–led cop comedy AND an early brand name for a dash-mounted radar detector.

ANSWERS - 1. James May Day - **2.** Little Richard the Lionheart - **3.** Smokey Bear Bryant - **4.** Joseph Smith & Wollensky - **5.** S Club 7 for All Mankind - **6.** Oceans 12 Monkeys - **7.** Selena Gomez Addams - **8.** First Battle of Bull Run Forrest Run - **9.** John Cougar Town - **10.** Hot Fuzz Buster

Dogs!

1 Before he died at a record age of 26 years, 8 months, Shiba Inu mix Pusuke lived in this country.

2 Most experts agree that this breed of working dog is the most intelligent.

3 A condition that results from inbreeding, dysplasia affects this portion of a dog's anatomy and causes dislocations, arthritis, and other health defects.

4 This famous sled dog led the last leg of diphtheria serum deliveries to Nome, Alaska, during a 1925 epidemic.

5 King Charles Spaniels, Yorkshire terriers, and Chihuahuas are all classified by this terminology.

6 Describing a dog and its relatives' genus, the word *Canis* was coined by this 18th-century Swedish inventor of taxonomy.

> **LOST IN TRANSLATION**
>
> *Inu* means "dog," so if you're saying "Shiba Inu dog," you're saying "Shiba dog dog," and you can take this advice all the way to the ATM machine.

7 Surprisingly, this diminutive breed of Tibetan monastery guard dog shows one of the purest genetic lineages to its wolf ancestors.

8 As head of CBS's children's programming, Fred Silverman invented this cartoon dog after listening to Frank Sinatra's version of "Strangers in the Night."

9 Harry Nilsson's song "One" was most famously performed in a 1969 cover by this band.

10 Decorated World War I hero dog Sergeant Stubby was found as a stray by troops outside Yale and, after the war, became one of the first canine mascots of this university.

8. Scooby-Doo - 9. Three Dog Night - 10. Georgetown

ANSWERS - 1. Japan - 2. Border Collie - 3. Hips - 4. Balto - 5. Toy - 6. Carl Linnaeus - 7. Lhasa Apso -

Random Stuff You Might Know

1 This longtime Celtic's nickname is "The Truth."

2 His screen debut was as Boo Radley in 1962's *To Kill a Mockingbird*.

3 What is the capital of Serbia?

4 This word describes a "shell-less terrestrial gastropod mollusk."

5 Shakespeare's King Henry V decides to wage war upon France after the dauphin's ambassador gives this sarcastic sporting-good gift to the crown of England.

6 Used unofficially by the Italian national football team, AC Roma, Baltimore Ravens, and USC, this song has been a sports stadium staple since 2003.

7 He became the president of the People's Republic of China in 2012.

DID YOU KNOW?

Usage of Winnie the Pooh's imagery in the People's Republic of China is severely censored, as bloggers have used Winnie to ridicule and caricature the Chinese president, and by mentioning it, this book will not be sold in the People's Republic of China.

8 *Data*, *Divisions of Figures*, and *Catoptrics* are three of the surviving works by this third-century BCE Greek mathematician.

9 This *Beverly Hills, 90210* star is the youngest of seven siblings.

10 One point for each of the 12 most popular girls' names from 1900 to 1909.

ANSWERS - 1. Paul Pierce - 2. Robert Duvall - 3. Belgrade - 4. Slug - 5. Tennis Balls - 6. "Seven Nation Army" - 7. Xi Jinping - 8. Euclid - 9. Jennie Garth - 10. Ethel, Florence, Alice, Mildred, Marie, Dorothy, Elizabeth, Ruth, Anna, Margaret, Helen, Mary

20th-Century Literature

1 President Barack Obama modeled his book *Dreams of My Father* on this 1952 Ralph Ellison novel.

2 Popocatépetl and Iztaccíhuatl are the two mountains of this type that overshadow the characters of a 1947 Malcolm Lowry novel.

3 In 1938, this novel won the Pulitzer Prize for best fiction; in 1940, its film adaptation won the Oscar for Best Picture.

4 In 1969, this Philip Roth novel was declared by the Australian government a prohibited import, probably because of the monologue about masturbating with the liver.

PRO TIP

If anyone ever says "literature" and "Mississippi," the answer is probably going to be Answer #7. That's the rule.

5 While filming a scene, Humphrey Bogart suggested a line based on Prospero's in *The Tempest* ("We are such stuff as dreams are made on"), which doesn't appear in this Dashiell Hammett novel.

6 Saleem Sinai discovers that anyone born in India between midnight and 1:00 a.m. on August 15, 1947, has supernatural powers in *Midnight's Children*, written by this *Satanic Verses* author.

7 The poverty-stricken Bundren family attempt to bury the remains of Addie Bundren in her hometown of Jefferson, Mississippi, in *As I Lay Dying*, written by this southern author.

8 This 1947 Pulitzer Prize–winning novel's name is taken from the nursery rhyme "Humpty Dumpty."

9 European cousin Countess Olenska disrupts Newland Archer and May Welland's perfect marriage in this 1920 Edith Wharton novel.

10 "On Friday noon, July the twentieth, 1714, the finest bridge in all Peru broke and precipitated five travelers into the gulf below" begins *The Bridge of San Luis Rey* by this author.

Before and After

See page 2 if you need a refresher on the rules.

1 Dorothy marries Blanche's uncle in the series finale of this show AND Joe Francis's soft-core porn franchise.

2 The hero of *Talladega Nights* AND "Across 110th Street" songwriter and singer.

BEHIND THE STICKS

In a modern bar, the cocktail in Question #9 is typically Guinness over hard cider, preferably draft. I prefer Crispin's. It's drier, more tart, and less syrupy-sweet than some other ciders.

3 The cocreator of Rocawear AND the third dimension in Cartesian coordinates.

4 Willie Mays's nickname AND the stars of the *House Party* film franchise.

5 The Fresh Prince's surrogate father figure AND former 11-time championship-winning NBA head coach nicknamed the Zen Master.

6 Many sources cite this 1959 Miles Davis classic as the best-selling jazz album of all time AND the highest-priced Johnnie Walker product.

7 The winner of 1973's Battle of the Sexes tennis match AND from 1998 until 2007, Patton Oswalt played Spence Olchin on this sitcom.

8 The queen of soul AND founded in 1964, this Pennsylvania-based company specializes in commemorative coins.

9 This beer cocktail was originally stout and champagne AND Lou Reed and John Cale's 1960s band.

10 The Murano's slightly smaller crossover SUV sibling AND the first stand-alone *Star Wars* anthology film.

ANSWERS - 1. Golden Girls Gone Wild - 2. Ricky Bobby Womack - 3. Jay Z Axis - 4. Say Hey Kid N Play - 5. Uncle Phil Jackson - 6. Kind of Blue Label - 7. Billie Jean King of Queens - 8. Aretha Franklin Mint - 9. Black Velvet Underground - 10. Nissan Rogue One

World Currencies

1 Meaning "let it become," this word describes a currency issued by government law.

2 Sweden was the first European country to issue paper currency, because an overabundant supply of this metal would've caused devalued coins to weigh several kilograms.

3 This four-letter word or its derivations describe the most popular fractional currency category name in the world.

4 By percentage of daily trading, this is the world's third-most-valuable currency after the US dollar and the euro.

5 The anonymous programmer or group of programmers going by the name Satoshi Nakamoto invented this cryptocurrency.

6 Named after a place rich with gold deposits, this currency is a shortening of the Dutch word for "Ridge of White Waters."

7 On April 2, 1792, the US dollar was officially defined as 371¼₆ grains of pure silver in a report to Congress by this man.

8 The Overseas Exchange Office of this continent issues nonlegal tender dollars, the purchase of which help fund scientific endeavors.

9 In 2013, the time on the clock featured on the reverse of this American bill was changed from 4:10 to 10:30.

> **NOBODY KNOWS**
> ....
> Answer #9 is the only US currency depicting a building outside of Washington, DC, but that's got an obvious reason. What nobody actually knows is why the time was changed, or what the significance of either time was. The bureau has no record of an answer to either question.

10 By not participating in the FOREX market, the North Korean won and Cuban peso are classified as this 14-letter word starting with *N*.

ANSWERS - 1. Fiat - 2. Copper - 3. Cent - 4. Japanese Yen - 5. Bitcoin - 6. Rand - 7. Alexander Hamilton - 8. Antarctica - 9. $100 Bill - 10. Nonconvertible

Random Stuff You Might Know

1 She is the protagonist of *The Scarlet Letter*.

2 A support team consisting of a dynamic go-getter, a genius, and a man from Ireland from the core of this Channel 4 sitcom.

3 Commissioned by dictator Nicolae Ceaușescu in 1986, the world's largest palace, world's most expensive building, and world's heaviest building is the Palace of Parliament of this country.

NOBODY NOSE

Legend has it that the Danish duelist's prosthetic nose in Question #6 was gold or silver but lost to history. His remains were exhumed in 2010 to discover his cause of death (it was uremia, but really everyone knew they were looking for the nose). Though it had been missing since at least his first exhumation in 1901, scientists concluded that the nose was brass from trace chemical amounts of the alloy on his skull.

4 The Haupt Conservatory, Stone Mill, and Peggy Rockefeller Rose Garden are features of this verdant New York landmark.

5 This year marked Joe DiMaggio's last season, Mickey Mantle's first season, and announcer Bob Sheppard's first year as Yankee Stadium PA announcer.

6 This Danish astronomer famously lost his nose in a duel.

7 He was the first cast member of *Beverly Hills, 90210* to direct an episode.

8 Electro is a supervillain nemesis of this superhero.

9 Groom Lake is another name for this US Air Force facility.

10 One point for each of the nine members of the Fellowship of the Ring.

ANSWERS - 1. Hester Prynne - 2. *The IT Crowd* - 3. Romania - 4. New York Botanical Garden - 5. 1951 - 6. Tycho Brahe - 7. Jason Priestley - 8. Spider-Man - 9. Area 51 - 10. Frodo, Samwise, Merry, Pippin, Gandalf, Gimli, Legolas, Aragorn, Boromir

Animals

1. John Calipari has coached this college basketball team since 2009.

2. This animal's extant species are the white, black, Indian, Javan, and Sumatran.

3. Bergmann's rule dictates that the body mass of an animal increases with this change in environment.

4. This was the most prominent physical feature of the pre-dinosaur, mammal-like reptile Dimetrodon.

5. This is the largest dolphin.

6. He was the lead singer of the Animals.

7. A recently discovered amber specimen for the first time displayed intact examples of this physiological feature of dinosaurs.

8. This mammal has killed more people than any other wild mammal.

9. Al Kaline spent his entire career on this baseball team.

10. New York City boasts the world's densest population of this fastest animal on Earth.

DID YOU KNOW?

Despite generating billions of dollars in revenue, college football and basketball players are not paid salaries. What a crazy fact! That people aren't paid even though they make billions of dollars for corporations, states, and institutions. Insane, right?

ANSWERS - 1. Kentucky Wildcats - 2. Rhinoceros - 3. Colder Temperatures - 4. Sail Back - 5. Orca - 6. Eric Burdon - 7. Feathers - 8. Tiger - 9. Detroit Tigers - 10. Peregrine Falcon

57

Science

1 With an increase in enthalpy, the melting of an ice cube is a physical manifestation of this kind of thermal process.

2 The Calvin cycle describes the chemical reactions that turn CO_2 into glucose during this plant process.

DID YOU KNOW?

Unlike the rather scientific Calvin cycle, the Hobbes cycle is actually a red wagon with a stuffed tiger in it pushed down a hill into a pond or evil snowman or imaginary dinosaur.

3 This word describes the agent upon which an enzyme acts.

4 This word refers to a macromolecule that comprises repeating subunits.

5 Since 1919, the IUPAC has standardized the definitions and nomenclature in English-language chemistry; the *P* stands for this.

6 In geology, egg-shaped ridges called drumlins are created by this force of nature.

7 As the universe's rate of expansion is accelerating, current cosmology theorizes that the universe will end in either the Big Chill or the Big Rip, not this "Big" theory of ultimate contraction and collapse.

8 This word describes either heredity or something that should be taxed at like 95 percent to eliminate generational wealth.

9 Many languages, including French, Italian, and Russian, call this abundant gas *azote*, which refers to its properties and is Greek for "no life."

10 French Parliament's ban on inoculation prompted this author in 1734 to write that his countrymen had so little regard for their children that "had inoculation been practiced in France, it would have saved the lives of thousands."

ANSWRS - 1. Endothermic Process - 2. Photosynthesis - 3. Substrate - 4. Polymer - 5. Pure (International Union of Pure and Applied Chemistry) - 6. Glaciers - 7. Big Crunch - 8. Inheritance - 9. Nitrogen - 10. Voltaire

World Capitals

I name the country, you give the capital. That's it. No room for error. Either you got it, or you don't.

1 Azerbaijan

2 Senegal

3 Zambia

4 Sudan

5 New Zealand

6 Kyrgyzstan

7 Honduras

8 Democratic Republic of the Congo

9 Republic of the Congo

10 Papua New Guinea

> **PRO TIP**
>
> Use free flashcard app Anki to memorize things with finite sets, like Oscar winners, countries, and capitals.

ANSWERS - 1. Baku - 2. Dakar - 3. Lusaka - 4. Khartoum - 5. Wellington - 6. Bishkek - 7. Tegucigalpa - 8. Kinshasa - 9. Brazzaville - 10. Port Moresby

59

Random Stuff You Might *Not* Know

1 In copyright infringement parlance, *DRM* stands for this.

2 Steubenville, Ohio, has a massive mural in tribute to this hometown crooner, born Dino Paul Crocetti.

3 Since 1994, this party has won every one of South Africa's elections.

4 Thomas Jefferson University is a private college in this city, where its namesake did his most famous writing.

5 Beck designed glasses for Warby Parker in a promotion with this Dave Eggers–founded publishing house and online literary portal.

6 This is the title of Salvador Dalí's famous painting of melting clocks, which are actually melting pocket watches.

7 This element, with atomic number 101, is named after the creator of the periodic table of elements.

WHEN YOU WISH UPON A STAR

Winnie the Pooh is currently the final Disney animated film made with traditional, hand-drawn animation techniques rather than 3D computer animation.

8 The West Slavic linguistic subgroup of Lechitic includes Kashubian, Pomeranian, Silesian, and—with 45 million native speakers, which is by far the most numerous—this language.

9 This MP from Islington North was the leader of the UK's Labour Party from 2015 to 2020.

10 One point for each of the nine feature films released by Walt Disney Animated Studios between 2010 and 2020. (Note: not Pixar.)

ANSWERS – 1. Digital Rights Management – 2. Dean Martin – 3. ANC, African National Congress – 4. Philadelphia – 5. McSweeney's – 6. Persistence of Memory – 7. Mendelevium – 8. Polish – 9. Jeremy Corbyn – 10. Tangled, Winnie the Pooh, Wreck-It Ralph, Frozen, Big Hero 6, Zootopia, Moana, Ralph Breaks the Internet, Frozen II

Philosophy

1 All humans are mortal; all Greeks are humans; therefore all Greeks are mortal is an example of this argument of deductive reasoning.

2 Thomism refers to the philosophy of this Dominican friar and saint.

3 Attributed to Laozi, this Chinese work's title translates to *The Great Book of the Way*.

4 Although he had two teachers before him, medieval Muslim intellectuals referred to this Greek philosopher as the "First Teacher."

5 While finishing his *Phenomenology of Spirit*, Hegel's city of Jena was besieged and captured by this individual, who "astride a horse, reaches out over the world and masters it."

6 According to Guinness, this Robert Pirsig book, of which 5 million copies have been sold, holds the record of 121 publisher rejections for a worldwide best seller.

> **HERE YOU GO**
>
> Hegel is arguing that reality is merely an a priori adjunct of non-naturalistic ethics, Kant via the categorical imperative is holding that ontologically it exists only in the imagination, and Marx is claiming it was offside.

7 Schopenhauer was an important influence on such historical greats as Einstein, Nietzsche, Freud, and this "Ride of the Valkyries" composer.

8 Literally defined as "to join or unite," this word got its more relevant meaning of "steady control of senses" in the fifth-century BCE religious texts *Katha Upanishad*.

9 *Love, ideal, solid*, and *crystal* can all be preceded by this three-syllable philosophical description.

10 This branch of philosophy is centered on the critical reflection on art, culture, and nature.

10. Aesthetics
6. *Zen and the Art of Motorcycle Maintenance* - 7. Richard Wagner - 8. Yoga - 9. Platonic -
- Napoleon - 5. Napoleon -
ANSWERS - 1. Syllogism - 2. Saint Thomas Aquinas - 3. *Tao Te Ching* - 4. Aristotle - 5. Napoleon -

Before and After

See page 2 if you need a refresher on the rules.

1 The subtitle to 2004's *Team America* AND this six-episode show spawned the successful *Naked Gun* series of movies.

2 "Izzo (H.O.V.A.)" and "Takeover" are both Jay-Z songs by this producer AND Yul Brynner plays a violent theme park android in this movie.

3 Rapper who has starred in movies like *Any Given Sunday*, *SWAT*, and *Deep Blue Sea* AND this reclusive author's last published work was a 1965 New Yorker novella called *Hapworth 16, 1924*.

4 Rick James and Kevin Johnston cowrote this Eddie Murphy song AND Captain Lou Albano appears in the videos for both "Girls Just Wanna Have Fun" and this Cyndi Lauper song.

FUN FACT

Wyoming's largest airport is also the only airport located inside a National Park. So green!

5 He played Pacey Witter on *Dawson's Creek* and Peter Bishop on *Fringe* AND the largest airport in Wyoming is in this town.

6 A 1943 Betty Smith novel about the Irish American Nolan family's ordeals in Williamsburg AND Coney Island's NY Mets affiliate.

7 This structure's official paint color is international orange AND children reach a mythical kingdom across a creek in this book.

8 TV show featuring Dennis, Dee, Charlie, Mac, and Frank AND Connie Mack's team from 1901 to 1950.

9 He plays *Law and Order SVU*'s Fin Tutuola AND Deutsche Telekom's mobile subsidiaries outside of Germany.

10 Contrary to popular belief, this company's logo is not a spinning propeller AND "Once, on a trek through Afghanistan, we lost our corkscrew and were forced to live on food and water for several days," quipped this vaudevillian and screen star.

ANSWERS - 1. World Police Squad - 2. Kanye West World - 3. LL Cool J. D. Salinger - 4. Party All the Time after Time - 5. Joshua Jackson Hole - 6. A Tree Grows in Brooklyn Cyclones - 7. Golden Gate Bridge to Terabithia - 8. It's Always Sunny in Philadelphia Athletics - 9. Ice T Mobile - 10. BMW. C. Fields

Game Shows

16

1 In 1938, the very first television game show consisted of one of these grade school contests.

2 Although the dollar values changed throughout the years, he was the only host of *Pyramid* from 1973 to 1988.

3 First running on ABC in the 1960s, then revived in the 1990s by Lifetime, this show consisted of a series of questions to determine the amount of time contestants could spend in the aisles of a grocery store.

4 Along with *Let's Make a Deal*, this is the only daytime nonsyndicated network game show currently on the air.

5 This game show is derived from a 1990s Swedish show called *Expedition Robinson*.

6 From 1998 to 2001, she was the permanent center square on *Hollywood Squares*.

7 The 1986 debut of this game show tripled the ratings of the then-fledgling Nickelodeon Network.

8 When host Ralph Edwards announced he would host his game show in the first town to change its name, Hot Springs, New Mexico, became this.

9 In 1992, Samsung Electronics was sued for creating an ad with a robot replicating this TV host's signature move.

10 In *Cheers*, what was Cliff Clavin's answer to the *Jeopardy!* question, "Archibald Leach, Bernard Schwartz, and Lucille LeSueur."

DID YOU KNOW?

"Civil Servants,"
"Stamps from
Around the World,"
"Mothers and Sons,"
"Beer," "Bar Trivia,"
and "Celibacy" were
Cliff Clavin's *Jeopardy!*
categories.

ANSWERS - 1. Spelling Bee - **2.** Dick Clark - **3.** Supermarket Sweep - **4.** The Price Is Right - **5.** *Survivor* - **6.** Whoopi Goldberg - **7.** *Double Dare* - **8.** Truth or Consequences - **9.** Vanna White - **10.** "Who are three people who have never been in my kitchen?"

Random Stuff You Might Know

1 Comedian T. D. "Daddy" White's 1828 blackface minstrel character bore this name, later synonymous with racist legislation.

2 Chennai, Kolkata, Chittagong, and Yangon are all major port cities on this body of water.

3 Although unrelated, a former Philadelphia Eagles Pro Bowler and current NBA All-Star point guard share this last name.

4 *The Black Candle*, narrated by Maya Angelou, is a 2012 documentary on the founding and tenets of this American holiday.

5 Quebecois for a dish containing fries, gravy, and cheese curds.

6 To protect their anonymity, Lenin, Trotsky, Golda Meir, and Tito are all adopted pseudonyms described by this bellicose three-word term.

7 Since 2008, Ralph Wilson Stadium, Wrigley Field, Fenway Park, Heinz Field, and Citizens Bank Park have all hosted this New Year's Day (or thereabouts) sporting event.

FUN FACT

One time I asked Question #10 and one team exclaimed, "How should we know? We're Jews!" and I replied, "So were most of them!"

8 This capital city is 50 miles north of Tallinn, 250 miles east of Stockholm, and 190 miles west of St. Petersburg.

9 What is the first name of Britney Spears's first child?

10 One point for each of the top 10 most-often-mentioned people or entities in the Bible.

James Bond

17

1 Author Kate Westbrook has written three novels based on the diaries of this Bond secretary.

2 Ian Fleming chose the name James Bond, the "dullest name I have ever heard," from an author on books about this subject.

3 Ian Fleming's Jamaican estate GoldenEye was—after his death—sold to this music star.

BUZZER BEATER

No amount of preparation for *Jeopardy!* can prepare you for having to say the answer to Question #7 with a straight face.

4 Goldfinger was employed by the evil organization SMERSH, based on this real-life spy agency.

5 Starring Jane Seymour as Solitaire, this 1973 feature was the first Bond movie with Roger Moore.

6 *GoldenEye, Tomorrow Never Dies*, and *The World Is Not Enough* featured Bond driving or riding products by this auto and motorcycle maker.

7 James Bond says, "I must be dreaming" after hearing this Bond girl's incredibly unsubtle name.

8 The surfing scene in *Die Another Day* was performed by this pro surfer and husband to volleyball star Gabrielle Reece.

9 Audiences cheered at the premiere of *The Spy Who Loved Me* when after skiing off a cliff, Bond deploys a parachute with this on it.

10 Seven-foot, one-inch actor Richard Kiel was famous as Bond villain Jaws and as Mr. Larson in this 1996 comedy.

Before and After

See page 2 if you need a refresher on the rules.

1 James Todd Smith's stage name AND the creator of *Alias*.

2 The man in the yellow hat was the steward of this character AND this leader of the US Third Army during World War II was nicknamed Old Blood and Guts.

3 In Greek mythology, the kidnapped sister of Castor, Pollux, and Clytemnestra AND the MVP of 1992's Super Bowl XXVII.

DID YOU KNOW?

The Beatles famously performed Answer #6 for the satellite-transmitted television special *Our World*, to which Pablo Picasso and Maria Callas also contributed.

4 The voice of *Kung Fu Panda*'s Po AND a sap, card game, or General Pershing's nickname.

5 Chris Elliott plays creepy Woogie in this movie AND this monarch's head was presented after her 1587 execution, revealing her long auburn hair to be a wig.

6 In a 1971 interview, John Lennon admitted that this 1967 Beatles' hit was a propaganda song AND the newly elected UK prime minister is caught kissing his former maid at a school play in this movie.

7 Since 1998, he has filed over 20 suits for defamation, which included allegations of homosexuality and slander of his religion AND the McDonnell Douglas AGM 109 Tomahawk.

8 Because of a song, this phone number has been the subject of countless suits and bidding wars AND Morris the Cat's preferred brand of cat food.

9 From 1833 to 1835, this figure of folklore was the first representative from Tennessee's 12th district AND Miami detectives Sonny and Rico, respectively.

10 The recording of the heart's electrical activity, abbreviated AND *Beg for Mercy* was the 2003 debut album of this Jamaica, Queens, rap crew.

ANSWERS - 1. LL Cool J, J. Abrams - 2. Curious George Patton - 3. Helen of Troy Aikman - 4. Jack Black Jack - 5. There's Something about Mary Queen of Scots - 6. All You Need Is Love, Actually - 7. Tom Cruise Missile - 8. 867-5309 Lives - 9. Davy Crockett and Tubbs - 10. EKG-Unit

Bartending

1 On a soda gun, the letter Q indicates this beverage.

2 *Blind Pig* and *Blind Tiger* are synonyms for this type of establishment.

3 In 1988, Roger Ebert said, "The more you think about what happens in it, the more you realize how empty and fabricated it really is" about this movie.

4 In 1875, writer Horatio Alger popularized this word for forcibly evicting someone from the premises.

5 Falling out of favor in the 1860s, this drink got its name in the 1880s after coming back into style.

6 Daisuke Inoue invented this machine in Japan in 1971—but never patented it.

7 Take a jigger of cognac, a sugar cube, and Peychaud's Bitters, stir it over ice, and pour it into a second glass swirled with a dash of absinthe and you have this classic New Orleans cocktail.

8 No longer used, the term *fern bar* referred to preppy singles bars that were popularized in the 1970s by this Manhattan bar that later became a national chain.

9 A Gibson is gin and vermouth garnished with this item.

10 Elijah Craig is said to be the inventor of this spirit.

> **BEHIND THE STICKS**
>
> The Q on the soda gun stands for "quinine," an antimalarial bark extract, once a prominent ingredient in Answer #1. Quinine was first isolated in 1823 and drunk throughout the British Empire—mixed with gin, of course—to stave off tropical sicknesses.

ANSWERS - 1. Tonic Water - 2. Speakeasy - 3. Cocktail - 4. Bounce - 5. Old-Fashioned - 6. Karaoke - 7. Sazerac - 8. TGI Fridays - 9. Pickled Onion - 10. Bourbon Whiskey

Random Stuff You Might Know

1 This famous Algonquin-speaking historical figure's name, given by her father, Powhatan, was a nickname meaning "little playful and annoying one."

2 Although cited as early as 1939, the 1950 NCAA basketball champions from City College of New York popularized this underdog sports term.

LUCK OF HISTORY

Answer #8 ended up being synonymous with destruction and chaos, but the Goths ended up being synonymous with Skyler, who now goes by Dark Storm, but he'll grow out of it when he gets to college.

3 Viral photo website theCHIVE sells "BFM" T-shirts that feature a picture of this actor in 3D glasses.

4 This city is the county seat of Cook County.

5 Jazz composer and bandleader Charles Mingus played this instrument.

6 Who is the number-one employer in the People's Republic of China?

7 The company founded by Milanese fashion partners Domenico and Stefano.

8 Popular for destroying artwork, this tribe in fact helped maintain and spread Roman artwork into the Middle Ages, according to modern historians.

9 Famous for playing a TV doctor, this British comedian's writing and acting partner for nearly 20 years was Stephen Fry.

10 One point for each of the top 12 players with the most career MLB plate appearances.

Famous Quotes

1 This FDR quote was said about the Great Depression and not World War II, as many believe.

2 "A horse, a horse, my kingdom for a horse!" is from this Shakespeare play.

3 "There's snakes out there this big" is a quote of seminal cinematic importance from this 1997 artistic tour de force.

4 These three words were said by John Wilkes Booth after shooting President Lincoln.

5 In what year did Ronald Reagan say, "Mr. Gorbachev, tear down this wall!"?

6 *"Alea iacta est"*—translation: "The die is cast"—said Julius Caesar upon crossing this river.

7 "I was free, and they should be free also; I would make a home for them in the North, and the Lord helping me, I would bring them all there," said this American hero in 1886.

THE PROBLEM WITH QUOTES . . .

. . . is everyone has one. So many quotes are so hard to verify because they've been taken out of context, perverted, altered, misattributed, stolen, and meme-ified until the original source is lost to the mists of the Internet.

8 "I don't think there will be a woman prime minister in my lifetime," said this leader in 1973, just six years before she attained the position.

9 This quote, apparently of unknown folk origin, was first recorded in Jean-Jacques Rousseau's *Confessions* when Marie Antoinette was nine years old.

10 "The Ballot or the Bullet" speech by Malcolm X on March 29, 1964, features a famous quote about this American landmark.

ANSWERS - 1. "The only thing we have to fear is fear itself." **- 2.** *Richard III* **- 3.** *Anaconda* **- 4.** *"Sic semper tyrannis"* (thus always to tyrants) **- 5.** 1987 **- 6.** The Rubicon **- 7.** Harriet Tubman **- 8.** Margaret Thatcher **- 9.** "Let them eat cake." **- 10.** Plymouth Rock

ROUND 2 / DIFFICULTY LEVEL 1 2 3 **4** 5 6

Cartoons

1 The zoetrope, an early animation device, is this shape.

2 This 1940 Disney release was the first animated movie presented in stereophonic sound.

3 In 2020, Steven Spielberg developed a reboot of this beloved nineties cartoon.

FUN FACT
....

American Zoetrope is Francis Ford Coppola and George Lucas's film-production company based in San Francisco.

4 In 1991, the avant-garde assassin story *Æon Flux* premiered on this MTV animation showcase.

5 Name two out of three Belcher children from an animated sitcom that first aired in 2011.

6 These animated corporate mascots are variously known as Knisper, Knasper, and Knusper in Germany and Pif, Pof, and Paf in Italy.

7 The workplace of Tex Avery, Chuck Jones, and Bob Clampett, Termite Terrace is the famed animation backlot bungalow of this studio.

8 Dr. Drakken and Shego are the archvillains of this Disney Channel heroine.

9 A 1999 BBC special paid tribute to Monty Python's "Dead Parrot" sketch by having Eric Cartman attempt to return this fellow *South Park* character.

10 Baba Looey was the sidekick of this 1950s and '60s animated equine sheriff.

ANSWERS - 1. Cylinder - 2. *Fantasia* - 3. *Animaniacs* - 4. *Liquid Television* - 5. Tina, Gene, Louise - 6. Snap, Crackle, and Pop - 7. Warner Bros. - 8. Kim Possible - 9. Kenny - 10. Quick Draw McGraw

Famous Deaths

1 John McClane unclasps a watch, causing this villain to plummet to his death from the top of Nakatomi Plaza.

2 Despite being frozen by liquid nitrogen, this machine is finally killed after falling into a vat of molten steel.

3 He was killed by DEVGRU operators as part of Operation Neptune Spear.

4 He is trampled by wildebeests after hanging from a cliff by his paws and getting knocked off by his brother.

5 While sitting on the toilet, he is shot with a crossbow by his unloved son.

6 Alongside her boyfriend, she was killed in an ambush in Bienville Parish, Louisiana, on May 23, 1934.

7 He was hanged on December 2, 1859, less than a month after his failed raid on the Harper's Ferry arsenal.

8 Returning from a stay at her royal summer residence Roc Agel, she had a stroke, lost control of her car, and succumbed to her injuries on September 13, 1982.

9 A year and a half after he ordered the attack on Pearl Harbor, he was shot down over Bougainville by First Lieutenant Rex Barber on April 18, 1943.

10 Fifteenth-century executioner Geoffroy Thérage said he "greatly feared to be damned for he had burned" this holy woman.

> **THE 27 CLUB**
>
> The conceit that famous musicians tend to die at age 27—including counterculture luminaries like Brian Jones, Jim Morrison, Janis Joplin, and Jimi Hendrix, and later icons like Kurt Cobain and Amy Winehouse—is all a myth. In 2011, *The British Medical Journal* stated that there is no increased risk of death for musicians at age 27.

ANSWERS - 1. Hans Gruber - 2. T-1000 - 3. Osama bin Laden - 4. Mufasa - 5. Tywin Lannister - 6. Bonnie Parker - 7. John Brown - 8. Grace Kelly - 9. Isoroku Yamamoto - 10. Joan of Arc

Random Stuff You Might Know

1 Almaty is the largest city in this country.

2 With more than 2,200 versions, this is the most covered copyrighted song in history.

3 Smithfield, Westphalian, and Serrano refer to specific regional preparations of this food.

4 The Hofmeister Kink is an iconic styling cue adorning the C-pillar of this brand of automobile.

5 *Univoltinism* refers to organisms that do this only once a year.

6 Billionaire Peter Thiel founded a business that later merged with Elon Musk's X.com to form this company.

7 What does *NASDAQ* stand for?

8 George Howell's Boston-area chain The Coffee Connection invented and trademarked this beverage.

9 Where in the body would you find metatarsal bones?

10 One point for each of the first 12 member states of the European Union.

WE LIKE CARS

In automotive design, the *A-pillar* refers to the structure at the leading edge of the cabin, i.e., what holds up the windshield. The *B-pillar* would be the middle of the cabin, i.e., between the doors of a sedan. The *C-pillar* is the rear of the greenhouse, sloping toward the trunk.

ANSWERS - 1. Kazakhstan - **2.** "Yesterday" - **3.** Ham - **4.** BMW - **5.** Breed - **6.** PayPal - **7.** National Association of Securities Dealers Automated Quotations - **8.** Frappuccino - **9.** The Foot - **10.** Belgium, France, Italy, Luxembourg, The Netherlands, Germany (founder), Denmark, Ireland, UK, Greece, Portugal, Spain

Football Season

1. The movie *The Damned United* follows a largely fictional account of Brian Clough's disastrous 1974 tenure managing this First Division club.

2. Formerly sponsored by Carling and then by this what's in-your-wallet company, the football League Cup is now sponsored by Carabao energy drink.

3. While Real Madrid leads with 12 Champions League titles, this Italian club is second with 7.

4. The MetroStars, Manchester United, Everton, Bolton Wanderers, Colorado Rapids, and the US men's national team are on the résumé of this goalkeeper.

5. The October 12, 1935, league match against Arsenal saw the highest-capacity crowd ever at this Chelsea home stadium, with 83,905 in attendance.

6. One of the Soviet era's most heated rivalries was between Spartak Moscow and this now Ukrainian club.

7. Gareth Bale's record 100-million-euro transfer fee came as he was purchased by Real Madrid from this club.

8. From 1982 to 1984, this Juventus attacking midfielder was the only person before Lionel Messi to receive three consecutive Ballon d'Or awards.

9. The professional players of Ipswich Town played footballers alongside actors in this 1981 World War II football movie.

10. Who was captain of England's 1966 World Cup champion side?

> **HAROLD GODWINSON, GODWINSOME, GODLOSESOME**
>
> In 1066, winning a battle with the same name as Answer #5, Harold repelled a Norwegian invasion, thus preserving Anglo-Saxon England—for three weeks. Harold tried to repel another invasion less than a month later by William of Normandy, better known as William the Conqueror, who, uh, conquered.

ANSWERS - 1. Leeds United - 2. Capital One - 3. A.C. Milan - 4. Tim Howard - 5. Stamford Bridge - 6. Dynamo Kyiv - 7. Tottenham Hotspur F.C. - 8. Michel Platini - 9. *Escape to Victory* - 10. Bobby Moore

73

Before and After

See page 2 if you need a refresher on the rules.

1 Frank Oz and Jim Henson originated the roles of these roommates AND the Hall of Famer nicknamed Mr. Cub.

2 Singers of "To Be with You" or Carrie Bradshaw's love interest AND this *Sesame Street* character revealed on Twitter that his international "cousins" are a variety of different colors (i.e., not yellow).

3 Dense Thomas Pynchon novel about the search for German V-2 rockets after World War II AND Twink, Starlite, and Lurky are this animated character's companions.

4 This corporation was created with the 1892 merger of the Edison Company and Thomson-Houston Electric AND Jeff Lynne's Beatlesque pop rock band.

5 On September 15, 2008, this company filed the largest bankruptcy in US history AND the compilers of "Rapunzel," "Rumpelstiltskin," and "Snow White."

6 The four primary voices in a chorus, abbreviated and from highest to lowest register AND Homer Simpson's barbershop quartet.

THE SIMMMMPPPSONNNNSSSS

The four items Homer finds at the swap meet in episode 9F21 "Homer's Barbershop Quartet" are the Declaration of Independence, Action Comics #1, Inverted Jenny stamps, and a "Strata-who-vius."

7 "The Heart of Rock and Roll" is the first track on *Sports* by this artist AND the leaders of 1804's Corps of Discovery.

8 "I'm Too Sexy" is their signature hit AND PBS's most famous Presbyterian minister.

9 This actor played the hero of the 2004 British film *Layer Cake* AND this Scottish talk show host rose to fame in *The Drew Carey Show*.

10 A B-list pop singer or ascorbic acid AND the author of *The Voyage of the Dawn Treader*.

ANSWERS - 1. Bert and Ernie Banks - 2. Mr. Big Bird - 3. Gravity's Rainbow Brite - 4. General Electric Light Orchestra - 5. Lehman Brothers Grimm - 6. S A T B Sharps - 7. Huey Lewis and Clark - 8. Right Said Fred Rogers - 9. Daniel Craig Ferguson - 10. Vitamin C. S. Lewis

Bravo TV

1 Bravo's first major broadcast was the 1992 Texaco-sponsored adaptation of this Shakespeare play.

2 *Don't Be Tardy* stars this *Real Housewives of Atlanta* personality.

3 Harold Dieterle is the very first winner of this Bravo reality competition.

4 Bravo's *Married to Medicine* follows the lives of female doctors and doctors' wives in this southern state capital.

5 From 1982 until 2007, *Project Runway*'s Tim Gunn rose from teacher to associate dean to chair of the fashion department of this art and design college.

6 At more than four hours, the longest *Inside the Actors Studio* interview ever became two one-hour episodes of conversation with this film director.

7 *Watch What Happens Live* is hosted by this Bravo personality.

8 Patti Stanger is better known by this nickname, the title of her show.

9 *Real Housewives of New York*'s Luann de Lesseps claims she is a countess because her ex-husband's great-grandfather received a title for building this artificial maritime thoroughfare.

10 "Land Ahoy Finally," "Naughty Yachties," and "Shut Your Porthole" are all clever episode titles for this Bravo series about chartered yachts.

THAT'S A LOTTA WIVES!

There have been 10 American and 13 international installments of the *Real Housewives* franchise. *Real Housewives of Bangkok* is slated to be the next international version. Since you're reading this in the future, can you tell me if the ladies ever settle their beef after that incident in the lobby of the Anantara Siam Hotel? You know, THAT incident.

Random Stuff You Might Know

1 This British overseas territory is thought to be the last known location of Neanderthals before their extinction.

2 This Paul Simon song was inspired by the name of an egg and chicken dish on a Chinese menu.

3 This 1955 play is a fictional account of the famous Scopes Monkey Trial.

4 This is the 1895 trademark for diacetylmorphine by Bayer Pharmaceuticals.

5 Running from 2007 to 2009, this ABC fantasy-comedy centered around supernatural, life-giving powers of pie maker Ned.

6 What is the second-most-populous city in Japan?

7 An alkaloid is a naturally occurring organic compound containing at least one atom of this element.

8 Whereas Luciano Pavarotti was from Italy, his fellow members of the Three Tenors, Carreras and Domingo, are from this country.

9 This food's name is Mexican Spanish slang for "light lunch," but it literally means a plug or wadding to fill a hole.

10 One point each for the 10 most populous cities in the US in 1880.

ANSWERS - 1. Gibraltar - **2.** "Mother and Child Reunion" - **3.** *Inherit the Wind* - **4.** Heroin - **5.** *Pushing Daisies* - **6.** Yokohama - **7.** Nitrogen - **8.** Spain - **9.** Taco - **10.** New Orleans, San Francisco, Cincinnati, Baltimore, St. Louis, Boston, Chicago, Brooklyn, Philadelphia, New York

The 2000s

1. With 32.2 million units sold, he was the highest-selling music artist of the 2000s.

2. This former *View* and *Fox and Friends* personality was the fourth-place finisher on the second season of *Survivor*.

3. Tom Cruise used this four-letter word, meaning "fluent but shallow and insecure," to confront Matt Lauer during an interview.

4. What was the highest-grossing movie of the 2000s?

5. In 2004, armed gunmen stole *Madonna* and this other famous Edvard Munch painting from a Norwegian museum.

6. On September 15, 2008, MTV aired a three-hour series finale for this long-running afternoon show.

7. Russell Simmons and his then wife, Kimora Lee Simmons, founded this women's and girl's fashion line.

8. This was the only team to win two World Series in the 2000s.

9. This *NSYNC album was the best-selling album of the 2000s.

10. A 2004 made-for-TV movie subtitled *The Dale Earnhardt Story* bore this single digit as its title.

AGE IS JUST A NUMBER

Diversify your trivia experience—and enhance your inclusion—by spreading out the years. Yeah, a round on 1988 might be lost on someone born in the 1990s, but it goes both ways. If you go for a round on 1960s sitcoms, for example, balance your evening out with something on Number-One Hits of 2018. That'll teach 'em.

Before and After

See page 2 if you need a refresher on the rules.

1 AC/DC's megahit follow-up album to *Highway to Hell* AND a *Latrodectus hesperus*, or Scarlett Johansson in the Marvel Universe.

2 In 2016, Steven Spielberg directed a film adaptation of this Roald Dahl book AND the leader of Special Sauce.

3 Christopher Walken received an Oscar nomination for Best Supporting Actor as a con man's father in this movie AND an energetic concert hall dance popularized in 1840s Paris.

4 This Quaker landowner founded Philadelphia AND this comedy magic duo appeared in the video for Run DMC's "It's Tricky."

5 This R&B singer's biggest hit was 1991's "Everybody Plays the Fool" AND although this prime minister was infamous for appeasing Hitler, modern historians think his delay allowed the UK to prepare.

6 The directors of *Fargo* and *The Big Lebowski* AND this Irish family comedy drama was Edward Burns's 1995 directorial debut.

7 Father of Jaden and Willow AND alma mater of Barbara Bush and Sylvia Plath.

8 The singer of "Take Me Home, Country Roads" AND Chauncey Billups and Carmelo Anthony were the late 2000s core of this franchise.

9 A hedonist remains unchanged while his portrait deteriorates in this Oscar Wilde novel AND the nickname for the *New York Times*.

10 "Git 'er done" is the catchphrase of this stand-up comic AND the actor who played the villain of *Iron Man 3* and antihero of *Memento*.

BEHIND THE STICKS

Please don't order a "Black and Tan"—it was the nickname for the Royal Irish Constabulary, a brutal British organization that committed crimes against humanity on the Irish people during the Irish War of Independence. (It would be like ordering a "Nathan Bedford Forrest" cocktail.) Ask for a "Half and Half" instead.

ANSWERS - 1. Back in Black Widow - 2. The B F G Love - 3. Catch Me If You Can Can - 4. William Penn and Teller - 5. Aaron Neville Chamberlain - 6. The Coen Brothers McMullen - 7. Will Smith College - 8. John Denver Nuggets - 9. The Picture of Dorian Gray Lady - 10. Larry the Cable Guy Pearce

Clothing and Fashion

1 Counterfeits of this Italian high-fashion brand are easily spotted because fakes do not have a deep cutout in the middle of the letter *R* in the logo.

2 Madisar, Kodagu, Karnataka, and Nivi are but four of the 80 recorded ways one can wear this subcontinental garment.

3 This is the name for the small plastic or metal sheath at the ends of a shoelace.

BIG MONEY

Notwithstanding Drake's estimated $2 million solid-gold Air Jordans, Kanye West's $1.8 million pair of Yeezys were the first pair of sneakers to break the $1 million barrier at auction.

4 "Li Co Ri Lo Ci Ro Li Co T" is shorthand for the instructions to tie a tie in this style.

5 In 1904, Paris shirtmaker Charvet invented a version of this men's shirt accessory using knotted silk, sometimes referred to as a monkey's fist.

6 After freelance work for Chanel and Yves Saint Laurent, this shoe designer became a landscape gardener until opening a shoe salon in 1991 for Princess Caroline of Monaco, his first customer.

7 In 1989, Hall of Fame forward Dominique Wilkins appeared in the first commercial for this popular Reebok sneaker.

8 A part of military uniforms from the mid-19th century until just after World War I, puttees were worn on what part of the body?

9 With a logo featuring two women sitting back-to-back, this Italian company is famous for their football gear and tracksuits.

10 "Never stop exploring" is the slogan of this favorite outdoor company of both adventurers and junior-level analysts.

7. The Pump - 8. Legs - 9. Kappa - 10. The North Face
ANSWERS - 1. Prada - 2. Sari - 3. Aglet - 4. Windsor Knot - 5. Cuff Links - 6. Christian Louboutin -

Random Stuff You Should Know

1 This famous Austrian crystal company and its Kahles subsidiary made rifle scopes and binoculars for the German army in World War II.

2 In 2016, at age 18, Max Verstappen became the youngest person ever to win one of these races.

SO ANIMATED!

Inspired by a routine in the film *Anchors Aweigh*, Paula Abdul choreographed, and Disney artists animated, the cat in "Opposites Attract." The character later released its own single that went to Number 9 in Norway. Animated cats are HUGE in Norway.

3 What was the name of Paula Abdul's animated feline partner in the video to 1989's "Opposites Attract"?

4 This former Gawker Media sports blog broke stories on Manti Te'o girlfriend hoax and Brett Favre's scandalous texts to Jenn Sterger.

5 What is the sequence of buttons in the "Konami code" in many video games?

6 Bratislava is the capital of this country.

7 While Beethoven went famously deaf, this German composer spent the last 50 years of his life in England, growing nearly completely blind.

8 This former CEO of Yahoo! was Google employee number 20.

9 George Clooney rocks this royal haircut in 1996's *From Dusk till Dawn*.

10 One point for each Best Picture Oscar winner from 1970 to 1979.

ANSWERS - 1. Swarovski - 2. Formula One - 3. MC Skat Kat - 4. Deadspin - 5. Up Up Down Down Left Right Left Right B A - 6. Slovakia - 7. George Frideric Handel - 8. Marissa Mayer - 9. Caesar - 10. Kramer vs. Kramer, The Deer Hunter, Annie Hall, Rocky, One Flew over the Cuckoo's Nest, The Godfather Part II, The Sting, The Godfather, The French Connection, Patton

The Renaissance

1 Describing geniuses such as Leonardo da Vinci, this eight letter *P*-word is a synonym for Renaissance man.

2 *The Birth of Venus* is by this Renaissance artist.

3 Cosimo, Piero, and Lorenzo were the first names of three generations of this famous family.

4 On May 6, 1527, after a war with France and the papacy, the forces of Holy Roman Emperor Charles V sacked this city.

5 How many theses did Martin Luther write?

6 Jeremy Irons starred as Pope Alexander VI, the patriarch of this Italian family in a Showtime series of the same name.

7 The four largest moons of Jupiter are collectively referred to in honor of their discoverer, this astronomer

8 The term *New World* was coined by this continental namesake.

9 This Spanish work is often credited as the first Western novel.

10 The Galleria dell'Accademia is home to this world-famous statue.

OUT OF THIS WORLD

Jupiter's four largest moons are, in order of size, Ganymede, Callisto, Io, and Europa. Of Jupiter's 79 known moons, the first was discovered in 1610.

Before and After

See page 2 if you need a refresher on the rules.

1 These plugs come in Types A, B, and C, Mini A and B, and Micro A and B AND 1956 Marilyn Monroe mass-transit-titled movie.

2 Disney Channel comedy about teens living in a hotel AND 2017 NL Rookie of the Year and 2019 NL MVP.

3 Kawasaki's trademarked brand name for personal watercraft AND Bombardier's trademarked brand name for snowmobile.

4 The first film in the *Chucky* franchise AND a man fantasizes that Bogey's ghost gives him dating advice in this 1972 comedy.

5 Also representing Team GB, this tennis great's older brother has seven Grand Slam titles in doubles AND this waterway runs 3,750 km from near Melbourne to its mouth near Adelaide.

6 A Seattle tavern owner was so fond of one barbershop song that he gave his fast-casual restaurant this name AND in 1974, this Brewer became the last MLB player to hit a home run at age 18 or younger.

7 Parodied in *Zoolander*, this compact transportation was 2000's toy of the year AND this mega-manager organized the March for Our Lives student protest and clashed with Taylor Swift.

BRING IT UP-TO-DATE

10 Things I Hate about You is an adaptation of Shakespeare's *The Taming of the Shrew*, and *The Lion King* is basically *Hamlet*. There are a lot of these.

8 Emma Stone's Hawthorne-inspired teen comedy AND England's most difficult GCE testing, abbreviated.

9 Jackson Browne song and album AND Richard Mulligan's *Golden Girls* spin-off.

10 The Darkness's falsetto-heavy hit AND the infamous Niagara Falls, New York, environmental disaster-zone neighborhood.

ANSWERS - 1. Universal Serial Bus Stop - 2. The Suite Life of Zack and Cody Bellinger - 3. Jet Ski Doo - 4. Child's Play It Again, Sam - 5. Andy Murray River - 6. Red Robin Yount - 7. Razor Scooter Braun - 8. Easy A Levels - 9. Running on Empty Nest - 10. I Believe in a Thing Called Love Canal

Sports Rules

1 "LBW," "stumped," and "handled the ball twice" are ways to get out in this sport.

2 Although once legal, the "fake to third, throw to first pickoff" move has since 2013 been classified as what?

3 Introduced in 1993 and completely abolished by 2004, this was the two-word name of FIFA's failed sudden-death experiment.

> **PRO TIP**
> ....
> Learn at least the most basic football facts so you won't be utterly humiliated on your *Jeopardy!* appearance.

4 Although the NFL play clock is 40 seconds, a play clock of this duration is imposed on the offense after penalty delays.

5 A 1945 NCAA basketball game between Columbia and Fordham saw the first test, but not widespread adoption, of this type of field goal.

6 An interference penalty will be assessed to those who interrupt wave priority in professional competitions in this sport.

7 The sliotar must be between 69 and 72 mm in diameter and Gaelic Athletic Association–approved in this sport.

8 The 3 rings of the house are 12, 8, and 4 feet in diameter in this sport.

9 Known as the piste, a strip that is 1.5 to 2 meters wide and 14 meters long is the competitive setting for this sport.

10 After being called on by the home plate umpire, the first- or third-base ump will make this gesture to signal a strike should a batter fail to check their swing.

ANSWERS - 1. Cricket - 2. Balk - 3. Golden Goal - 4. 25 Seconds - 5. Three-Pointer - 6. Surfing - 7. Hurling - 8. Curling - 9. Fencing - 10. Clenched Fist

Random Stuff You Might *Not* Know

1 This former longtime CNN personality traveled with the Beatles on their second American tour.

2 According to a 2006 experiment, clicking the first link in the body text of every Wikipedia article will eventually lead you to this page, 95 percent of the time.

3 This famous character was four years old in 1950, six years old in 1957, and remained eight(?) years old from 1979 until February 13, 2000.

4 A Xerces Blue, Duke of Burgundy, and Plum Judy are all species of this animal.

5 Also known as a Norwegian omelette or *glace au four*, this dessert bears the name of a US state.

6 In 1967, Pronto Markets were rebranded as this grocery chain in a parody of the name of the famous tiki bar at the Beverly Hilton.

7 In flight, this is the word for a loss in aerodynamic lift caused by exceeding a wing's angle of attack.

8 Although most of this city is in County Antrim, small portions are in County Down.

AIN'T NOTHIN' TO F WITH

Killah Priest, Busta Rhymes, and Redman are also not members of Wu-Tang.

9 McDonald's acquired this national restaurant chain in 1998 and had divested its stake by 2006, having expanded it from 16 to 500 locations.

10 One point for each of the nine original, official members of the Wu-Tang Clan. (Hint: Cappadonna is out. He's the unofficial 10th member.)

ANSWERS - 1. Larry King - 2. Philosophy - 3. Charlie Brown - 4. Butterfly - 5. Baked Alaska - 6. Trader Joe's - 7. Stall - 8. Belfast - 9. Chipotle - 10. RZA, GZA, Method Man, Ol' Dirty Bastard, Raekwon, Ghostface Killah, Inspectah Deck, U-God, Masta Killa

European Cities

1 The International Court of Justice, better known as the World Court, is in The Hague in this country.

2 This fragrant city's cathedral is Germany's most visited landmark.

3 From 1038 until 1569, this southern Polish city, and not Warsaw, was the capital of the Kingdom of Poland.

4 Juventus F.C. is based in this Italian Winter Olympics host city.

5 This Scottish city lends its name to British slang for a headbutt.

6 Vaduz is the capital of this European nation.

7 Gibraltar's iconic rock, also known as the Jabal-al-Tariq, is the logo of this insurance company.

8 Copenhagen's widely visited *Little Mermaid* statue was commissioned by the son of the founder of this brewery.

9 The Sea of Marmara forms the southern border of this transcontinental city.

10 For 2,500 years, this Spanish city has been a famed center for high-quality steelmaking.

DID YOU KNOW?

Construction on the cathedral in Question #2 started in 1248, but all work ceased in 1473. For the next four centuries, the city's skyline was dominated not by the unfinished spires but by the massive 15th-century crane, left in place by the workmen at the top of the edifice.

Pooches

Name the dog breed for each photo!

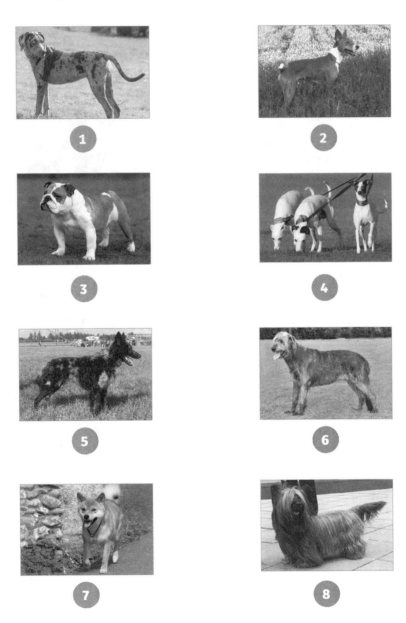

1

2

3

4

5

6

7

8

Sequels

1 While attending Windsor College, Sidney and Randy are confronted with a copycat killer inspired by their horrifying high school experience in this sequel.

2 This was the first sequel to ever win the Best Picture Oscar.

3 *Patch's London Adventure* was the subtitle to the direct-to-video sequel of this 1961 Disney animated classic.

4 A supernatural portrait of this Carpathian is the villain of *Ghostbusters II*.

5 *Unchained* was supposed to be the subtitle of the fifth film in this superhero series, but it was canceled after the terrible reception of the fourth film in 1997.

6 This notoriously bad 1993 video game movie's closing scene teased a sequel that fortunately never happened.

7 Released in 1916, *The Fall of a Nation* was the world's first sequel, following up on *The Birth of a Nation* by this director.

8 The second and third installments of this Robert Zemeckis trilogy were filmed concurrently.

9 This was the 1967 sequel to *A Fistful of Dollars*.

10 In a 2008 movie, Steve Coogan stars as a high school drama teacher who attempts to produce an impossible sequel to this Shakespeare play.

> **DID YOU KNOW?**
> ....
>
> Max von Sydow provided the voice of the Carpathian in *Ghostbusters II*. The actor portraying him, Wilhelm von Homburg (real name Norbert Grupe!) was so incensed he was overdubbed that he left the film's premiere.

ANSWERS - 1. Scream 2 - 2. The Godfather Part II - 3. 101 Dalmatians - 4. Vigo - 5. Batman - 6. Super Mario Bros. - 7. D. W. Griffith - 8. Back to the Future - 9. For a Few Dollars More - 10. Hamlet 2

Random Stuff You Might Know

1 Also called the Saltire, St. Andrew's Cross is the national flag of this country.

2 This country's Althing is the oldest body of parliamentary governance in the world.

3 Formerly 7 Race Course Road, 7 Lok Kalyan Marg is the official residence of the prime minister of this country.

4 What is the newest Ivy League school?

5 Who is writer-director Judd Apatow's wife?

6 Jesse Eisenberg, Anne Hathaway, and Jamie Foxx provide voices for this animated bird movie.

7 Invented in 1830 and used for bone surgery, the osteotome was the first recorded example of this device, now used in the lumber industry.

8 At 13,207 feet, the Argentine Pass is the highest vehicle-accessible pass in this US state.

9 Monasteries known as abbeys are under the authority of a person bearing this religious title.

10 One point for each of the top 12 NFL quarterbacks with 300 or more passing touchdowns.

> **NAME THAT BODY**
>
> Tricky trivia contests will often mention national governments. So, remember the Dáil (pronounced *Doyle*) is in Ireland, the Diet usually refers to Japan, the Knesset is in Israel, and "useless" is the United States Senate.

ANSWERS - 1. Scotland - 2. Iceland - 3. India - 4. Cornell - 5. Leslie Mann - 6. *Rio* - 7. Chain Saw - 8. Colorado - 9. Abbot - 10. Tom Brady, Drew Brees, Peyton Manning, Brett Favre, Philip Rivers, Dan Marino, Aaron Rodgers, Ben Roethlisberger, Eli Manning, Matt Ryan, Fran Tarkenton, John Elway

The Colonial Era

1 The British American colonies traded exclusively with and received enslaved people and exports from the mother country in this kind of economic system.

2 The 1675 atrocity known as the Great Swamp Massacre during King Philip's War saw colonial militia and Pequot allies slaughter members of this Rhode Island–based Algonquian tribe.

3 Sounding similar to a tequila brand, this was the Dutch word to describe feudal-type settlers and enslavers with huge land holdings and immense power in the colony of New Netherland.

> **PRO TIP**
> ....
> Benjamin Franklin was appointed the first postmaster general in 1775.

4 This 1693 institution is the oldest university in the southern colonies.

5 Bacon's Rebellion of 1676 diminished this white labor practice in order to permanently isolate enslaved people.

6 The 18th-century social elite of New York, Charleston, Boston, and Philadelphia built stately homes in this British architectural style.

7 With the help of his cousin, a Nantucket whaler, Benjamin Franklin charted this ocean current to increase the speed of mail.

8 Enslaved people living in the South Carolina coastal region retained more African language and cultural identity than those on the mainland, in part because of the specialized knowledge necessary in farming this cereal crop.

9 Although most famous as a minister with involvement in the Salem witch trials, this New England Puritan also experimented with agriculture and inoculation.

10 At the time of the Revolution, 85 percent of white Americans were descended from the British Isles, and at 8.8 percent, settlers from this country were the second most populous.

ANSWERS - 1. Mercantilism - 2. Narragansett - 3. Patroon - 4. College of William and Mary - 5. Indentured Servitude - 6. Georgian - 7. Gulf Stream - 8. Rice - 9. Cotton Mather - 10. Germany

Before and After

See page 2 if you need a refresher on the rules.

1 Netflix original focused on the now-adult Tanner children and their own families AND group best known for "Jump Around."

2 Eddie, Mike, Stone, Jeff, and Matt AND Run DMC's DJ.

3 Until moving to VH1 for its ninth season, this was Logo's highest-rated show AND 1996 Halle Berry and Jim Belushi movie about a high school's participation in a professional solar car competition.

4 This Puerto Rican pop star's career began at age 12 in Menudo AND the director of *The Departed*.

5 This Elle Woods movie had a successful Broadway adaptation AND Bob Dylan album featuring "Visions of Johanna."

6 Will.i.am cowrote this Black Eyed Peas hit with Justin Timberlake AND Gabriel García Márquez's most famous novel.

FUN FACT

That *Whiplash* star and I appeared on the same episode of *The Tonight Show*. Didn't get to meet him but my family talked about cats with Billy Corgan, so that was cool.

7 The star of *Whiplash* and *Divergent* AND famous skeptics and Vegas resident comic magicians, reversed.

8 Douglas, Turner, and DeVito star in this Indiana Jones–esque rip-off AND this beer-swilling wrestler regularly antagonized his boss Vince McMahon.

9 Derek Waters created this inebriated Comedy Central series from his "Funny or Die" sketches AND Mel Brooks's 1981 anthology film featuring "Jews in Space" and "Hitler on Ice."

10 He has feuded with Drake and was released from an unjust prison term in 2018 AND two-word phrase for what groups of people do when they circulate aimlessly.

ANSWERS - 1. Fuller House of Pain - 2. Pearl Jam Master Jay - 3. RuPaul's Drag Race the Sun - 4. Ricky Martin Scorsese - 5. Legally Blonde on Blonde - 6. Where Is the Love in the Time of Cholera - 7. Miles Teller and Penn - 8. Romancing the Stone Cold Steve Austin - 9. Drunk History of the World Part I - 10. Meek Mill Around

Rhyme Time

The answer to each clue is two words that rhyme. A quick example: A Disney chipmunk's water buckets = "Dale's Pails." Get it?

1 *Dharma*'s Mehndi ink

2 Forrest's baby mama's lucky coin

3 "Die Kunst der Fuge" writer's chronometer

4 A tubular float used during a seasonal wind reversal

5 An Anglo-Saxon town official appointed by Wooster's valet

6 Maize core-related employment

7 A short tune about a municipality

8 The most resourceful Sagarmatha

9 A bright and cheerful Henson character

10 The Canadian PM on overcranked film, shortened

FAST AND LOOSE
....

When hosting with this round, it's up to you how much of a disciplinarian you want to be. If you've got a stickler crowd, make sure the tenses and possessives match up. If you're low-key, it's all up to you.

ANSWERS - 1. Jenna's Henna - 2. Jenny's Penny - 3. Bach's Clock - 4. Monsoon Pontoon - 5. Jeeves's Reeves - 6. Cob Job - 7. City Ditty - 8. Cleverest Everest - 9. Pert Bert - 10. Slo-Mo Trudeau

Random Stuff You Might *Not* Know

1. In 1919, Sir Barton became the first of 13 to accomplish this difficult sporting feat.

2. Who shot Mr. Burns?

3. If you had one lakh rupees, you would have this many rupees.

4. The day after being canceled by Fox, *Brooklyn Nine-Nine* was picked up by this network.

5. *The Economist* famously demonstrates purchasing-power parity, or PPP, with an index based on this popular food item.

6. Addis Ababa is the location of the headquarters of this 55-member state supranational entity.

7. Paige joins Piper and Phoebe in the Power of Three after the death of this original *Charmed* sister.

8. Born Maksymilian Faktorowicz, businessman Max Factor marketed his products with this six-letter hyphenated synonym for cosmetics.

9. This word originates in medieval spiked barriers and the men who moved them to restrict access to roads.

10. One point for each of the Seven Summits, or the highest peaks on each of the seven continents.

PRO TIP

Memorize the answers to Question #10 before your *Jeopardy!* appearance. They come up all the time. (Except for the peak on the Australian continent. Every time that comes up, it's about its location in Papua New Guinea.)

ANSWERS - 1. Triple Crown - 2. Maggie - 3. 100,000 - 4. NBC - 5. Big Mac - 6. The African Union - 7. Prue - 8. Make-Up - 9. Turnpike - 10. Denali, Elbrus, Kilimanjaro, Aconcagua, Carstensz Pyramid or Puncak Jaya, Everest, Vinson

Musical Instruments

1 Contrary to popular stories, this tuba relative was not initially invented as a marching band instrument.

2 Greek god Apollo is often depicted with this two-stringed folk harp.

3 This woodwind's name is a corruption of the French for "high [or loud] wood."

4 Jazz artist Dave Brubeck played this instrument.

5 Used in both period-correct performances and many popular songs, this plucked keyboard instrument saw a revival in the 1960s.

6 Wendy Carlos rose to fame for her interpretations of Bach using this instrument.

7 Beethoven's Symphony No. 9 is the first symphonic appearance of this high-pitched flute-family instrument.

8 According to George Harrison, this instrument gently weeps.

9 Performing in blackface in the 1840s and '50s, Joel Walker Sweeney is the earliest-documented white player of this five-stringed instrument.

10 Carnegie Hall's main auditorium is named for Isaac Stern, a virtuoso of this instrument.

IN THE PITS

Hautbols—meaning "high wood"—retained its French pronunciation as it entered the English language. But calling it *hawt boyz* isn't a bad idea either.

Before and After

See page 2 if you need a refresher on the rules.

1 The second book to star Katniss Everdeen AND "Lemme show ya something" was Jim Carrey's catchphrase for this accident-prone *In Living Color* character.

2 Despite inclusion on the Monopoly board, this railroad did not service Atlantic City AND Beck's fifth studio album.

3 This publisher owns Doubleday, Alfred A. Knopf, and Ballantine Books AND in 1839 Poe wrote of "The Fall of" this building and its family.

SWING AND A MISS

Lady Gaga's NYU classmates created a Facebook group called "Stefani Germanotta, you will never be famous." In a way, they were correct, as "Stefani Germanotta" is not famous. In another sense, HOLY CRAP THIS IS THE BIGGEST FAIL EVER. What a bunch of NOT-stradamuses. (Bad pun.)

4 Turntablist often ejected by Uncle Phil AND Hendrick Motorsports Number 24 Chevrolet SS.

5 Akon cowrote this Lady Gaga debut single AND many news outlets noted the aerobic benefits of this popular interactive arcade game.

6 Claiming the "World's Greatest Sandwiches," this franchise has grown from 500 stores in 2007 to more than 1,600 today AND the Bloomberg School of Public Health is part of this institution.

7 The military command to march in the opposite direction AND what Bill and Ted had to do in their third movie.

8 "Norwegian Wood (This Bird Has Flown)" and "In My Life" are off of this album AND singers of "Runaway Train."

9 In the 1970s and '80s, he wrote under the pen name Richard Bachman AND Robert Fripp's prog-rock band.

10 Beware Greeks bearing this gift AND this America hit was originally called "The Desert Song."

ANSWERS - 1. Catching Fire Marshall Bill - 2. B & Odelay - 3. Penguin Random House of Usher - 4. DJ Jazzy Jeff Gordon - 5. Just Dance Dance Revolution - 6. Jimmy Johns Hopkins - 7. About Face the Music - 8. Rubber Soul Asylum - 9. Stephen King Crimson - 10. Trojan Horse with No Name

Nineties Cartoons

1 Goliath, Brooklyn, Lexington, and Hudson were the heroes of this Disney animated series.

2 A young Seth MacFarlane wrote on a mid-1990s cartoon series based on this Jim Carrey character.

3 Sidekicks IQ and Gordo Leiter starred in a cartoon about the teenage nephew of this famous movie hero.

4 Appearing in an early nineties cartoon, Digeri Dingo and Wendell T. Wolf were sidekicks and sometimes enemies of this Warner Bros. animated character.

> **JUST THE FACTS**
>
> New *DuckTales* is amazing. So so so so so good.

5 What is the last name of Doug's crush Patti?

6 "Let's get dangerous" was the battle cry of this Disney cartoon character.

7 *X-Men: The Animated Series* helped create a momentarily popular superhero of this card-throwing Cajun.

8 A short called "Frog Baseball" on MTV's animation showcase *Liquid Television* was the debut appearance of these animated characters.

9 A demented Peter Lorre was the inspiration for the voice and character of this terrible Chihuahua.

10 What is the home city of the Powerpuff Girls?

Random Stuff You Might *Not* Know

1 Meaning "union of senses," this neurological condition can include symptoms like letters or numbers possessing inherent colors.

2 "I had a lover's quarrel with the world" is the epitaph engraved on the gravestone of this mid-20th-century American poet.

3 Folklore contends that the amount of brown on this animal larvae's coat is a predictor of winter severity.

BRING IN DA NOISE, BRING IN DEFUNCT

Question #5 is exemplary of "just tough enough" sports trivia. Asking about long-demolished Philadelphia venues (Shibe Park and the Baker Bowl) is too obscure.

4 This company, whose name is French for "the crucible," fabricates absurdly expensive cast-iron pots in a foundry that was established in 1925.

5 Before 1910, you could watch a game by parking your carriage or car in the outfield of this uptown Manhattan ballpark.

6 In 2001, by using Bose-Einstein condensates, physicist Lene Vestergaard Hau became the first person to slow, then eventually stop, this.

7 This husband of Sarah Michelle Gellar was once a producer and director for World Wrestling Entertainment.

8 *Broadway Bound, Biloxi Blues*, and this play make up Neil Simon's Eugene trilogy.

9 Which constituent emirate is the capital of the United Arab Emirates?

10 One point for each of the world's 10 busiest airports by international passenger traffic.

ANSWERS - 1. Synesthesia - 2. Robert Frost - 3. Woolly Caterpillar - 4. Le Creuset - 5. Polo Grounds - 6. Light - 7. Freddie Prinze Jr. - 8. *Brighton Beach Memoirs* - 9. Abu Dhabi - 10. Atatürk Airport, Incheon International Airport, Suvarnabhumi Airport, Frankfurt, Amsterdam, Singapore, Paris Charles de Gaulle, Hong Kong, London Heathrow, Dubai International Airport

Presidential Trivia

1 In 1877, this president's wife became the first to be officially referred to as First Lady.

2 "I don't remember that I was ever president," said this man, so happy with his second career as chief justice of the Supreme Court.

3 This president's private collection of 6,000 books became the foundation of the Library of Congress.

4 He was the only president to personally salvage a partially melted-down nuclear reactor.

> **PRO TIP**
>
> Only one man has ever served as both president and chief justice of the Supreme Court. Get this down

5 At 6 feet, 4 inches, or 193 cm, our tallest president, Abraham Lincoln, was just a centimeter taller than this president.

6 From 1782 until 1945, the eagle on the presidential seal faced the bundled arrows of war until President Truman changed it to face this item.

7 John F. Kennedy, at age 43, was the youngest person elected president, but who became president through other means at age 42?

8 This was the only president to serve his entire term as a bachelor.

9 Before becoming president, this American wrote the Monroe Doctrine as Secretary of State.

10 With immense personal wealth from mining and engineering, this president donated his salary to charity.

ANSWERS - 1. Rutherford B. Hayes - 2. William Howard Taft - 3. Thomas Jefferson - 4. Jimmy Carter - 5. Lyndon B. Johnson - 6. Olive Branch - 7. Teddy Roosevelt - 8. James Buchanan - 9. John Quincy Adams - 10. Herbert Hoover

Chemistry

1 The most powerful explosions—other than nuclear reactions—are a result of the output of the chemical reaction created when this abundant triradical element recombines into its stable 1:1 triple-bonded state.

2 In 1798, Henry Cavendish discovered the specific gravity of Earth and ascertained that the planet's core was 5.4 g/cm^3, or 80 percent the density of this element in liquid form.

IT'S THE BOMB

As the Cold War accelerated and the United States sought to flex its nuclear muscle, they detonated their Operation Crossroads' Able bomb on July 1, 1946. Four days later, designer Louis Réard named his racy new swimsuit after the location of the test: Bikini Atoll.

3 A *Miami Vice* episode, a Queens of the Stone Age song, a Fatboy Slim album, and an Olivia Wilde film all have this four-word title, a variant on a 1935 DuPont slogan.

4 Name this "Block Rockin' Beats" Mancunian electronic music duo.

5 The Arabic *al-qalyah*, meaning "plant ash," became *alkali*, which in 1809 was adapted into *Kalium*, the Neo-Latin name for this element.

6 Replacing just 1 percent of aluminum ions with chromium in the aluminum oxide of corundum yields a yellow-green absorption, creating the red color of this gem.

7 This scientist's got (atomic number) 99 problems, but a silvery element that glows blue in the dark and is named after him ain't one of them.

8 This ska punk band was named for the two 1952 atomic tests that discovered atomic element 99 and 100, Fermium.

9 "Beyond the Elements: Reactions" was a 2021 episode in the 47th season of this WGBH Boston–produced science program.

10 This six-letter mnemonic acronym tells us the six elements that make up the vast majority of covalent bonds in biological molecules.

ANSWERS - 1. Nitrogen - 2. Iron - 3. "Better Living through Chemistry" - 4. The Chemical Brothers - 5. Potassium - 6. Ruby - 7. Albert Einstein - 8. Operation Ivy - 9. *Nova* - 10. CHNOPS

Stanley Cup and NBA Finals

1 How many Stanley Cup trophies are there?

2 The phrase "Season Not Played" is engraved on the Stanley Cup for this season.

3 From 1976 to 1988, these were the only three teams to win the Stanley Cup.

4 Despite 13 Stanley Cup wins, this team has neither won nor appeared in a Stanley Cup final since 1967.

5 He is both the only player with three Conn Smythe trophies and multiple trophies from multiple teams.

6 The Boston Celtics won a record eight straight NBA championships in the 1950s and '60s, facing difficulties only when against the Warriors, the 76ers, or the Lakers when helmed by this player.

7 The first eighth seed to ever reach the NBA Finals came with this team's 1999 appearance.

8 After losing the 1976 ABA Championship to the New York Nets, this team joined the NBA and has never appeared in the NBA Finals.

9 The 1951 Rochester Royals won their only NBA Finals appearance and are today known as this team.

10 Who's better: LeBron or Jordan?

> ### THE VERY FIRST CUPS
>
> The original Stanley Cup was purchased in London in the late 1880s or early 1890s. The stewards of the cup feared for its welfare, and since 1970, it has been housed in the Hockey Hall of Fame. That cup number one is referred to as the Dominion Hockey Challenge Cup.

ANSWERS - 1. **Three** - 2. 2004–05 - 3. Canadiens, Islanders, Oilers - 4. Maple Leafs - 5. Patrick Roy - 6. Wilt Chamberlain - 7. Knicks - 8. Denver Nuggets - 9. Sacramento Kings - 10. This argument will never be settled. The real winner is basketball. (Just give yourself the point.)

Random Stuff You Might *Not* Know

1 The "Bridal Chorus," better known as "Here Comes the Bride," is from this Wagner opera.

2 According to Deadspin, the highest-paid public employees of 27 states have this same title.

3 What are yawls, pinnaces, and launches?

4 David Bowie wrote "All the Young Dudes" for this English glam rock band.

5 This American city was historically known as the Rubber Capital of the World.

6 In 1534, he founded the Society of Jesus, better known as the Jesuit Order.

7 Other than Sabrina, he was the only character to appear in every episode of *Sabrina the Teenage Witch*.

8 Stephen "the Rifleman" Flemmi was a key witness in testimony against this gangster.

9 From 1962 to 1969, he was the Yankees' first baseman and occasionally filled in at center field for the ailing Mickey Mantle.

10 One point for each of the 15 departments within the executive branch's cabinet.

FUN FACT

According to his autobiography, Answer #9 ran up such a bill at the Copacabana that the owners sent a couple of bouncers to collect money from him outside Yankee Stadium. The wayward first baseman skipped out on the bill and just avoided the Copa for a couple of months until they forgot.

ANSWERS - 1. *Lohengrin* - **2.** College Football Head Coach - **3.** Types of Boats - **4.** Mott the Hoople - **5.** Akron, Ohio - **6.** Ignatius of Loyola - **7.** Salem the Cat - **8.** Whitey Bulger - **9.** Joe Pepitone - **10.** Homeland Security, Veterans Affairs, Education, Energy, Transportation, Housing and Urban Development, Health and Human Services, Labor, Commerce, Agriculture, Interior, Justice, Defense, Treasury, State

Heroes and Heroines

1. Edward Taylor's work on mythology and Joseph Campbell's work comparing Jesus, Moses, and the Buddha led to the creation of the theory of the monomyth, or this two-word term.

2. With a complete absence of sympathetic characters, this 1848 William Makepeace Thackeray novel is subtitled *A Novel without a Hero.*

3. The polyamorous relationship between William Moulton Marston; his wife, Elizabeth Holloway Marston; and their life partner, Olive Byrne, inspired the 1941 creation of this comic book Amazon.

4. On July 7, 1456, an appellate court declared this heroine of medieval France innocent of the charges that had led to her execution 25 years earlier.

5. The archetype of the reluctant hero is typified by this everyman, a persistent nuisance to the would-be robbers of Nakatomi Plaza.

6. Awarding more than $38 million in scholarships and awards for civilian heroism, the Carnegie Hero Fund has been based for 114 years in this steel city.

7. Germanic heroic narratives follow a warrior and his heroic death and are epitomized by this circa 1000 CE Old English epic.

8. Asimov's *Foundation* series, Card's *Ender's Game* series, and Lucas's *Star Wars* franchise exemplify this two-word cosmic musical term.

9. Beethoven's Symphony No. 3 (*Eroica*), or the heroic symphony, was originally dedicated to this man until he proclaimed himself emperor.

10. This ancient hero was the Sumerian king of Uruk and was immortalized in a 2000 BCE Akkadian epic bearing his name.

> **BEHIND THE SCENES**
>
> *Die Hard* was contractually offered as right of first refusal to Frank Sinatra; he had starred in *The Detective*, a 1968 movie based on a book by Roderick Thorp, and *Die Hard* was based on its sequel, *Nothing Lasts Forever.* The producers hoped the 73-year-old Sinatra would decline. Good thing he did.

ANSWERS - 1. Hero's Journey - 2. Vanity Fair - 3. Wonder Woman - 4. Joan of Arc - 5. John McClane - 6. Pittsburgh - 7. Beowulf - 8. Space Opera - 9. Napoleon - 10. Gilgamesh

Before and After

See page 2 if you need a refresher on the rules.

1 "Four legs good, two legs bad" Orwell novella AND Willie Nelson, John Mellencamp, and Neil Young's eighties agricultural relief benefit concert.

2 Robert Heinlein's 1961 novel about a Martian named Valentine Michael Smith AND orphaned Littlefoot joins Cera, Ducky, Petrie, and Spike in the search for the Great Valley in this animated dinosaur movie.

3 *Master of the Senate* is Robert Caro's narrative of this future president's work on the Civil Rights Act of 1957 AND the makers of Band-Aids.

4 A straight male comic book artist pursues a lesbian comic book artist in this now sorta problematic 1997 Kevin Smith movie AND in 2008, she became the first British woman to win five Grammys.

5 Clive Owen assists a pregnant refugee in this dystopian movie AND Will Smith goes extraterrestrial in this song.

6 This Naughty by Nature hit on infidelity samples the Jackson 5's "ABC" AND gym class, abbreviated.

7 The author of *The Waste Land* AND the leader of the Untouchables.

TRAITOR TRAITOR

In a final "f— you" to the treasonous loser in Answer #9, former enslaved persons buried in Arlington National Cemetery are forever honored with the word "CITIZEN" engraved on their headstones.

8 A-ha's biggest hit AND Britney and Madonna's 2003 dance hit duet.

9 This traitor accepted the 13th Amendment and "the extinction of slavery" but publicly opposed Black political and voting rights AND this star of *The Dirty Dozen* was a distant relative to the guy in the first half of the question and is buried on his estate, which is today Arlington National Cemetery.

10 In the early days of television, networks assigned the number 13 would adopt one of these bad-luck animals as mascot AND a Ted Nugent hard-rock song.

ANSWERS - 1. Animal Farm Aid - 2. Stranger in a Strange Land before Time - 3. Lyndon B. Johnson & Johnson - 4. Chasing Amy Winehouse - 5. Children of Men in Black - 6. O. P. P. E. - 7. T. S. Eliot Ness - 8. Take on Me Against the Music - 9. Robert E. Lee Marvin - 10. Black Cat Scratch Fever

Eighties Sitcoms

1 Played by actor Andrew Koenig, this best friend of Mike Seaver on *Growing Pains* moved away to join the US Marine Corps.

2 This actor was the only one of the Golden Girls to not previously star or costar in a sitcom.

3 This sitcom's opening credits featured a beat-up van driving from New York to a Connecticut autumnal landscape.

4 Although prolific in the 1970s, sitcom creator Norman Lear produced only this Valerie Bertinelli show in the 1980s.

5 Constantly breaking the fourth wall, this landmark Showtime series was Garry Shandling's first sitcom.

6 In season two of *Full House*, Danny Tanner becomes host of this morning show.

7 This *Mr. Belvedere* star's paltry stats for his five seasons playing on the Milwaukee and Atlanta Braves were a .200 average, 14 home runs, and 74 RBIs.

8 In the third and fourth series of *Blackadder*, this actor and comedian played Prince George, the prince regent, and Lieutenant George, respectively.

9 December 17, 1989, was the debut of this smoking pair of *Simpsons* twins.

10 What was the actual name of the pub featured on the opening credits of *Cheers*?

FUN FACT

Lori Loughlin, the actor who played Danny's conost in Answer #6, ended up getting caught bribing her children's way into a safety school. Whoops.

ROUND 4 / DIFFICULTY LEVEL 1 2 3 4 5 **6**

Random Stuff You Might *Not* Know

1. Since at least 1894, a 22-mile bridge has been proposed but never built to effectively join the city of Chennai with this island nation.

2. This name can refer to either a suburb of Seattle or the oldest public hospital in the US.

3. The Catskill Mountain House, Kaaterskill Falls, and Cold Spring, New York, were favorite subjects of this English-born Hudson Valley painter.

4. This third-largest city in Arkansas is home to the University of Arkansas.

5. Located in southwest Siberia on the Ob River, this is Russia's third-largest city after Moscow and St. Petersburg.

6. This is the Spanish word for "song."

7. The five beaches in Normandy, France, invaded by American, British, and Canadian forces on D-Day were Utah, Omaha, Gold, Juno, and this one.

8. Thomas Piketty, Amartya Sen, and Joseph Stiglitz all have this career.

9. Respectively, William Bradford and Myles Standish were the second and sixth signatories of this document.

10. One point for each of the 12 most visited cities by international tourists in 2019, according to CNN.

AROUND THE WORLD

With more arrivals to its international airport than Istanbul, the city of Antalya, Turkey, is known as the Capital of Turkish Tourism. Beaches, mountains, an Ottoman-era walled city, and what looks like a really cool toy museum grants Antalya 30 percent of Turkey's foreign visitation. Probably not just the toy museum, but that's what I'd see.

ANSWERS - 1. Sri Lanka - 2. Bellevue - 3. Thomas Cole - 4. Fayetteville - 5. Novosibirsk - 6. Canción - 7. Sword - 8. Economist - 9. Mayflower Compact - 10. Antalya, Delhi, Istanbul, Kuala Lumpur, New York City, Dubai, Paris, Singapore, Macau, London, Bangkok, Hong Kong

Baking

1. "Mark it with a *T*, put it in the oven for Tommy and me" ends this more than 500-year-old baker's man nursery rhyme.

2. In 1840, Anna Russell, the Duchess of Bedford, invented this afternoon meal of baked goods.

3. This is the name for a thick-walled, tightly sealed cast-iron pot used for open-flame baking.

4. Sodium bicarbonate, or baking soda, acts as a leavening agent by reacting with acids in batters and thus releasing this gas.

5. The ancient Roman baked good *spira* would be recognizable to consumers today as this German-named baked treat.

6. From 2010 to 2016, this food writer and TV personality was senior judge on the *Great British Bake Off*.

7. Cartoons frequently depict failure and collapse in the baking of these notoriously delicate egg dishes.

8. Naan is leavened. Name any of the three South Asian flatbreads that are unleavened.

9. Loose stool and abdominal discomfort were some of the side effects of eating baked potato chips made with this calorie-free fat substitute.

10. Dave Chappelle cowrote and starred in this 1998 stoner comedy.

> **WHEN IN ROME**
>
> In ancient Rome, bakers and pastry makers were so valued by a decadent society fixated on entertainment that the invention of a new style of pastry or baked good could prove a path for social advancement or manumission. In Pompeii, at least 33 bakeries have been discovered.

ANSWERS - 1. "Pat-a-Cake" - **2.** Teatime/Afternoon Tea - **3.** Dutch Oven - **4.** Carbon Dioxide - **5.** Pretzel - **6.** Mary Berry - **7.** Soufflé - **8.** Roti, Chapati, or Paratha - **9.** Olestra/Olean - **10.** Half Baked

Before and After

See page 2 if you need a refresher on the rules.

1 He played Smokey from *Friday* AND Jon Stewart has frequently clashed with this bow-tied former CNN *Crossfire* host.

2 Willie Mays was nicknamed this kind of "Kid" AND the subject of this 2006 song is a long-distance runner and graduate of Columbia University.

3 Since 2014, she's led the *NFL on Fox* sideline reportage team AND their biggest hit was the "Boogie Woogie Bugle Boy."

4 He played Bane in *The Dark Knight Rises* AND Franklin Dixon is the pseudonym for the authors of books about these child detectives.

WHAT ELSE CAN HE DO?

The first half of Answer #5 can also "fly like an eagle" and "reach out and grab ya."

---

5 His personas have included the Gangster of Love, the Space Cowboy, and Maurice AND the home stadium of the Milwaukee Brewers.

6 A 1974 John le Carré novel about a retired intelligence officer reinstated to unravel a Soviet mole AND these black-and-white comic nemeses debuted in the January 1961 issue of *Mad* magazine.

7 Mikey Walsh considers this pirate the "original Goonie" AND 1971 Gene Wilder musical fantasy film.

8 As player-manager from 1916 to 1926, he led the Cleveland Indians to their first-ever World Series title AND Nancy Pelosi's job title.

9 His mother was a "15-year-old French prostitute named Chloe with webbed feet" AND this 1987 horror film ends with its hero and his Oldsmobile transported to 1300 CE.

10 Nicknamed Dutch, this Pittsburgh Pirate was called the greatest star to ever take the diamond by Ty Cobb AND this educational institution is atop Staten Island's Grymes Hill.

ANSWERS - 1. Chris Tucker Carlson - 2. Say Hey There Delilah - 3. Erin Andrews Sisters - 4. Tom Hardy Boys - 5. Steve Miller Park - 6. Tinker Tailor Soldier Spy vs. Spy - 7. One-Eyed Willy Wonka & the Chocolate Factory - 8. Tris Speaker of the House - 9. Dr. Evil Dead 2 - 10. Honus Wagner College

Plants

1 This plant-created stimulant evolved as a natural pesticide to stun and kill insect predators.

2 Broccoli, cauliflower, brussels sprouts, Chinese cabbage, cabbage, and this currently in-vogue vegetable are all selectively bred varieties of the exact same species.

3 The Native American planting trio entailed corn for structure, squashes to prevent weeds, and beans to add this element to the soil.

> **PRO TIP**
> ....
> Methuselah is more than 4,800 years old; born in 2832 BCE, it's 300 years older than the Sphinx and the domestication of the camel (both kinds—dromedary and Bactrian).

4 Pando, an entire forest of quaking aspen, is considered one organism with 80,000-year-old roots, weighs more than 6 million kgs, and takes up 106 acres in this southwestern state.

5 Other than both being in California, what do Methuselah, the world's oldest tree, and Hyperion, the world's tallest tree, have in common?

6 This is the only fruit that bears its seeds on the outside.

7 Under what kind of tree was Siddhartha Gautama sitting when he gained enlightenment and became the Buddha?

8 This is the name of the plant cellulose fiber material used to make paper.

9 Unlike its smaller cousins, poison ivy and poison oak, this poison plant can grow up to 30 feet tall.

10 Yew, willow, and olive branches are acceptable climate-appropriate substitutes used to celebrate this Christian movable feast.

ANSWERS - 1. Caffeine - 2. Kale - 3. Nitrogen - 4. Utah - 5. Their exact locations are kept secret. - 6. Strawberry - 7. Fig or Bodhi - 8. Pulp - 9. Poison Sumac - 10. Palm Sunday

Random Stuff You Might *Not* Know

1 On car exteriors, spoilers and air dams create additional grip on the road through this aerodynamic thrust.

2 Sana'a is the capital of this country.

3 Debuting in 1965, Masanori Murakami became the first Japanese major leaguer as a pitcher for this team.

4 In 1930, this country hosted and won the very first FIFA World Cup.

5 Until 2004, Macallan scotches were exclusively aged in barrels that once held this liquor.

6 What is the largest city in Alabama?

7 The Hogan, Whitehurst, Burke, Scott, Paramount, and Hatch amendments have all unsuccessfully attempted to overturn this Supreme Court decision.

8 Alice Springs, Australia, is halfway between Port Augusta in the south and this city on the north coast.

9 Boutros is Arabic for this Christian name.

10 One point for each of the 12 countries with a higher hourly minimum wage in US dollars than the US.

DID YOU KNOW?

Boutros Boutros-Ghali was the only UN secretary-general whose reelection was vetoed by the Security Council. Fourteen members voted for his reelection, while one with veto power voted against. Guess who it was? It was the US.

ANSWERS - 1. Downforce - 2. Yemen - 3. San Francisco Giants - 4. Uruguay - 5. Sherry - 6. Birmingham - 7. *Roe v. Wade* - 8. Darwin - 9. Peter - 10. Japan, Canada, UK, Netherlands, Ireland, San Marino, New Zealand, Belgium, France, Monaco, Luxembourg, Australia

108

Late-Night Talk Shows

1 On February 1, 1982, this show replaced *The Tomorrow Show* with Tom Snyder and has remained in NBC's lineup over the course of four different hosts ever since.

2 *Saturday Night Live*, *The Tonight Show with Jimmy Fallon*, and *Late Night with Seth Meyers* are all produced by this Lorne Michaels production company.

3 A precursor to late-night TV was radio's *The Pepsodent Show*, hosted by this golfing comedian.

4 Beginning in 1971, NBC remained on air an hour later, creating late-night shows to recoup advertising revenue lost after a ban on TV ads for these products.

5 *Saturday Night with Miriam*, *The Ray D'Arcy Show*, and *The Late Late Show* are all late-night talk shows on this Irish state-owned network.

6 "Mount Baldy—what did Yul Brynner's wife do on their wedding night?" was a joke by this Carson psychic.

> **FUN FACT**
>
> I have beaten Amy Poehler at darts, and I can't remember if I got a beer poured on me by Amy Poehler or if I poured a beer on Amy Poehler as a result of the victory. Lost to the sands of time, this story is.

7 Carson Daly, Lilly Singh, and Amber Ruffin have all hosted shows in the 1:37 a.m. ET/PT time slot on this network.

8 Before *The Arsenio Hall Show*, Arsenio Hall took over for the unpopular Joan Rivers on Fox's *The Late Show* until he left to film this Eddie Murphy movie.

9 Running for two seasons, *The Jon Stewart Show* aired on MTV and gained momentary notoriety when this goth rocker piggybacked Stewart off stage.

10 Trevor Noah speaks English, Zulu, Sotho, Tswana, Tsonga, Afrikaans, German, and this language of his mother.

ANSWERS - 1. Late Night with David Letterman - **2.** Broadway Video - **3.** Bob Hope - **4.** Cigarettes - **5.** RTÉ - **6.** Carnac the Magnificent - **7.** NBC - **8.** Coming to America - **9.** Marilyn Manson - **10.** Xhosa

ROUND 2 / DIFFICULTY LEVEL 1 2 **3** 4 5 6

Before and After

See page 2 if you need a refresher on the rules.

1 *The Mutiny of the Hispaniola* is the subtitle to this Robert Louis Stevenson novel AND Marlon Brando got a Razzie for Worst Supporting Actor for his role in this H. G. Wells–adapted film.

2 Site of the 1994 FIFA World Cup Final AND in *George White's Scandals of 1931*, Ethel Merman sang that "Life Is Just a . . . " this.

3 Matthew McConaughey coaches college football after a plane crash in this movie AND Alexander Grant, Holly Haferman, and this artist are the credited songwriters of the hit song "Love the Way You Lie."

4 The cartoon character based on Art Carney and named after a New York Yankee AND the host of *Man vs. Wild.*

5 *XXL* is the subtitle to the sequel of this movie AND in 2008, this former Yankee became the second pitcher to retire after a 20-win season.

6 The nickname of William Frederick Cody AND he was the 42nd president of the United States.

7 The second film in the Hunger Games series AND the subtitle to the *Twin Peaks* feature film.

8 "Homemade Home Video," "Portrait of a Virgin," and "A Family Business" are segments from the first episode of this HBO documentary series AND Andie MacDowell stars in this 1989 Steven Soderbergh film.

9 Fred Willard's commentary as Buck Laughlin is a highlight of this canine comedy movie AND Missouri's nickname.

10 The author of the poem "Defence of Fort M'Henry" AND a ceremonial civic honor presented to welcome visiting dignitaries.

ANSWERS - 1. Treasure Island of Doctor Moreau - 2. Rose Bowl of Cherries - 3. We Are Marshall Mathers - 4. Yogi Bear Grylls - 5. Magic Mike Mussina - 6. Buffalo Bill Clinton - 7. Catching Fire Walk with Me - 8. Real Sex, Lies, and Videotape - 9. Best in Show Me State - 10. Francis Scott Key to the City

Animals

1. Behind the University of Michigan and Notre Dame, this Connecticut canine team is the third-winningest team in the history of college football.

2. Close to 70 percent of the 334 species of this mammalian infraclass live on the Australian continent.

3. This amphibian song by the Doors references Jim Morrison's arrest in New Haven.

4. Bearing little resemblance to modern species, the snapping turtle, hoatzin, horseshoe crab, and coelacanth are all described with this two-word term.

5. Pycnofibers were the small, hairlike, furry coats covering the bodies and wings of these flying reptiles of the Triassic through Cretaceous periods.

6. Beatrix "the Bride" Kiddo and a Los Angeles Laker both have this reptilian nickname.

7. This 13th-century traveler mistook the Asian rhinoceros for a unicorn.

8. According to the Family Guy Wiki, Brian Griffin is this breed of dog.

9. This Manhattan institution is home to a 94-foot-long, 21,000-pound model of a cetacean.

10. The theory of natural selection was formulated by observing the differences in beak shape and purpose among a species of birds from the Galápagos Islands that came to bear this name.

UNICORNS, EVERYWHERE

Also mistaken for unicorns: narwhals, oryx, your start-up.

ANSWERS - 1. Yale Bulldogs - 2. Marsupial - 3. "Peace Frog" - 4. Living Fossil - 5. Pterosaurs - 6. Black Mamba - 7. Marco Polo - 8. Labrador - 9. American Museum of Natural History - 10. Darwin's Finches

ROUND 4 / DIFFICULTY LEVEL 1 **2** 3 4 5 6

Random Stuff You Should Know

1 This New York neighborhood's name means "the Neighborhood."

2 Ljubljana is the capital of this country.

3 Billy Joel, Garth Brooks, and Adele have all charted with cover versions of this Bob Dylan song.

4 This former manager of Manchester United was recently voted the Portuguese Coach of the Century.

5 Irish slang for "a brawl," this word originated at an annual Dublin fair held from 1204 until the 19th century.

6 Betty Crocker, Green Giant, Pillsbury, and Häagen-Dazs are all brands of this Minnesota-based corporation.

7 This outlaw country artist is the only son of Waylon Jennings and Jessi Colter.

8 Daly City, 16th Street Mission, and Fremont are all stations in this American municipal transit system.

9 Robyn Fenty is the given first and last name of this music artist.

10 One point for each of the first 12 elements on the periodic table.

Shakespearean Dictionary

1 The title of this Aldous Huxley novel comes from Shakespeare's play *The Tempest*.

2 Shakespeare gets credit for first using this Spanish-derived word for a small dried fish.

3 Shakespeare was the first person to use this word, often paired with *carry-on* or *rolling*, as a noun.

4 Neil Young may not know that this term used to describe a person of pure intentions originates in *Henry V*.

5 *Richard II* is the first documented usage of these two words describing the visible path of a meteoroid.

6 Meaning "an impossible or foolish quest," this three-word term is from *Romeo and Juliet*.

7 In *Hamlet*, this is the soul of wit.

8 This cool phrase, meaning "to initiate social conversation at a first meeting," originated in *The Taming of the Shrew*.

9 Often used in conjunction with military aircraft, this word meaning "covert" is from *Macbeth*.

10 Green Day could not have had the time of your life without these two words from *Troilus and Cressida*.

> **DID YOU KNOW?**
>
> Shakespeare used 31,534 unique words. Scholars estimate that English in his time included another 35,000 words that he did not use, putting his theoretical maximum vocabulary at around 66,000 words. Eminem holds the Guinness World Record for vocabulary of a recording artist at 8,818. That's a lot of Mom's spaghetti.

ANSWERS - 1. *Brave New World* **- 2.** Anchovy **- 3.** Luggage **- 4.** Heart of Gold **- 5.** Shooting Star **- 6.** Wild Goose Chase **- 7.** Brevity **- 8.** Break the Ice **- 9.** Stealthy **- 10.** Good Riddance

Fruits and Veggies

1 This psychedelic group had a *Billboard* number-one hit in 1967 with "Incense and Peppermints."

2 Nicknamed "Cubby," he produced *Chitty Chitty Bang Bang* and a whole bunch of other Ian Fleming film adaptations.

3 Formerly France Télécom S.A., this is Europe's fourth-largest—and the world's tenth-largest—wireless provider.

4 *Kripik teripang* and *haisom cah jamur* are Indonesian preparations of this leathery maritime echinoderm.

5 Professional pyrotechnicians refer to this consumer firework as a "globe salute."

6 Near the extreme western tip of England, a small island in Cornwall is home to—and named after—a rare wild breed of this young shoot spring vegetable.

7 In 1976, the first product by this company went on sale for $666.66; its designer was unaware of the biblical reference and said he liked "repeating digits."

8 With domestication origins in prehistory, this bulb vegetable's relationship with humankind is so ancient that remnants of it were found in the eye sockets of the mummified Ramses IV.

9 Freezing, sinking, or smacking are three ways to separate the edible seeds from the inedible pulp of this fruit.

10 In 2021, this prop comedian—born Scott Thompson—began a six-night-a-week residency at the Luxor Hotel in Las Vegas.

ANSWERS - 1. Strawberry Alarm Clock - 2. Albert R. Broccoli - 3. Orange S.A. - 4. Sea Cucumber - 5. Cherry Bomb - 6. Asparagus - 7. Apple Inc. - 8. Onion - 9. Pomegranate - 10. Carrot Top

US Constitution

1 The Third Amendment to the Constitution prohibits these people from boarding in private homes.

2 The 18th Amendment enacting Prohibition was repealed by the 21st Amendment in this year.

3 On August 22, 1978, an amendment was proposed to allow two senators, a voting representative, and de facto statehood for this federally controlled city.

FUN FACT

Wyoming has nearly 130,000 fewer residents than Washington, DC, yet still has two senators and DC has none, which makes total sense.

4 The Supreme Court's 1803 *Marbury v. Madison* decision established the tradition of judicial review of the Constitution under the leadership of this chief justice.

5 From 1781 until 1789, the United States was governed by this predecessor to the Constitution.

6 The Constitution's principle of due process was a common-law legacy of this 1215 document.

7 The Founding Fathers were partly inspired to write the Constitution based on the experiences of a confederacy formed by this upstate New York group of Indian nations.

8 What is the 15th word of the Constitution's preamble?

9 How many pages is the original, parchment-written Constitution of the United States?

10 In 2013, 148 years late, this state finally ratified the 13th Amendment, which abolished slavery.

ANSWERS - 1. Soldiers - **2.** 1933 - **3.** Washington, DC - **4.** John Marshall - **5.** Articles of Confederation - **6.** Magna Carta - **7.** Iroquois - **8.** Union - **9.** Four - **10.** Mississippi

Random Stuff You Might *Not* Know

1 All Souls, Hertford, and Merton are 3 of the 38 constituent colleges of this university.

2 The island of Komodo is in this nation.

3 Despite Mel Gibson's film portrayal, this historical figure was minor nobility and not a rural farmer.

4 Used to stop bleeding, this medical device and procedure's name is derived from the French word for "to turn."

5 The Four Noble Truths are the basic philosophical orientation of this religion.

6 What was Britney Spears's character name in her two cameos in *How I Met Your Mother*?

7 Heat, Pulse, and Rise are celebrity-branded fragrances by this singer.

8 Riyad Mahrez and Jamie Vardy played together on this Premier League championship–winning club.

9 Which of the eye's photoreceptor cells is responsible for processing color in relatively bright light?

10 One point for each of the 12 buildings to hold the title of world's tallest since 1901.

PRO TIP

The Great Pyramid of Giza was the world's tallest structure for 3,871 years, surpassed by England's Lincoln Cathedral in 1311, which held the record for 238 years until its spire was destroyed in 1549. But the 28-foot-tall Tower of Jericho held the record for 4,000 years. It was the world's tallest structure from 8000 to 4000 BCE. There. Like 15 *Jeopardy!* responses in that one.

ANSWERS - 1. Oxford - **2.** Indonesia - **3.** William Wallace - **4.** Tourniquet - **5.** Buddhism - **6.** Abby - **7.** Beyoncé - **8.** Leicester City - **9.** Cones - **10.** One Times Square (Allied Chemical, Times Building), Singer Building, Met Life Tower, Woolworth, Bank of Manhattan (40 Wall Street/Trump Building), Chrysler Building, Empire State Building, World Trade Center, Sears Tower (Willis), Petronas, Taipei 101, Burj Khalifa

China

1. When translated from English to Mandarin, the famous slogan of this company became "Eat your fingers off."

2. For the last time, you can't see this from near-Earth orbit.

3. Popular among marines for "to be enthusiastic," this Chinese-adapted phrase means "work together."

4. The Fujianese dialect for either "fish sauce" or "eggplant sauce" is the origin of the name of this condiment.

5. This is the largest country that borders China.

6. This former Houston Rocket is both the owner of another of his former teams, the Shanghai Sharks, and the chairman of the Chinese Basketball Association.

7. Beijing, Tianjin, Shanghai, and this city are directly controlled by the Chinese government.

8. The highest-grossing American film in China's box office history is this superhero saga conclusion.

9. Traditional values, deemed regressive and harmful or vestiges of feudalism, were purged during this late 1960s and early '70s period in Chinese history.

10. The three teachings of China are Confucianism, Buddhism, and this third religious philosophical tradition.

> **BOX OFFICE JUGGERNAUT**
>
> *Wolf Warrior 2* (2017) is China's highest-grossing film of all time, pulling in $874 million. It was written, produced, and directed by Wu Jing, who also played the starring role. That's like if James Cameron went, "Sure, I'll be the *Avatar* blue people, too!"

ANSWERS - 1. KFC - 2. Great Wall - 3. Gung Ho - 4. Ketchup - 5. Russia - 6. Yao Ming - 7. Chongqing - 8. *Avengers: Endgame* - 9. Cultural Revolution - 10. Taoism

117

Before and After

See page 2 if you need a refresher on the rules.

1. He ate 50 hard-boiled eggs in an hour AND Jessica Jones's husband.

2. An outfield out committed by this scoring play does not affect the hitter's batting average AND Jennifer Lopez was the most famous of these *In Living Color* background dancers.

FROM BACKGROUND TO FOREGROUND

FKA Twigs, Tupac, Left Shark, and Michael K. Williams all got their starts as backup dancers.

3. "Macarena" singers AND Wayne, Martin, and Nelson hold off a gang of ranchers in this 1959 classic western.

4. The face that launched a thousand ships AND former shortstop for the Rockies, Blue Jays, and Yankees.

5. The former head coach of the Jets and Bills AND star of 2016 superhero film.

6. Spanish Mexican friars in California were the first to make this cheese AND this fictional character's daughter Kim spent like six whole days in perilous situations.

7. SpongeBob's best friend AND alter ego of Guardian of the Galaxy Peter Quill.

8. She gained 30 pounds to play frumpy Martha in *Who's Afraid of Virginia Woolf?* AND the youngest-ever winner of a Grammy for Album of the Year.

9. The two comforting words on the cover of *The Hitchhiker's Guide to the Galaxy* AND "I Write Sins Not Tragedies" band.

10. Rupert Murdoch bought this Alexander Hamilton–founded product in 1976 AND the WHO describes this period as the most crucial yet most neglected part of a child's development.

ANSWERS - 1. Cool Hand Luke Cage - 2. Sacrifice Fly Girls - 3. Los del Rio Bravo - 4. Helen of Troy Tulowitzki - 5. Rex Ryan Reynolds - 6. Monterey Jack Bauer - 7. Patrick Star-Lord - 8. Elizabeth Taylor Swift - 9. Don't Panic! at the Disco - 10. New York Post Partum

Movie Math

See the explanation on page 7 if you need a refresher on the rules.

1 *Less Than* ___ PLUS ___ *Hours: The Secret Soldiers of Benghazi*

2 *Another* ___ *Hours* MINUS ___ *Men Out*

3 ___ *Rise of an Empire* PLUS ___ *Days Later*

4 *13 Going On* ___ MINUS ___ *Grams*

5 *The Hateful* ___ TIMES ___ *Crazy Nights*

6 ___ *Mile* DIVIDED BY ___ *Weeks Notice*

7 ___ *Days of Night* MINUS ___ *Minutes or Less*

8 *Stalag* ___ MINUS *Apollo* ___

9 *Passenger* ___ DIVIDED BY ___ *Amigos*

10 *Winchester* ___ TIMES *House of* ___ *Corpses*

> **BEHIND THE SCENES**
>
> One of the "Men Out" in the 1919 Chicago "Black Sox" scandal was "Shoeless" Joe Jackson, also ostensibly the subject of another baseball film, *Field of Dreams.*

ANSWERS - 1. **13** (0 + 13 = 13) - 2. **40** (48 - 8 = 40) - 3. **328** (300 + 28 = 328) - 4. **9** (30 - 21 = 9) - 5. **64** (8 × 8 = 64) - 6. **4** (8 ÷ 2 = 4) - 7. **0** (30 - 30 = 0) - 8. **4** (17 - 13 = 4) - 9. **19** (57 ÷ 3 = 19) - 10. **73,000** (73 × 1000 = 73,000)

119

Random Stuff You Might Know

HOW :) BECOMES AN EMOJI

Anyone can submit a proposal for a new emoji to the consortium in Answer #2. You just need to write it up, design it, describe it, prove through five different searches that there's a need for it, use it in context, use it with other emojis, and you know what, it's not worth it. The world can go without a quiz host emoji.

1 What is the largest city in Iran?

2 This seven-letter word starting with *U* is the name of the computer industry's consortium for standards in representation of text and symbols.

3 This is Aziz Ansari's acclaimed Netflix series.

4 In 1173, King Henry II of England, ruler of England, Normandy, and Anjou, faced a rebellion instigated by three of his sons and their mother, this ruler of Aquitaine.

5 After claiming $13,000 in a gold stake, a Swedish immigrant named Johan founded a shoe store in Seattle that would become this eponymous department store.

6 The border between these two nations is the most frequently crossed international boundary in the world.

7 This four-letter word for a deep pile carpet is derived from the Norse word for "beard."

8 In humans and other mammals, the ceruminous and sebaceous glands secrete this protective substance.

9 This word can refer to either a medium-sized watercraft built for speed or Mariano Rivera's fastball.

10 One point for each of the 10 most abundant elements in the universe.

ANSWERS - 1. Tehran - **2.** Unicode - **3.** *Master of None* - **4.** Eleanor - **5.** Nordstrom - **6.** US and Mexico - **7.** Shag - **8.** Earwax - **9.** Cutter - **10.** Sulfur, Magnesium, Silicon, Nitrogen, Iron, Neon, Carbon, Oxygen, Helium, Hydrogen

Urban Dictionary

1 According to Urban Dictionary, this is defined as a vast array of pornography and advertisements.

2 Sharing its name with a pop-punk band, this Urban Dictionary entry describes 24 hours of smoking marijuana.

3 Urban Dictionary defines this nation as "the country Hitler wasn't born in."

4 This Urban Dictionary entry is defined as "an individual who believes that the white male Christian god should be the only object of worship on the planet."

5 This word is described by Urban Dictionary as "it's uncomfortable and there's this big hot thing in the sky and there are other people that you sometimes have to talk to."

6 According to Urban Dictionary, this is "a failed experiment in preparing young people for the adult world . . . built around 1960."

7 Urban Dictionary says that 10 minutes is the maximum attention span for this Google-owned website.

> **DID YOU KNOW?**
>
> Urban Dictionary was founded by Aaron Peckham in 1999. It has since accumulated more than 7 million definitions with roughly 2,000 new entries added daily.

8 This EDM genre is described by Urban Dictionary as "the music created from transformers having sex."

9 Used in *Straight Outta Compton*, these two words are defined by Urban Dictionary as a farewell to someone even though you couldn't give two shits less that they're leaving.

10 An entry in Urban Dictionary paraphrases James Nicoll to describe this language as one that "lurks in dark alleys, beats up other languages, and rifles through their pockets for spare vocabulary."

ANSWERS - 1. The Internet - 2. Green Day - 3. Germany - 4. Republican - 5. Outside - 6. High School - 7. YouTube - 8. Dubstep - 9. Bye Felicia - 10. English

Before and After

See page 2 if you need a refresher on the rules.

1 Scotland's mythical plesiosaur AND motorized arena favorite Grave Digger.

2 Legendary son of Uther Pendragon AND the US Open's venue is named for this sports star and activist.

3 Fictional nineties hairstyle icon AND garment for Masters Tournament winner.

4 Home Run Derby champion in 2017 AND before gaining TV fame, she served in Manhattan Family Court.

5 "I have come here to chew bubblegum and kick ass, and I'm all out of bubblegum" movie AND a hit for Moore and McCartney in two different mediums.

6 Betting jargon for first; first or second; or first, second, or third AND 1927 Kern and Hammerstein American musical.

7 A Packers fan AND "You never get a second chance to make a first impression" hair care product.

8 Frontier item made by a wright or an Old Crow song AND Pat Sajak's workplace.

9 Anne Brontë's debut novel AND the leader of the Unsullied.

10 The full name of the main character in TV's *The Nanny* AND "She Drives Me Crazy" band.

ANSWERS - 1. Loch Ness Monster Truck - 2. King Arthur Ashe - 3. Rachel Green Jacket - 4. Aaron Judge Judy - 5. They Live and Let Die - 6. Win Place or Show Boat - 7. Cheese Head & Shoulders - 8. Wagon Wheel of Fortune - 9. Agnes Grey Worm - 10. Fran Fine Young Cannibals

Saved by the Bell

1 *Saved by the Bell's* precursor, *Good Morning, Miss Bliss,* took place in Indianapolis; when retooled, the action took place in this fictional California town.

2 Appearing in the final season, this character was named after the daughter of a famous television producer.

3 *Saved by the Bell's* classroom set was later used by *That's So Raven* and this Miranda Cosgrove show.

4 Before achieving stardom, this *Wild Things* actor had a cameo in *Saved by the Bell.*

5 What company manufactured Zack Morris's enormous cell phone?

6 What was A. C.'s nickname for Jessie?

7 What was the name of Screech's anthropomorphic robot?

8 Above a filing cabinet near his desk, Mr. Belding has a diploma in this martial art.

9 Although Tiffani Amber Thiessen was cast as Kelly Kapowski, both Elizabeth Berkley and this *Beverly Hills, 90210* actor auditioned for the role.

10 In 2009, this talk show mounted an unsuccessful campaign to make a *Saved by the Bell* reunion.

BEHIND THE SCENES

A decade later, *Saved by the Bell* was rebooted. Now do *F Troop,* cowards!

Random Stuff You Might Know

1 In 2007, open-source advocate Chris Messina is credited with introducing the use of this symbol on Twitter.

2 St. Francis of Assisi is the first in recorded Christian history to receive on his body these marks of the crucified body of Jesus Christ.

3 St. John's, the capital of Newfoundland and Labrador, marks its founding year as 1497, when this Italian explorer, under contract to England, first landed in its harbor.

DID YOU KNOW?

Three 6 Mafia was the first hip-hop *group* to win the Academy Award for Best Original Song. The first hip-hop *song* to win the award, however, was Eminem's "Lose Yourself" from *8 Mile* in 2002.

4 With 87.6 percent of the vote, this Washington Senators pitcher received the least number of votes of the first five inaugural members of the Baseball Hall of Fame.

5 Performed by Three 6 Mafia, this song from *Hustle & Flow* won the 2005 Oscar for Best Original Song.

6 Beverly Cleary created Ralph S. Mouse and nine novels starring this annoying little sister.

7 After the United States, this is the second-most-populous member of NATO.

8 Sooner and this other crème white Welsh pony are matching mascots of the University of Oklahoma.

9 By number of supporters, this is Ukraine's most popular football club.

10 One point each for the 10 Academy Award Best Picture winners for the decade of 2000 to 2009.

Departed, No Country for Old Men, Slumdog Millionaire, The Hurt Locker
10. *Gladiator, A Beautiful Mind, Chicago, LOTR: Return of the King, Million Dollar Baby, Crash, The*
- **5.** "It's Hard out Here for a Pimp" - **6.** Ramona Quimby - **7.** Germany - **8.** Boomer - **9.** Dynamo Kyiv -
ANSWERS - **1.** Hashtag (or Number or Pound Sign) - **2.** Stigmata - **3.** John Cabot - **4.** Walter Johnson -

US Army Ranks

Ten-hut! Name the US Army ranks by their insignia.

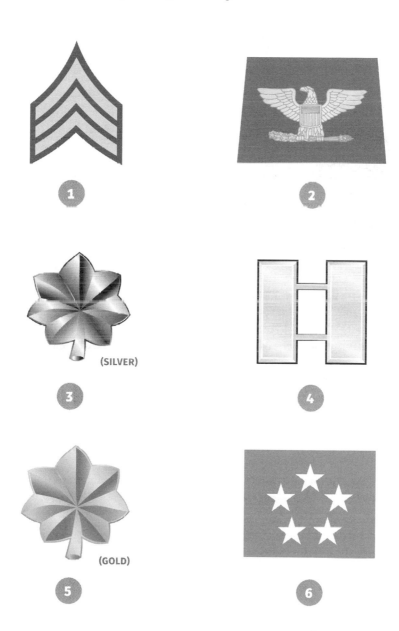

(SILVER)

(GOLD)

The United Kingdom

1 After booking a one-way ticket to LA, English singer-songwriter Ed Sheeran was discovered by this Oscar-winning actor, singer, and comedian.

2 Beginning with earthen mounds in 3100 BCE, scientists theorize that this world monument was continually altered for the next 1,000 years.

IT'S THE UK, OK?

Remember this: The UK is properly the United Kingdom of Great Britain and Northern Ireland. So that's a state, an island, and a country.

3 The English Bill of Rights of 1689 prevents people of this faith from ever ascending the throne of England.

4 The area known as Holyrood is the home to this country's autonomous Parliament.

5 Wings and engines for planes made by this European multinational aircraft company are manufactured in the UK.

6 James Watson is an American, but this co-discoverer of DNA was British.

7 In 1922, five-sixths of this island seceded from the United Kingdom.

8 The national anthem of the United Kingdom provided the melody for this American patriotic song.

9 Music artists from this English city claim the most number-one singles (54) of any city per capita in the world.

10 *Rain, Steam and Speed, Wreckers Coast of Northumberland*, and *The Fighting Temeraire* are famous paintings by this English Romantic artist.

ANSWERS - 1. Jamie Foxx - 2. Stonehenge - 3. Catholicism - 4. Scotland - 5. Airbus - 6. Francis Crick - 7. Ireland - 8. "My Country, 'Tis of Thee" - 9. Liverpool - 10. J. M. W. Turner

Middle Ages

32

1 On Christmas Day, 800 CE, he was crowned Holy Roman Emperor.

2 Featuring rounded arches, barrel vaults, and narrow windows in robust walls, this is the name given to the architectural style immediately preceding Gothic.

3 Nearly 70 meters long, this tapestry depicts the events leading to and culminating in the Norman invasion.

4 The first documented use of this foreign military technology by Europeans against Europeans took place in 1304 when it was used by the English against the Scots.

5 Jan van Eyck's famous *Ghent Altarpiece* was one of the artistic masterworks seized by the Nazis and recovered as depicted in this movie starring and directed by George Clooney.

6 Most likely introduced from Baghdad in the mid-13th century, this device tripled the wool output of medieval Europe.

7 This Benedictine abbess of Bingen wrote music, studied natural history, and produced visionary works of Christian mysticism.

8 The Danelaw refers to the 9th- and 10th-century Viking-dominated territories of this island.

9 Robin Hood and Maid Marian were depicted as this kind of animal in Disney's 1973 *Robin Hood.*

10 He wrote the 1485 epic *Le Morte d'Arthur.*

> **PRO TIP**
>
> There are basically only three French cathedrals for trivia purposes. Memorize them. Reims was liberated by Joan of Arc and is the traditional location of the coronation of French kings. Notre Dame de Paris is in Paris and flammable. The third one is Chartres. (Nothing really ever happened at Chartres.)

ANSWERS - 1. Charlemagne - 2. Romanesque - 3. Bayeux Tapestry - 4. Gunpowder - 5. *The Monuments Men* - 6. Spinning Wheel - 7. Hildegard - 8. Great Britain - 9. Fox - 10. Thomas Malory

Random Stuff You Might Know

1. Modern pizza was invented in this city during the late 19th century.

2. This pop singer's evangelical upbringing included eating "angeled" eggs and a ban on Lucky Charms (because the word *luck* is reminiscent of Lucifer).

3. This is the title of the crown prince of the royal family of France.

4. Canon cameras began in 1933 with a copy of this German company's 35 mm film camera.

5. What was Hungarian classical composer Bartók's first name?

6. He was the only US president alumnus of Amherst College.

7. This 1803 Supreme Court case defined the boundary between the judicial and executive branches.

8. Meaning "military observation," this word derives from the French word for "to recognize."

AROUND THE COUNTRY

In the downstairs men's bathroom of Macalester College's music building, the farthest stall was graffitied "Bartok Rulez!" I can't remember if I did it or not.

9. Originally thought to be a fig, more recent scholarship says that the apple of the Adam and Eve fable was most likely this Mediterranean fruit.

10. One point for each of the 15 officially recognized current sovereign states that directly succeeded the 15 Soviet Socialist Republics of the USSR.

ANSWERS - 1. Naples - 2. Katy Perry - 3. Dauphin - 4. Leica - 5. Béla - 6. Calvin Coolidge - 7. *Marbury v. Madison* - 8. Reconnaissance - 9. Pomegranate - 10. Armenia, Azerbaijan, Belarus, Estonia, Georgia, Kazakhstan, Kyrgyzstan, Latvia, Lithuania, Moldova, Russia, Tajikistan, Turkmenistan, Ukraine, Uzbekistan

Germany

33

1 In 2017, the American-built Tesla Model S outsold in Europe BMW's flagship 7 Series and this Mercedes-Benz flagship model.

2 Oktoberfest takes place in this German state.

3 Many middle-class and working-class Germans emigrated to the United States after the aristocracy regained control following the 19th-century European revolutions that began in this year.

4 Duisburg, Oberhausen, Essen, Hagen, Dortmund, and others are collectively referred to as a conurbation in this river valley.

5 This is the name in German of the German federal parliament.

6 Germany never lost a game in which this top scorer in both the history of German national football and the World Cup scored.

7 Nearly all American Christmas traditions— including wreaths and trees—were German traditions popularized by this German-born consort of Queen Victoria.

8 In 1895, this German physicist discovered X-rays.

9 The scores to *The Dark Knight* trilogy, *Gladiator*, and *The Lion King* were composed by this German composer.

10 In 1919, Walter Gropius founded this German design and architecture school.

> **DID YOU KNOW?**
>
> BMW's iconic blue-and-white logo is *not* a spinning propeller. Although there was a spinning propeller ad from 1929, the BMW logo predates that by more than a decade. Instead, the blue and white is an homage to the colors of the flag of the company's home state, Answer #2.

Before and After

See page 2 if you need a refresher on the rules.

1 According to official lore, this starship commander was born March 22, 2233, in Iowa AND born-again Christian former star of *Growing Pains*.

2 The creator of Sansa and Arya AND Emilio Estevez's dad.

3 Two-word slang for "Australia" AND the battleship's cook is a former Navy SEAL in this 1992 action flick.

4 He was shot and killed by his former friend on April 3, 1882, in St. Joseph, Missouri, AND from 2013 to 2016, this Alex Cross author was the country's highest-paid author.

5 She haunts the Hogwarts girls' lavatory AND the 29-floor Margate hotel is the tallest building in this South Carolina tourist town.

6 Building wherein John Hancock signed his "John Hancock" AND signing location of the Treaty of Versailles.

7 He gained his lofty title after the death of Saul and Jonathan AND he is the voice of *Planet Earth*.

8 The English nickname for the last movement of Beethoven's Ninth AND based on Psalm 98, Psalm 96, and Genesis 3:17, this is the most published Christmas carol in North America.

9 This video game franchise, unabbreviated, began in 1999 with eight playable characters; as of 2018, it has 74 AND musing on God, free will, and patricide, this was Dostoyevsky's final novel.

10 Played by Bubba Smith, "Spare Tire" Dixon was the nemesis to the former Polk High School football star of this sitcom AND Stephen King's *Night Shift* featured this story of terrifying Amish-dressed juveniles.

ANSWERS - 1. Captain Kirk Cameron - 2. George R. R. Martin Sheen - 3. Down Under Siege - 4. Jesse James Patterson - 5. Moaning Myrtle Beach - 6. Independence Hall of Mirrors - 7. King David Attenborough - 8. Ode to Joy to the World - 9. Super Smash Brothers Karamazov - 10. Married with Children of the Corn

Plant Kingdom

1 Often used in traditional medicine and unproven in its efficacy toward improving memory, this Chinese- and Japanese-cultivated tree is the only species in its taxonomic division.

2 Whereas the flag of Canada features a maple leaf, the flag of this nation features a cypress tree.

3 In 2005, a Judean date palm sprang from a 2,000-year-old seed and was thus given this biblical name synonymous with longevity.

PRO TIP

Hong Kong, South Carolina, FIJI, Mexico, and many others have plants on their flags. Study these, all you budding vexillologists.

4 Pamela Lillian Isley is the alter ego of this Batman supervillain.

5 A single variety of hair grass and a single variety of pearlwort are the only two flowering plants on this continent.

6 "Green Onions" was a 1962 instrumental hit by this band.

7 Although they visually resemble land-based plants, these maritime plants are actually multicellular algae.

8 He's the lead singer of Led Zeppelin.

9 Alien seedpods create doppelgängers in a small California town in this 1956 horror classic.

10 Rousseau said, "I know no greater man on earth," and Goethe said, "I know no one among the no longer living who has influenced me more strongly" of this Swedish botanist.

10. Carl Linnaeus
6. Booker T. and the MG's - 7. Seaweed - 8. Robert Plant - 9. *Invasion of the Body Snatchers* -
ANSWERS - 1. Ginkgo Biloba - 2. Lebanon - 3. Methuselah - 4. Poison Ivy - 5. Antarctica -

ROUND 4 / DIFFICULTY LEVEL `1` `2` `3` `4` **5** `6`

Random Stuff You Might *Not* Know

1 Plus or minus 10, how many symphonies did Franz Joseph Haydn write?

2 Synonymous with the state, this is the Russian word for "fortress."

3 Aardman Animations is best known as the creator of this Plasticine duo.

4 The Hebrides are an archipelago on the west coast of this constituent country.

5 In 1955, the Mercedes-Benz 300 SLR of Pierre Levegh crashed and exploded, killing more than 80 spectators at this famed auto race.

6 With a coal mine burning underneath it since 1962, Centralia is a ghost town in this US state.

IN THE PITS

Young People's Concerts are excellent entry points into classical music if you've ever been curious. Entertaining and educational for adults, too!

7 Featuring St. Louis athletes like Marshall Faulk, "Air Force Ones" was a number-three hit by this rapper in 2002.

8 Airing from 1958 to 1972, the New York Philharmonic and CBS television's *Young People's Concerts* was hosted by this conductor.

9 What is the name of Toronto's Canadian Football League team?

10 One point for each of the 12 smallest sovereign nations on Earth by area.

ANSWERS - 1. 104 (Between 94 and 114 gets a point!) - 2. Kremlin - 3. Wallace and Gromit - 4. Scotland - 5. Le Mans - 6. Pennsylvania - 7. Nelly - 8. Leonard Bernstein - 9. Argonauts - 10. St. Vincent and the Grenadines, Grenada, Malta, Maldives, St. Kitts and Nevis, Marshall Islands, Liechtenstein, San Marino, Nauru, Tuvalu, Monaco, Vatican City

New York Neighborhoods

1 The Belmont neighborhood of the Bronx is most famous for this Little Italy thoroughfare.

2 The Staten Island Ferry, Staten Island Yankees, and Staten Island Borough Hall are all in this neighborhood.

3 While serving at Fort Hamilton, Robert E. Lee was on the vestry of St. John's Episcopal Church—also the site of Stonewall Jackson's baptism—in this southwest Brooklyn neighborhood.

4 This Queens neighborhood's name is the anglicization of the name of the Dutch port city of Vlissingen.

5 This is the only inhabited island of the Bronx's Pelham Islands.

6 McLean Avenue creates the border between the Woodlawn neighborhood in the Bronx and this fourth-most populous city in New York State.

> **NYC LOCAL TIP**
>
> Any clue that mentions a US city's population prior to 1898 is probably trying to trick you, but the answer is likely Brooklyn. On January 1, 1898, New York City absorbed the independent city of Brooklyn (as well as the other three boroughs). The residents of Brooklyn gathered in front of their former city hall and held a mock funeral for their city.

7 Dutch for "Dead Hill," this Staten Island neighborhood is named after the highest point in New York City.

8 In 1978, the artists living in this neighborhood created its terrible acronym name on purpose to deter real estate developers. (It didn't work.)

9 This Queens neighborhood was named after one of its first developers, the Real Good Construction Company.

10 W. E. B. Du Bois, Thurgood Marshall, Duke Ellington, and Cab Calloway are among the many prominent and wealthy Black residents who lived in the elegant row houses of this Harlem neighborhood.

ANSWERS - 1. Arthur Avenue **- 2.** St. George **- 3.** Bay Ridge **- 4.** Flushing **- 5.** City Island **- 6.** Yonkers **- 7.** Todt Hill **- 8.** DUMBO **- 9.** Rego Park **- 10.** Sugar Hill

Before and After

See page 2 if you need a refresher on the rules.

1 This character has appeared in the most Disney animated movies ever AND in the climactic battle scene of this 1933 movie, the hero Rufus T. Firefly wears a different uniform in every take.

2 Viola, Duke Orsino, and Countess Olivia form a cross-dressing love triangle in this Shakespeare play AND the band behind the hit "Sister Christian."

FUN FACT

Totoro, from the classic Japanese animated film *My Neighbor Totoro*, makes a nonspeaking cameo appearance in the first part of Answer #7.

3 A 19th-century Speaker of the House, US senator, secretary of state, and failed presidential candidate AND in 2008 this Idol made his Broadway debut as Sir Robin in *Spamalot*.

4 Despite being the villain, Arnold Schwarzenegger got top billing in this 1997 movie AND Mork from Ork.

5 A special wager question on *Jeopardy!* AND a staple item of the In-N-Out Burger menu.

6 In 2003, New York governor George Pataki issued the state's first-ever posthumous pardon for this notorious comic AND the actor who played Ash Williams in the *Evil Dead* franchise.

7 Lotso is the villain of this animated movie AND Leonard Nimoy directed this Guttenberg, Selleck, and Danson hit.

8 The full name of this comic strip that ran from 1924 to 2010 about a fatherless ginger-haired girl AND exhibition shooter known as Little Miss Sure Shot.

9 This 18.5-ton coelurosaurian theropod was one of the world's last non-avian dinosaurs AND Donald Trump's (and Exxon's) first secretary of state.

10 This San Francisco Giants first baseman led the 1984 US Olympic team in batting average, hits, and RBI AND a famous *Daily Planet* reporter.

ANSWERS - 1. Donald Duck Soup - 2. Twelfth Night Ranger - 3. Henry Clay Aiken - 4. Batman & Robin Williams - 5. Daily Double Double - 6. Lenny Bruce Campbell - 7. Toy Story 3 Men and a Baby - 8. Little Orphan Annie Oakley - 9. Tyrannosaurus Rex Tillerson - 10. Will Clark Kent

Commodities

1 The property of an individual unit of a commodity that is interchangeable with another is known as this *F* word.

2 This two-word holly plant, endemic to South America, lends its second word to the caffeinated drink made from its leaves.

3 "From the taste of wheat, it is not possible to tell who produced it; a Russian serf, a French peasant, or an English capitalist," wrote this German philosopher and economist in 1859.

4 This is the *M* in the full name of the commodity-trading, food-processing, multinational ADM.

5 This Emmy-winning actor is the great-great-granddaughter of the founder of the world's largest trader of cotton and rice.

6 The world's exclusive trading exchange of palm oil, Bursa Malaysia, operates in this currency.

7 Random length lumber, hardwood pulp, and softwood pulp are traded alongside, more famously, lean hogs, live cattle, and feeder cattle in this city's mercantile exchange.

8 The two main benchmarks for crude oil are the West Texas Intermediate and this type of North Sea crude, sharing its name with the surname of a famous Ricky Gervais character.

9 Cooling superconductor magnets in MRI machines are the single-largest worldwide use for this gas in its liquid form.

10 Once a premium industrial product, this word describes the rapidly commodifying synthetics with units measured between 1 and 100 nm.

> **PRO TIP**
>
> To be a great host—not just a good one—you gotta keep up the banter. There's gonna be dead air, and if your audio system isn't up to par to pipe in some fadeable background music, keep your guests entertained with some light jokes. Trivia folks are pretty easy to please, so groan-worthy puns or pointing out obviously incorrect answers are fast ways toward a cheap laugh.

ANSWERS - 1. Fungibility - 2. Yerba Maté - 3. Karl Marx - 4. Midlands (Archer-Daniels-Midlands) - 5. Julia Louis-Dreyfus - 6. Malaysian Ringgit (RM) - 7. Chicago - 8. Brent Crude - 9. Helium - 10. Nanomaterials

Random Stuff You Might Know

1 The opening credits of *Gilligan's Island* feature an American flag at half-staff because the filming occurred days after this event.

2 What is the currency of Indonesia?

3 Blame a 1974 prank by Danish theater group Solvognen for the inspiration for the 1994 creation of this annual holiday-themed public nuisance.

4 PeoplesBank Park in York, Pennsylvania, is the only ballpark in the United States with a field boundary higher than this baseball landmark.

5 The first-run episodes of this children's show moved to subscription-only HBO in 2016.

6 He was the first casualty of the Boston Massacre.

7 This district of Tokyo is internationally known as the nexus of Japanese youth style and culture.

8 This American cultural icon was a dancer, singer, performer, cook, actor, and prostitute until, in 1969, at the age of 41, she rose to international stardom with the publication of her first of seven autobiographies.

9 This Greek goddess's Roman analogue is Diana.

10 One point for the top 12 characters to appear in the most Marvel Comics.

ANSWERS - 1. JFK Assassination - **2.** Rupiah - **3.** SantaCon - **4.** Fenway Park's Green Monster - **5.** *Sesame Street* - **6.** Crispus Attucks - **7.** Harajuku - **8.** Maya Angelou - **9.** Artemis - **10.** Beast, Invisible Woman, Hulk, Human Torch, Cyclops, Mr. Fantastic, Thor, The Thing, Iron Man, Wolverine, Captain America, Spider-Man

Fictional Geography

1. The ruins of a statue likened to Tawaret, the Egyptian goddess of childbirth, and a lighthouse are two of the landmarks on the island in this TV series.

2. Located near Sumatra, Mildendo is the capital of this tiny fictional island created by Jonathan Swift.

3. This fictional dystopia's name is derived from the Latin term for "bread and circuses."

4. Over time, this fictional Thomas More locale went from his original satirical meaning of Greek for "not a place" to today's meaning of "perfect society."

5. The volcano Amon Amarth rises from the desert plain Gorgoroth in this fictional land.

6. This film opens on Tatooine and concludes on the Forest Moon of Endor.

> **AN OLD TRIVIA STANDBY**
>
> The death of C. S. Lewis, the author of one of the answers in this round, was largely overshadowed. On any other day, his death would have been front-page news. Unfortunately for Mr. Lewis, he died on November 22, 1963, the same day as John F. Kennedy.

7. From a creator of *Rick and Morty*, Planet Schlorp is the home world of Korvo and Terry in this Hulu show.

8. Cair Paravel is the seat of High King Peter and his siblings, who are the rulers—for a time—of this fictional land.

9. Only officers are allowed to visit the fictional island Bali Ha'i in this musical.

10. The students of Seven Seas High School, a school aboard the SS *Tipton*, visit Parrot Island in this Disney Channel sequel/spin-off series.

ANSWERS - 1. Lost - 2. Lilliput - 3. Panem (*The Hunger Games*) - 4. Utopia - 5. Mordor - 6. Return of the Jedi - 7. *Solar Opposites* - 8. Narnia - 9. *South Pacific* - 10. *The Suite Life on Deck*

Before and After

See page 2 if you need a refresher on the rules.

1 The singers of "Hold On, I'm Comin'" and "Soul Man" AND "Eat Drink Play" is the slogan of this chain of entertainment restaurants.

2 This 1902 comic character later became famous as the mascot for a shoe company AND this LA restaurant is the purported birthplace of the Cobb salad.

3 This model and actor starred in *Pearl Harbor* and *Sin City* AND this Philadelphia edge city is famous for the country's third-largest shopping mall.

PENNSYLVANIA FEELIN'

The city in Question #3 is named after a popular inn that is one day's journey from colonial Philadelphia.

4 Frederick Law Olmsted and Calvert Vaux designed this Brooklyn landmark after finishing Central Park AND the second-highest-priced Monopoly property.

5 A songwriter for *The Lion King* soundtrack AND the economist who theorized that state intervention is necessary to mitigate boom-and-bust cycles.

6 Rosalind and Celia find love in the Forest of Arden in this Shakespeare comedy AND Bugs Bunny was inspired by Clark Gable's carrot-eating character nicknamed Doc from this movie.

7 After their lifelong feud is resolved, elderly rivals Max and John hunt a giant catfish in this 1993 sequel AND the singers of "The Safety Dance."

8 *The Carrie Diaries* is a spin-off of this show AND according to "California Love," Tupac represents LA, good ol' Watts, and this location.

9 King Nebuchadnezzar II allegedly built this botanical Wonder of the Ancient World to please his homesick wife AND this ensemble cast sci-fi drama ran in syndication from 1994 to 1998.

10 He starred with Jack Lemmon and Marilyn Monroe in *Some Like It Hot* AND he is perhaps best known for the *Superfly* soundtrack.

ANSWERS - 1. Sam & Dave & Buster's - 2. Buster Brown Derby - 3. Jaime King of Prussia - 4. Prospect Park Place - 5. Elton John Maynard Keynes - 6. As You Like It Happened One Night - 7. Grumpier Old Men without Hats - 8. Sex and the City of Compton - 9. Hanging Gardens of Babylon 5 - 10. Tony Curtis Mayfield

Extreme Sports

1 The famous quote, "There are only three sports: bullfighting, motor racing, and mountaineering, the rest are merely games" has been frequently—and erroneously—attributed to this author.

2 A participant in this French vaulting, rolling, and climbing movement sport is called a *traceur*.

3 Embracing the thrills of outdoor activity with the satisfaction of a well-pressed shirt, Englishman Phil Shaw founded an extreme version of this household activity in 1997.

4 In 1981, the Specialized Stumpjumper became the first mass produced model utilized by followers of this outdoor sport.

5 Former Alaskan Governor Sarah Palin's ex-husband Todd is a four-time winner of the Tesoro Iron Dog, the world's longest race for these vehicles.

6 In mountaineering, these multispiked items affix to your boots to aid in climbing during icy conditions.

7 Discovered in Sweden in 1924 and carbon-dated to 3200 BCE, the Kalvträskskidan is thought to be the oldest surviving example of this equipment used for both sport and transport.

8 On June 19, 2002, Texan Michael Barber set this unpowered air sport's world record by covering 437 miles.

9 Featuring Tony Alva and Tony Hawk, the 1986 skateboarding movie *Thrashin'* starred this actor famous for playing Thanos in the MCU series of films.

10 In 2009, Red Bull built a half pipe of natural snow on the backside of Colorado's Silverton Mountain specifically for this snowboarder.

LOST IN THE MISTS OF TIME

Oxford University's Dangerous Sports Club invented bungee jumping in 1979. Inspired by the vine-jumping and the land-diving rituals of Vanuatu, Oxford students jumped from Bristol, England's Clifton Suspension Bridge. Subsequently arrested, they nonetheless started a trend.

ANSWERS - 1. Ernest Hemingway - 2. Parkour - 3. Ironing - 4. Mountain Biking - 5. Snowmobiles - 6. Crampons - 7. Skis - 8. Hang Gliding - 9. Josh Brolin - 10. Shaun White

Random Stuff You Might *Not* Know

1 Chris Froome, a British winner of the Tour de France, was born in this country.

2 Muscat is the capital of this Arab sultanate.

3 Rapper Carlton Ridenhour is better known by this stage name.

4 This was the name of Felicity's unrequited love interest, played by Scott Speedman, in *Felicity*.

5 Who was elected mayor of London in 2016?

6 Babe Ruth, Lou Gehrig, Bob Meusel, and this second baseman formed the Yankees' Murderers' Row in the 1920s.

7 Because of his fear of flying, striker Dennis Bergkamp was nicknamed the Non-Flying Dutchman by supporters of this English Premier League club.

8 This word refers to an ancient practice of Christianity that actively shunned the material world to concentrate solely on spirituality.

9 Signed December 24, 1814, the Treaty of Ghent ended this conflict.

10 One point each for the titles of Bob Dylan's first 10 studio albums.

IT WAS A DIFFERENT TIME

The Battle of New Orleans—which shot genocidal racist Andrew Jackson to fame—was fought on January 8, 1815. News of the peace marked by the Treaty of Ghent didn't reach North America for another couple of weeks.

ANSWERS - 1. Kenya - 2. Oman - 3. Chuck D - 4. Ben Covington - 5. Sadiq Khan - 6. Tony Lazzeri - 7. Arsenal - 8. Gnosticism - 9. War of 1812 - 10. Bob Dylan, *The Freewheelin' Bob Dylan*, *The Times They Are A-Changin'*, *Another Side of Bob Dylan*, *Bringing It All Back Home*, *Highway 61 Revisited*, *Blonde on Blonde*, *John Wesley Harding*, *Nashville Skyline*, *Self Portrait*

Empires

1 In the 1780s, setting national policy, Thomas Jefferson said that the US should wait "till our population can be sufficiently advanced to gain it" before dismantling this country's empire piece by piece.

2 Some historians cite the true end of the Roman Empire not in 476 CE but instead with the 1453 CE fall of this city.

3 Although the British Empire had the highest population of any empire in history, with 458 million in 1938, this empire's 13th-century height boasted a higher proportion of the world population, with 25 percent of people on Earth under its rule.

> ° **I'LL RISK IT**
> ....
> Play Risk. You'll never know when it'll help you with the geography and provinces of long-dead empires. Isn't that right, Kamchatka?

4 Young staff attempt to save their store and dread Rex Manning Day in this 1995 movie.

5 The 1987 film *Empire of the Sun* stars this actor as a British child living in Japanese-occupied China.

6 At her empire's height in 1900, this queen's title was "Her Majesty by the Grace of God, of the United Kingdom of Great Britain and Ireland Queen, Defender of the Faith, Empress of India."

7 The credits of this band's second album, *Evil Empire*, lists personnel as the "guilty parties."

8 The 16th- to 18th-century Safavid Empire ruled over what today is this nation.

9 In 2007, the American Institute of Architects listed this structure as America's number-one favorite piece of architecture.

10 Lasting from 200 BCE to 200 CE, this Chinese empire was roughly contemporaneous with that of the Romans.

ANSWERS - 1. Spain - 2. Constantinople - 3. Mongol Empire - 4. *Empire Records* - 5. Christian Bale - 6. Victoria - 7. Rage Against the Machine - 8. Iran - 9. Empire State Building - 10. Han Dynasty

Oscars

1 Winning four Oscars in 1954 alone, this man has the record for most Academy Awards, with 22.

2 With 10 nominations, this 2000 movie holds the record for most nominations for a foreign language film.

3 Alan Menken won back-to-back best Oscars for the song "Beauty and the Beast" in 1991 and this song in 1992.

4 Appearing for only 16 minutes and 10 seconds, the actor who played this legendary 1991 character had the second-shortest screen time to earn the Best Actor award.

5 At 238 minutes with overture, entr'acte, and exit music, this is the longest movie to win Best Picture.

6 She's the only person to win an Academy Award for acting and another for writing.

7 In 1962, Omar Sharif became the first Middle Eastern actor nominated for an acting Oscar for his role in this David Lean film.

BEHIND THE SCENES

David Niven's 15-minute, 38-second appearance in *Separate Tables* (1958) is the shortest for Best Actor. The shortest Oscar-winning performance ever came with Beatrice Straight's 5-minute, 2-second Best Supporting Actress–winning performance from 1976's *Network*.

8 A. R. Rahman won the 2008 Oscar for Best Song for this *Slumdog Millionaire* song.

9 Luise Rainer won back-to-back Best Actress Oscars for 1936's *The Great Ziegfeld* and this 1938 movie based on a Pearl S. Buck novel.

10 In 1980, this actor won the Academy Award for Best Directing in his directorial debut for *Ordinary People*.

ANSWERS - 1. Walt Disney - 2. *Crouching Tiger, Hidden Dragon* - 3. "A Whole New World" - 4. Hannibal Lecter - 5. *Gone with the Wind* - 6. Emma Thompson - 7. *Lawrence of Arabia* - 8. "Jai Ho" - 9. *The Good Earth* - 10. Robert Redford

Chemistry

1 An organic compound must contain this element.

2 Focusing on elixirs and transmutation of base metals, this was the name of the protoscientific tradition that predated chemistry.

3 According to Aristotle, matter was made of these four elements.

4 An atom or molecule that has gained or lost electrons and is thus charged is known by this three-letter word.

5 Before being executed by guillotine, this French chemist debunked the phlogiston theory of combustion by discovering and naming oxygen and hydrogen.

6 In 1896, French chemist Henri Becquerel discovered this process by which an unstable nucleus loses energy by emitting particles like neutrinos.

7 In 1855, University of Heidelberg mechanic Peter Desaga helped design an open-gas-flame laboratory device for this man.

8 What is the formula in Avogadro's number?

9 What is the heaviest noble gas?

10 H_2SO_4 is this kind of acid.

> **PRO TIP**
>
> A trickier trivia test might try to slip you up, but don't fall for it: Although not popularly associated as such, helium is *also* a noble gas.

Random Stuff You Might *Not* Know

1 While Lingala, Kikongo, Swahili, and Tshiluba are recognized, this is the official language of the Democratic Republic of the Congo.

2 This spicy sauce is named for the eastern Thai city of its invention.

THAT'S SPICY

David Tran named his popular hot sauce company Huy Fong Foods after the Taiwanese freighter that took Tran and his family as refugees from war-torn Vietnam to Hong Kong. Although Huy Fong's green cap and rooster logo are trademarks, the word in Answer #2 has been deemed generic.

3 This number-one pick in the 2007 NBA draft is considered one of the biggest busts of all time.

4 The strong metamorphic bedrock of Manhattan is made of this kind of rock.

5 This bush ballad is often called the unofficial national anthem of Australia.

6 This Irish English rock band's name comes from the Irish phrase for "kiss my arse."

7 The companies that would later become Exxon and Mobil and ultimately ExxonMobil were the result of the breakup of this corporation.

8 William Daniels, the voice of *Knight Rider*'s K.I.T.T., is perhaps best known for this *Boy Meets World* role.

9 What is Turk's first name on *Scrubs*?

10 One point for each of *Rolling Stone* magazine's 10 greatest guitarists of all time.

ANSWERS - 1. French - 2. Sriracha - 3. Greg Oden - 4. Manhattan Schist - 5. "Waltzing Matilda" - 6. The Pogues - 7. Standard Oil - 8. Mr. Feeny - 9. Christopher - 10. Pete Townshend, Duane Allman, Eddie Van Halen, Chuck Berry, B. B. King, Jeff Beck, Keith Richards, Jimmy Page, Eric Clapton, Jimi Hendrix

Texas Sports

1 This Houston Oiler was both the first undrafted and first African American quarterback enshrined in the Pro Football Hall of Fame.

2 As part of the 1991 Twins and 1998 to 2000 Yankees, this former Texas A&M Aggie infielder has four World Series rings.

3 In 2004, Lone Star Park at Grand Prairie hosted this final race in the American Thoroughbred racing season.

THE MICK

On April 9, 1965, Mickey Mantle became the first player to get a single—and later in the game, a home run—at the Texas stadium in Answer #8.

4 FC Dallas plays in a soccer-specific stadium in Frisco, Texas, with naming sponsorship provided by this automaker.

5 This Texan won the gold medals in team, all-around, vault, and floor exercise gymnastic competitions in the 2016 Rio Olympics.

6 With a 102,512-person capacity, this stadium is Texas's largest sports venue.

7 This racer has won five of the eight United States Grand Prix held at Austin's Circuit of the Americas.

8 On December 17, 1965, Judy Garland, supported by opening act The Supremes, became the first musical artist to play this Texas sporting venue.

9 The Dallas Stars won their first and only Stanley Cup in this year.

10 The Texas Rangers were formed in 1971 as a relocation of the second iteration of this franchise.

ANSWERS - 1. Warren Moon - 2. Chuck Knoblauch - 3. Breeders' Cup - 4. Toyota - 5. Simone Biles - 6. Kyle Field - 7. Lewis Hamilton - 8. Houston Astrodome - 9. 1999 - 10. Washington Senators

Before and After

See page 2 if you need a refresher on the rules.

1. A 1977 Schwarzenegger and Ferrigno weightlifting movie AND Tony Stark's alias.

2. He received a knighthood for performing at Princess Diana's funeral AND in 1993, against Michael Jordan and Horace Grant, this Knicks guard made the play known only as "The Dunk."

AHH, THE KNICKS

In Game 7 of the 1994 Finals, that Knicks player in Question #2 missed 16 of 18 shots, 11 of which were from 3-point range. But everyone forgets he hit 16 points in the fourth quarter of Game 6. So . . .

3. By wins, poles, and laps led, she is the most successful woman ever in American open-wheeled racing AND the *Master and Commander* author.

4. Film and Broadway story of The Four Seasons AND "End of the Road" R&B group.

5. With 252, he has the most home runs as a Met in history AND Custard is this American Greetings character's cat.

6. This bovine animal tills the rice fields and provides dairy for much of the Indian subcontinent and Southeast Asia AND the losers of Super Bowls XXV, XXVI, XXVII, and XXVIII.

7. This actor played Spartacus AND acting as military governor from 1945 to 1951, he was known in Japan as Gaijin Shogun, or "the foreign general."

8. The subtitle added after the fact to a *Star Wars* movie AND the disgraced former goalkeeper of the US Women's National Team.

9. Rapper famous for "Ruff Ryders' Anthem" AND fans have divided this sci-fi TV show into Mytharc, Monster of the Week, and Syndicate episodes.

10. A British dried-fruit pudding with a silly name AND this 1930s character is torn between Tess Trueheart and Breathless Mahoney.

ANSWERS - 1. Pumping Iron Man - 2. Elton John Starks - 3. Danica Patrick O'Brian - 4. Jersey Boys II Men - 5. Darryl Strawberry Shortcake - 6. Water Buffalo Bills - 7. Kirk Douglas MacArthur - 8. A New Hope Solo - 9. DMX Files - 10. Spotted Dick Tracy

Alexander Hamilton

1 Hamilton wrote 51 of the 85 installments of this series of Constitutional interpretations.

2 The famous 1993 "Got Milk" TV commerical featuring a despondent Hamilton aficionado unable to pronounce the name Aaron Burr due to his lack of milk was directed by this blockbuster movie director.

3 Hamilton was born in Charlestown, the main town on this Caribbean island.

4 In February 2015, Lin-Manuel Miranda's *Hamilton* made its Off-Broadway debut at this arts venue.

5 Brokered between Madison and Jefferson with Hamilton, the Compromise of 1790 moved the capital of the United States to the District of Columbia in exchange for the federal government assuming this.

6 Founded by Hamilton, the very wordy New York Society for Promoting the Manumission of Slaves, and Protecting Such of Them as Have Been, or May Be Liberated was inspired by the work of this colleague and chief justice.

IT'S QUIET UPTOWN

Hamilton lived at Answer #8 for only two years before he was shot. Since then, the home has been physically moved twice. Once it was moved two blocks to accommodate the city's grid-plan orientation, and in 2006, it was moved off the grid into a city park so it could be fully restored.

7 In 1923, the south terrace of this Washington, DC, cabinet building unveiled a statue of Alexander Hamilton.

8 This is the name of Alexander Hamilton's mansion on West 141st and St. Nicholas Avenue in Manhattan.

9 Both Hamilton Hall and the ROTC program of this university are named after Alexander Hamilton.

10 "It's all about the Hamiltons, baby" is a line from this second-ever *SNL* Digital Short.

ANSWERS - 1. *The Federalist Papers* **- 2.** Michael Bay **- 3.** Nevis **- 4.** The Public Theater **- 5.** State Debt **- 6.** John Jay **- 7.** Department of Treasury **- 8.** The Grange **- 9.** Columbia **- 10.** *Lazy Sunday*

Random Stuff You Might *Not* Know

1 Persian for "seal," this bovine word refers to an edict issued by a pope.

2 The Black Paintings refers to a series of 14 works during the 1819 to 1823 late period of this Spanish painter.

3 Representing 38 percent of the population in the United States, the positive of this blood type is the most dominant blood type.

4 This is the name of the fictional last human city in the *Matrix* universe.

5 List the first name of three of the five former members of One Direction.

6 Fifth Generation Inc., Texas's first legal distillery, produces this award-winning, popular vodka brand.

7 The Cathedral of Learning, the tallest educational building in the Western Hemisphere, is the architectural centerpiece of this university's campus.

> **IN SOVIET RUSSIA, BUILDING MAKES YOU**
> ....
> The tallest educational building in the world is the Main Building of Moscow State University. It was built in the USSR between 1947 and 1953, so you know no one died making it.

8 This "double-O" word refers to a wilted and partially oxidized processing of tea.

9 The Continental Association, Declaration of Independence, Articles of Confederation, and Constitution are the great state papers of the United States; this Connecticut Founding Father is the only person to sign all four.

10 One point each for the 12 most populous cities in Texas.

ANSWERS - 1. Bull - 2. Francisco Goya - 3. O - 4. Zion - 5. Niall, Liam, Harry, Louis, Zayn - 6. Tito's - 7. University of Pittsburgh - 8. Oolong - 9. Roger Sherman - 10. Garland, Lubbock, Laredo, Plano, Corpus Christi, Arlington, El Paso, Fort Worth, Austin, Dallas, San Antonio, Houston

Mad Men

1 *Mad Men*'s tone is set in the pilot when Don Draper invents the "It's Toasted" slogan for this brand of tobacco.

2 In the episode "Maidenform," Sterling Cooper decides, much to the anger of Peggy and Joan, that every female consumer is either a Jackie, meaning Jackie Kennedy, or this fifties icon.

3 *Mad Men* spawned such short-lived period-inspired shows as *The Playboy Club* and this airline-based series.

4 The modern-day PR department of this English automaker was less than pleased with Joan's story line associated with their 1960s equivalents.

5 Betty and Don initially live in this town, the home to Sing Sing prison.

6 This character unsuccessfully attempts to blackmail Don Draper with evidence of his prior life as Dick Whitman.

7 Don's francophone second wife, Megan Calvet, is originally from this city.

8 According to *Mad Men*, these chips "are better than nuts."

9 Creator Matthew Weiner's son Marten plays this boy with an interest in Sally Draper.

10 This comedian was offered the role of Jewish department store owner Rachel Menken but declined because of conflicts with her own show.

BEHIND THE SCENES

In 1999, *Mad Men*'s Weiner wrote the show's spec script, the strength of which got him a job on *The Sopranos*. But HBO later passed on the show. AMC, which had never made a scripted original series, took the risk, and now we have Jon Hamm. So thank you for your service, Original Programming Executive Committee of AMC.

ANSWERS - 1. Lucky Strike - 2. Marilyn Monroe - 3. *Pan Am* - 4. Jaguar - 5. Ossining - 6. Pete Campbell - 7. Montreal - 8. Utz - 9. Glen - 10. Sarah Silverman

Before and After

See page 2 if you need a refresher on the rules.

1 Halliwell, Bunton, Beckham, Chisholm, and Brown starred in this 1997 movie AND 159 of the earth's nations are part of this international commercial supervisory body.

2 Tom Selleck's 1980s detective AND "Robbie," "Runaround," "Catch That Rabbit," and "Escape!" are some of the nine stories from this Isaac Asimov collection book.

3 The Voice Input Child Identicant, a.k.a. Vicki, was the robot star of this 1980s sitcom AND Joe Cocker's cover of "With a Little Help from My Friends" was the theme song of this 1980s and '90s show.

4 Mounds' sister candy AND novel about the Woo, Hsu, St. Clair, and Jong women.

5 Dylan song featuring a weatherman AND film featuring Joliet Jake and Elwood.

6 Rap and pop-punk artist famous for dating Megan Fox AND the captain of the volleyball, swim, and softball teams at Bayside High.

PRO TIP
....
Our ninth president was the shortest tenured; James Madison, at five feet, four inches, was the shortest.

7 The shortest tenured US president AND film actor who played Jones, Ryan, and Deckard.

8 Hollis, Queens, hip-hop legends AND the Soviet Union's abbreviation in Russian.

9 *Life among the Lowly* was the subtitle of this Harriet Beecher Stowe novel AND five unlucky college students are subjected to every horror film cliché in this 2011 dark comedy movie.

10 Sergei Prokofiev's musical story to introduce children to the symphony orchestra AND DiCaprio and Hill star in this Scorsese movie.

ANSWERS - 1. Spice World Trade Organization - 2. Magnum PI Robot - 3. Small Wonder Years - 4. Almond Joy Luck Club - 5. Subterranean Homesick Blues Brothers - 6. Machine Gun Kelly Kapowski - 7. William Henry Harrison Ford - 8. Run DMCCCP - 9. Uncle Tom's Cabin in the Woods - 10. Peter and the Wolf of Wall Street

Scientists

38

1 "The sea was angry that day, my friends," said this television character after pretending to be a marine biologist.

2 "The Scientist" is a song by this English band.

3 Before marrying her French husband, this scientist's maiden name was Skłodowska.

4 Satyendra Nath Bose—along with Albert Einstein—developed an eponymous theory of quantum mechanics resulting in the discovery of this subatomic particle named in his honor.

> **BEHIND THE SCENES**
>
> The speech in Question #1 was not in the original script—it was a late-night rewrite, but it took only one take to nail it.

5 Galileo rose to international fame with an analysis of a 1604 supernova first described by this German astronomer.

6 This father of the atomic bomb's most famous quote, "Now I am become Death, the destroyer of worlds" is paraphrased from the Bhagavad Gita.

7 When captured by the United States, this Nazi Sturmbannführer, who later created the moon landing's Saturn V rocket, lied by saying he wore his SS uniform only once.

8 From what disease did Stephen Hawking suffer?

9 In the third century BCE, this Syracusan calculated pi with remarkable accuracy to the ratio of 22/7.

10 In what field of science is the Fields Medal awarded?

ANSWERS - 1. George Costanza - 2. Coldplay - 3. Marie Curie - 4. Boson - 5. Johannes Kepler - 6. J. Robert Oppenheimer - 7. Wernher von Braun - 8. ALS (Lou Gehrig's Disease) - 9. Archimedes - 10. Mathematics

Random Stuff You Might *Not* Know

1 Producing 875,000 per day, this company manufactures the most tires in the world.

2 This downhill and slalom combination event made its debut at the 1983 skiing World Cup.

3 This is the most common first name in the world.

4 To a Canadian, the publication *THN* stands for this.

5 Fashion designer Lilly Pulitzer invented this breezy summer garment in the 1960s.

6 What kind of company was McKim, Mead & White?

7 The 1868 collapse of the 260-year-long Tokugawa Shogunate is known to historians as this "restoration."

8 Lithium is this atomic number.

9 Serving 18,804 days from 1959 to 2010, this West Virginian was the longest-serving US senator in history.

10 One point each for the 12 largest islands on Earth.

Famous Speeches

1. *Time*'s Man of the Year award and the youngest recipient ever to be awarded the Nobel Peace Prize were two of the immediate accolades for the orator of this August 28, 1963, speech.

2. Although employed 50 years earlier by Warren Harding, this two-word term was used to great effect by Richard Nixon in describing those voters who did not protest the Vietnam War.

3. "Atoms for Peace" was a 1953 speech to the United Nations by this world leader.

4. "Ask not what your country can do for you" is followed by these eight words.

5. "If the British Empire and Commonwealth last for a thousand years, men will still say" is followed by these five words.

6. Also written after a time of civil war, Pericles's 431 BCE funeral oration was used as the blueprint for this speech, more than 2,000 years later.

7. "The Fourth of July is yours, not mine. You may rejoice. I must mourn," said this abolitionist leader to a white audience in Rochester, New York, after the passage of the Fugitive Slave Act.

8. "Blessed are the meek, for they shall" do this, said Jesus Christ.

9. In 570 BCE, he gave his first sermon at Sarnath, spurring on a world religion.

10. "City upon a Hill" was a turn of phrase made popular by this Puritan leader's 1630 speech.

> **PRO TIP**
>
> *Jeopardy!* clues will often ask you to figure out—obliquely—what happened on certain dates, but usually it's only years. Some key ones to know: 1066, 1215, 1492, 1865, and 1918.

ANSWERS - 1. "I Have a Dream" - 2. Silent Majority - 3. Dwight D. Eisenhower - 4. "Ask what you can do for your country." - 5. "This was their finest hour." - 6. Gettysburg Address - 7. Frederick Douglass - 8. Inherit the Earth - 9. Buddha - 10. John Winthrop

Change a Letter, Change Everything

This is a fun wordplay round, wherein a clue is altered to reveal an unexpected answer solved by changing a single letter in what would otherwise be a rote question. Here's an example: Jagger and Richards band named after tumbling English teatime baked goods. Answer: Rolling Scones. (STONES ➡ SCONES)

1 Featuring the song "We Are Never Ever Getting Back Together," this Taylor Swift album reflects her love of 1980s BMX movies.

2 In this Bob Dylan song, the joker and the thief were very, very sick.

3 In this TV series, the survivors of an air crash must band together to deliver the mail.

4 In this first volume of three, Frodo sets out from the Shire with an ancient and powerful ladder step.

5 In this song, Beyoncé implores the listener: "If you like it, then you shoulda put some bells on it."

6 This 1787 Mozart opera tells the story of the arrogant titular character "Good John," albeit in two different languages.

7 This long-selling Pink Floyd album explores madness, greed, and a Canadian waterfowl.

8 Star of his own play, this Shakespearean character just can't stop creepily checking out people.

9 In this 1980s comedy, the titular character—in solidarity with labor— skips an entire month of school.

10 In this book, his final novel, James Joyce muses in a nonlinear fashion on Japanese fermented rice alcohol.

Movie Quotes

39

1 "Gentlemen, you can't fight in here. This is the war room!" is a quote from this 1964 satire.

2 "Mother of Mercy, is this the end of Rico?" is from this pizza-related 1930 gangster movie.

3 Jack Nicholson allegedly improvised this two-word line from *The Shining*.

4 This line from *The Graduate* is the only one-word quote on the American Film Institute's 100 best movie quotes of all time.

5 Amplifier maker Marshall made a special set of amps for actor Christopher Guest to thank him for this famous numerical movie quote.

6 The National Science Teachers Association encourages conversations on biology and self-image in response to the "I'm just one stomach flu away from my weight goal" quote from this movie.

7 Taken directly from declassified CIA reports, this profane, three-word catchphrase was used frequently in the 2012 movie containing its own name.

8 Springing it unscripted and without warning on his fellow actors in this movie, Joe Pesci improvised his famous "How am I funny?" dialogue, which was based on his experience as a waiter in a mob restaurant.

9 "Sayonara, baby" was used in the Spanish language releases of this movie, as the original quote wouldn't have been particularly memorable.

10 This word that does not appear in a quote from *Casablanca* is considered the most misremembered word in a movie quote of all time.

BEHIND THE SCENES

In a pivotal scene of *Casablanca*, the patrons of Rick's Café Américain band together to sing "La Marseillaise," the French national anthem, to drown out the exuberant singing of Nazi soldiers in attendance. In real life, many of the actors and extras singing were European refugees who had recently fled Nazi dominated Europe.

ANSWERS - 1. *Dr. Strangelove: Or, How I Learned to Stop Worrying and Love the Bomb* - 2. *Little Caesar* - 3. "Here's Johnny!" - 4. "Plastics" - 5. "These go to eleven." - 6. *The Devil Wears Prada* - 7. "Argo, fuck yourself" - 8. *Goodfellas* - 9. *Terminator 2* - 10. "Again"

Random Stuff You Might Know

1 The Year of Three Kings, 1936, resulted in Edward VIII of England succeeding the deceased George V, only to abdicate in favor of this English monarch.

2 In 2014, this American automaker dropped the iconic laurel wreath that ringed its logo.

3 *The Big Bang Theory*'s Penny is played by this actor.

4 Argentine NFL former placekickers Bill, Santiago, and Martín all have this last name.

5 This handheld weather protection's name is derived from the Latin word for "shadow."

6 The 755-student liberal arts school Bennington College is in this US state.

7 Soccer club Galatasaray S.K. is based in this country.

8 In 1927, a power struggle between Chiang Kai-shek and Wang Jingwei started the Chinese Civil War after this famous leader's death.

9 On what consumer item would you find an ISBN?

10 One point for the 12 cities with the world's *longest* metro and/or subway systems.

Stupid Laws

1 In Arkansas, a pinball machine is prohibited from awarding more than 25 free games to a winner, yet this children's restaurant is exempt from the law.

2 In Georgia, anyone engaging in activities with these South American livestock animals is accountable for any injury incurred, whereas professional trainers are immune from prosecution.

3 In Louisiana, this regional favorite dish is exempt from all sanitation laws.

4 In South Dakota, growers of this state flower of Kansas are allowed to use fireworks to scare off birds.

5 Anyone wishing to run for office in this state must acknowledge a supreme being or be barred from campaigning.

6 In West Virginia, you cannot use one of these domesticated polecats for hunting purposes.

7 In 2013, Oklahoma affirmed that there is an international conspiracy by these people to "overthrow the government of the United States and of the several states."

8 North Carolina prohibits these social games of chance from lasting more than five hours.

9 In Nevada, it is illegal to use this form of electromagnetic radiation to measure your shoe size.

10 In Missouri, if a bull or ram runs rampant for three or more days, anyone may do this to it without fear of prosecution.

> **I DON'T MAKE THE RULES**
>
> The oldest code of laws extant, the Code of Ur-Nammu (Mesopotamia, c. 2100 BCE), says that if you flooded another man's field, you owe that man three *kur* of barley per every *iku* of land you flooded. No idea what that means but if you cut off someone's foot, you'd owe them 10 shekels of silver.

ANSWERS - 1. Chuck E. Cheese - 2. Llamas - 3. Jambalaya - 4. Sunflowers - 5. Texas - 6. Ferret - 7. Communists - 8. Bingo - 9. X-Rays - 10. Castration

Before and After

See page 2 if you need a refresher on the rules.

1 The Gypsy Kings covered this Eagles mega-hit AND Katy Perry said that this song is her answer to Jay-Z's "Empire State of Mind."

PRO TIP

The Zeppelin line is based on "all that glisters is not gold" from *The Merchant of Venice*, Act 2, Scene 7.

2 Saint Peter's favorite Led Zeppelin song AND Diane Keaton directed the video for this 1987 Belinda Carlisle hit song.

3 This Coolio song was on the *Dangerous Minds* soundtrack AND writer Jim Steinman called this song "the ultimate car and sex song in which everything goes horribly wrong in the end."

4 This 1970 John Lennon single was written, produced, and released in just 10 days AND this Radiohead song concerns fate enforcement.

5 The lead single from Pink's 2008 album *Funhouse* AND Haddaway's "Roxbury Guys" dance hit.

6 This Elvis song features a prison dance party AND the Sharif don't like this song by the Clash.

7 Apparently, darkness has descended in this Bill Withers song AND Cream bassist Jack Bruce developed the riff of this song after seeing a Jimi Hendrix concert.

8 There are different strokes for different folks in this song by Sly and the Family Stone AND The Doors wrote this song after observing the pedestrians in Laurel Canyon.

9 A chant at a Parliament-Funkadelic concert inspired this Talking Heads song AND classic New Orleans ballad of woe.

10 This 1972 song was Neil Young's only number-one hit AND Kanye West added Jaime Foxx to this song after seeing *Ray*.

ANSWERS - 1. Hotel California Gurls - 2. Stairway to Heaven Is a Place on Earth - 3. Gangsta's Paradise by the Dashboard Light - 4. Instant Karma Police - 5. So What Is Love - 6. Jailhouse Rock the Casbah - 7. Ain't No Sunshine of Your Love - 8. Everyday People Are Strange - 9. Burning Down the House of the Rising Sun - 10. Heart of Gold Digger

Three of a Kind

40

Each of the words in these three-word sets may be combined with another word to form a familiar phrase or name. Find that common word.

1 Cheese, Bikini, and Theory

2 Armstrong, Bass, and Free

3 Buy, George, and Pete

4 Gay, Batten, and Dis-

5 Corner, High, and Ball

6 Penalty, Red, and Car

7 Home, Jump, and Ball

8 Back, Bag, and White

9 Six, Thought, and Throat

10 Buster, Town, and World

> **ETYMOLOGY INSANITY**
>
> Sir Walter Scott's *Ivanhoe* was the first work to mention a *Free Lance*, i.e., a medieval mercenary unallied with any specific lord.

Random Stuff You Might *Not* Know

1. This is the only state with a nonrectangular flag.

2. A subject of fictional medieval consternation, this 0.63-ounce passerine bird's airspeed velocity is actually 31 to 40 miles per hour.

EVERYONE KNOWS—OR DO THEY?

Remember: Barbie's full name is Barbara Millicent Roberts.

3. Carved into a post, "Croatoan" was the last known message from the settlers of this lost colony.

4. This *R* word describes a triangular fortification in front of the main wall of a fortress.

5. Lent to a popular toy, this name originally belonged to the son of the cofounder of Mattel toys.

6. On March 7, 1945, Karl Timmermann became the first American army officer to cross this river in more than four years.

7. Although officially listed as unknown, the *Oxford English Dictionary* suggests that the name of this bat used for baseball fielding practice is derived from the Old Scottish for "to fling."

8. He composed *Pictures at an Exhibition*.

9. Both Greenland and this group of islands north of Scotland are autonomous regions of Denmark.

10. One point for each of the 10 nations on which the United States has officially declared war.

ANSWERS - 1. Ohio - 2. Unladen Swallow - 3. Roanoke - 4. Ravelin - 5. Ken - 6. The Rhine - 7. Fungo - 8. Modest Mussorgsky - 9. Faroe Islands - 10. United Kingdom, Mexico, Spain, Germany, Austria-Hungary, Japan, Italy, Bulgaria, Hungary, Romania

Famous Dishes

Here are some foods from 'round the world, typically identified as their country's "national dish"—how many can you name?

Before and After

See page 2 if you need a refresher on the rules.

1 Band famous for "Rikki Don't Lose That Number" AND outspoken LGBTQ+ activist and nationally syndicated sex advice columnist.

2 The author of 1881's *The Portrait of a Lady* AND this 1961 Roald Dahl novel follows the adventures of an English orphan and a magical stone fruit.

3 Abbott and Costello's famous baseball comedy routine AND subtitle of the 2011 X-Men movie set during the Cuban missile crisis.

4 The performers of "Psycho Killer" and "Once in a Lifetime" AND Biden, Merkel, and Macron, collectively.

5 The owner of the Dallas Mavericks AND ham, roasted pork, Swiss cheese, pickles, and mustard, pressed and toasted.

6 The makers of Trivial Pursuit and Risk AND Fyodor Dostoyevsky's final novel.

7 The foundational ingredient of s'mores AND this American chain restaurant was sued in the 1990s by the Department of Justice for segregating Black customers from white customers.

DID YOU KNOW?

Gladys Williams's 1920s *A Book of 150 Recipes Prepared with Campfire Marshmallows* includes the first written recipe for s'mores and HOW ARE THERE 149 MORE DIFFERENT THINGS?

8 The premier yachting race trophy in the world AND Nissin's foam-containered ramen product.

9 Actor who portrayed the titular Uncle Buck AND a children's board game or Leonardo DiCaprio's plantation in *Django Unchained*.

10 Ned Stark's allegedly illegitimate son AND band famous for "Chasing Cars."

It's Football Season

1 In 1886, munitions workers in Woolwich, today's South East London, formed the Dial Square Football Club; one month later, they would rename themselves "The Royal" this, the club's name to this day.

2 With 260 goals, he is the all-time leader in goals scored in Premier League history.

3 For the 2017–18 season, Newcastle returned to the Premiership alongside Brighton & Hove Albion and this promoted club.

4 Scoring a record 13 goals in 11 consecutive matches, this striker led surprise Premier League champions Leicester City.

5 Although their crest has an elk upon it, supporters of this club call them the Hornets, Yellow Army, or Golden Boys.

6 Played for a variety of charities, the annual Football Association Community Shield match pits against one another the prior season's winners of the Premier League and this competition.

7 The 2016–17 season was the last year Tottenham played at this home ground.

8 Businessmen Joel and Avram Glazer own both the Tampa Bay Buccaneers and this club.

9 Before signing at DC United, Wayne Rooney briefly returned to this hometown club.

10 This club is named after the centerpiece feature of the Great Exhibition of 1851.

> **GOING OUT IN STYLE**
>
> When a legendary player retires in English football, they often receive the honor of a "testimonial match," a relic from when players were amateurs or only semiprofessional. To both honor the retiree and help finance a post-sporting career, the players' club stages a noncompetitive exhibition match and donates a portion of the box office to the retiring player.

ANSWERS - 1. Arsenal - 2. Alan Shearer - 3. Huddersfield Town - 4. Jamie Vardy - 5. Watford - 6. The FA Cup - 7. White Hart Lane - 8. Manchester United - 9. Everton - 10. Crystal Palace

Random Stuff You Might Know

1 In what professional field is the Pritzker Prize awarded?

2 This city is home to the UK's National Football Museum.

3 With 63 million riders annually, this is the busiest station in the New York City subway system.

4 This hit single was the first track on Ricky Martin's 1999 eponymous English-language debut album.

5 In 1884, Republican defectors known as Mugwumps supported this Democratic presidential candidate.

6 This country is second to Australia in global production of wool.

7 Where does ABC's *Revenge* take place?

8 In 1936, Bausch + Lomb created this brand name for its aviator sunglasses.

9 Action sequences, establishing shots, and cutaways are filmed by this group within a film production.

10 For 2020, the most recent year with complete data, one point for each of the top 12 retail banks in the United States by deposits.

ANSWERS - 1. Architecture - **2.** Manchester - **3.** Times Square 42nd Street - **4.** "Livin' La Vida Loca" - **5.** Grover Cleveland - **6.** New Zealand - **7.** The Hamptons - **8.** Ray-Ban - **9.** Second Unit - **10.** Charles Schwab Bank, State Street Bank and Trust, Capitol One, TD Bank, PNC Bank, Bank of New York Mellon, Truist Bank (formerly SunTrust), US Bank, Citibank, Wells Fargo Bank, Bank of America, JPMorgan Chase Bank

Recipes

For each question in this round, name the dish containing these ingredients.

1 Spaghetti, olive oil, onion, garlic, eggs, bacon, parmesan, pepper, and parsley.

2 White sugar, eggs, sweetened condensed milk, evaporated milk, vanilla extract; bake for 60 minutes and then invert dish to serve.

3 Salt, self-rising flour, butter, and water for dough; potatoes, peas, onion, garlic, ginger, turmeric, garam masala, red chili pepper, and coriander for filling; serve with chutney.

4 Eggs, cornstarch, chicken, dried red pepper pods, rice vinegar, rice wine, sugar, soy sauce; fry in vegetable oil; serve with rice.

5 Boneless chicken, salt, pepper, vegetable oil, flour, onion, margarine, bell pepper, celery, Worcestershire sauce, bouillon cubes, smoked sausage, stewed tomatoes, okra, shrimp, green onions

6 Unsalted butter, flour, milk, kosher salt, black pepper, nutmeg, Gruyère, Parmesan, Dijon mustard, Virginia ham; broil on crustless toasted white bread.

> **ON THE MIC**
>
> When hosting pub trivia, Recipes is a particularly great round for diverse groups of participants. And for heated disputes, because everyone always says, "No, that's not in that dish!" to which you say, "I don't care—did you get it right? Yes? Then don't complain."

7 Ice, diced pineapple, pineapple juice, Coco López coconut cream, white rum, dark rum; blend; garnish with pineapple slice.

8 Gosling's or Myers's rum, ginger beer, lime wedge.

9 Vegetable oil, pork shoulder roast, barbecue sauce, apple cider vinegar, chicken broth, brown sugar, chili powder, Worcestershire sauce, onion, garlic, dried yellow mustard; serve on hamburger bun.

10 Potatoes, canola oil, soybean oil, hydrogenated soybean oil, natural beef flavor, citric acid, sodium acid pyrophosphate, dextrose, and salt.

ANSWERS - 1. Spaghetti Carbonara - 2. Flan - 3. Samosas - 4. General Tso's Chicken - 5. Gumbo - 6. Croque Monsieur - 7. Piña Colada - 8. Dark and Stormy - 9. Pulled Pork Sandwich - 10. McDonald's Fries

Before and After

See page 2 if you need a refresher on the rules.

1 Wisconsin's former Speaker of the House AND Macklemore's partner.

2 Tompkins Square Park and the Nuyorican Poets Café are landmarks in this Manhattan neighborhood AND the Goo Goo Dolls' "Iris" and Alanis Morissette's "Uninvited" were hits off this terrible movie's soundtrack.

SOMEBODY ONCE TOLD ME

I just watched the video for that Smash Mouth tune in Question #7. Watch it, too. That song is . . . well, it's pretty damn good! Dated, but good.

3 Named after an American patriotic icon, this Sousa march was the theme song to *Monty Python's Flying Circus* AND this vegetable is known as a Jon's head in the UK and capsicum in Australia.

4 This firm unsuccessfully attempted a merger with KPMG in 1997 AND Tom Cruise had an uncredited cameo in this 1988 western.

5 This Jamaican crime film has been eclipsed by the fame of its soundtrack, recorded by star Jimmy Cliff AND "Take your time, hurry up," implores this Nirvana hit.

6 Paul McCartney and Stevie Wonder's 1982 number-one single AND soccer players Didier Drogba and Yaya Toure are from this nation, in English.

7 *Mystery Men, Digimon: The Movie*, and *Shrek* all prominently feature this Smash Mouth song AND a Jeff Bridges movie or David Bowie song.

8 Portia de Rossi played a cold corporate boss in this late-2000s ABC sitcom AND baseball player known as the Splendid Splinter.

9 Two brothers with the same name were the stars of this nineties Nickelodeon show AND baseball player known as Charlie Hustle.

10 Vermont dairy purveyors Cohen and Greenfield AND the actor who played NYPD detective Lenny Briscoe.

ANSWERS - 1. Paul Ryan Lewis - 2. Alphabet City of Angels - 3. Liberty Bell Pepper - 4. Ernst & Young Guns - 5. The Harder They Come as You Are - 6. Ebony and Ivory Coast - 7. All Star Man - 8. Better Off Ted Williams - 9. The Adventures of Pete & Pete Rose - 10. Ben and Jerry Orbach

Stage Names

1. Born Demetria Guynes, this actor's equally famous ex-husbands' real names were Walter and Christopher, respectively.

2. Letters from this *M*A*S*H* actor's real name of Alphonso d'Abruzzo form his shorter stage name.

3. Born Maurice Micklewhite, this iconic British actor took his stage name from a character played by Humphrey Bogart.

4. African American actor Caryn Johnson took this stage name after her mother argued that she'd get more parts if people thought she was Jewish.

5. Frederick Austerlitz and Virginia Katherine McMath are better known as this dancing duo.

6. Comedian Jacob Cohen took this stage name ostensibly to get some respect.

7. John Charles Carter is the real name of this gun-loving actor.

8. This rapper chose his stage name from his cousin's nickname for him based on Fozzie Bear's catchphrase.

9. This rapper's mother named him after a famous Incan revolutionary who sought to overthrow Spanish rule in South America.

10. The *B* stands for Bush, but what do the *J* and *E* of Jeb Bush stand for?

> **DID YOU KNOW?**
>
> George Oscar Bluth's nickname GOB in *Arrested Development* is inspired by the equally ridiculous nickname JEB Bush.

ANSWERS - 1. Demi Moore - 2. Alan Alda - 3. Michael Caine - 4. Whoopi Goldberg - 5. Fred Astaire and Ginger Rogers - 6. Rodney Dangerfield - 7. Charlton Heston - 8. Waka Flocka Flame - 9. Tupac Shakur - 10. John Ellis

ROUND 4 / DIFFICULTY LEVEL 1 2 3 4 **5** 6

Random Stuff You Might *Not* Know

1 This contemporary furniture store is an upscale retail subsidiary of Williams Sonoma.

2 Winning 52 US Swimming National Championships, Olympic swimmer Johnny Weissmuller is remembered today for portraying this fictional character.

PRO TIP

Unless you're really wrong or specifically instructed otherwise, spelling doesn't count on *Jeopardy!*, but try to get it close in pub trivia.

3 What do the towns and cities of Urayasu, Marne-la-Vallée, Hong Kong, Shanghai, Lake Buena Vista, and Anaheim all have in common?

4 What is the official language of Andorra?

5 Alaska's at-large congressional district is the largest by area, but this state's congressional district is both the country's second largest by area and the largest by population.

6 What is the last word of the Aladdin song "A Whole New World"?

7 The Dutch word for "coarse fabric," *piijakker*, and the American term *pilot cloth* are both possible origins for this naval-inspired overgarment.

8 Bruce Springsteen granted permission for this rap group to sample his song with 1990's "Banned in the USA."

9 What is the capital of Malta?

10 One point each for the 10 top-paid female actors in the world for 2020.

Blunt, Meryl Streep, Melissa McCarthy, Gal Gadot, Angelina Jolie, Sofia Vergara

8. 2 Live Crew - 9. Valletta - 10. Viola Davis, Elisabeth Moss, Ellen Pompeo, Nicole Kidman, Emily

ANSWERS - 1. West Elm - 2. Tarzan - 3. Disney Parks - 4. Catalan - 5. Montana - 6. "Me" - 7. Pea Coat -

Connecticut

1 A curiosity of postcolonial geography led to the creation of the Connecticut Western Reserve, which explains the prevalence of Connecticut settlers and duplicated place-names in this midwestern state.

2 Known as the father of American education, this famous dictionary compiler was born in what is today West Hartford.

3 Connecticut's largest factory is in Stratford and manufactures helicopters for this aircraft company.

> **DID YOU KNOW?**
> ....
> The father of Answer #10 was born in Massachusetts.

4 With 340,000 square feet of gaming, this is the largest casino in the United States.

5 Founded in 1843, this top-ranked all-girls school broke new barriers by insisting that its students learn chemistry, geology, and botany in addition to traditional subjects like Latin and arithmetic.

6 The only colonial governor to side with the American Revolution, Connecticut's Jonathan Trumbull issued the commission for this famously executed colonial spy.

7 Before becoming the Huskies in 1934, the University of Connecticut, then known as Connecticut Agricultural College, used this appropriate nickname.

8 Although never explicitly set at Yale, this terrible Joshua Jackson and Paul Walker movie heavily implies that it is.

9 In 2015, this Connecticut-born pop and blues guitarist and singer formed the touring band Dead & Company with three members of the Grateful Dead.

10 He was the only US president born in Connecticut.

43 Black American History

1 Carter G. Woodson's precursor to Black History Month, "Negro History Week," began on February 12, the birthday of Abraham Lincoln, and concluded on February 20, the birthday of this abolitionist.

2 In the 1920s, Jamaican-born Pan-Africanist Marcus Garvey had ideological clashes with this NAACP cofounder.

SISTER ACT

The Williams sisters are undefeated in Doubles Grand Slam Finals matches. FOURTEEN TIMES. Fourteen separate duos made it all the way to the final, and already knew that they lost. Demoralizing.

3 "She is one of the greatest players who ever lived.... I think she'd beat the Williams sisters," said Serena and Venus's former coach Bob Ryland on this 1957–58 Wimbledon and US Championship back-to-back winner.

4 This Alice Walker novel was awarded the 1983 Pulitzer Prize for fiction and was adapted into an 11-time Academy Award–nominated film.

5 On March 5, 1770, he became the first casualty of the American War of Independence.

6 John Lewis and Cory Booker discover their heritage in an episode of *Finding Your Roots*, a PBS series hosted by this Harvard professor.

7 Playwright Tarell Alvin McCraney adapted his Yale drama school project into this 2016 Best Picture awardee.

8 The National Gallery's attendance went up 300 percent after the 2017 unveiling of Kehinde Wiley's and Amy Sherald's portraits of two people with this last name.

9 Satchel Paige said, "[He] was the greatest hitter I ever pitched to," and Roy Campanella said, "Everything I could do, [he] could do better" about this legendary, slugging catcher.

10 Name either of the two American athletes to iconically raise a gloved fist while up on the medal podium at the 1968 Summer Olympics.

ANSWERS - 1. Frederick Douglass - 2. W. E. B. Du Bois - 3. Althea Gibson - 4. *The Color Purple* - 5. Crispus Attucks - 6. Henry Louis Gates Jr. - 7. *Moonlight* - 8. Obama - 9. Josh Gibson - 10. Tommie Smith and John Carlos

Children's Games

1 Once popular in Ireland and Britain, conkers is a game of slamming two of these nuts together to see whose is stronger.

2 In some parts of the United States, the penalty for breaking the silence of this game is to owe the winner a Coke.

3 No longer prevalent for obvious reasons, mumblety-peg involved throwing this object into the ground and then challenging the loser to pull it out with their mouth.

4 "Forcing the city gates" and "octopus tag" are alternative names for this breaking-the-chain running game.

5 On East 109th Street between Second and Third Avenues is the honorary Hall of Fame street for this New York City game.

6 "You know, for kids" is the Hula-Hoop-inventing catchphrase from this Coen brothers movie starring Tim Robbins.

> **LESSER-KNOWN SEQUELS**
> ....
> In *Tom Sawyer, Detective*, a sequel to *Tom Sawyer* and *Huckleberry Finn* I literally just learned about, Tom Sawyer says mumblety-peg is the favorite game of his childhood friends.

7 Thought to date to the Renaissance, prisoner's base involved creating a human chain from a safe base; these Louisiana Purchase explorers played the game against the Nez Perce.

8 Invented to teach the fundamentals of baseball to children—but subsequently becoming popular among young urban adults—this game originated in Cincinnati in 1917.

9 Leapfrog, king of the hill, and hide-and-seek are some of the many games in the 1560 painting *Children's Games* by this "the Elder" Flemish artist.

10 What is the very first item placed on the board to assemble the contraption in the game Mouse Trap?

Random Stuff You Might *Not* Know

1 The guidebook published annually from 1936 to 1966 was designed to help Black motorists find safe businesses and towns in Jim Crow–era America bore a cover of this color.

2 Passing by Earth in July 2015, the half-mile-wide Asteroid 2011 UW-158 is thought to have a 100-million-ton core of this metal, worth $5.4 trillion.

3 Chiang Mai is the most populous city and cultural capital of the northern hill region of this country.

4 In the 1930s, the Swiss Cheese Union promoted this dish as the national dish of Switzerland.

5 "Everybody has a plan until they get punched in the mouth" is a famous quote attributed to this boxer.

6 In 1997, the Hartford Whalers became this NHL franchise.

7 This 1994 movie broke new ground through its extensive use of CGI and digital editing, which inserted its main character into dozens of scenes of stock and historical footage.

AD MEN

When the Hartford Whalers joined the NHL, an ad executive noted that the team's logo was a harpoon and the mascot was a whale. He said that they couldn't go around killing their own mascot, so they rightfully changed the logo.

8 Borrowed from Sanskrit and meaning "enclosure," this three-letter Thai word now means "temple" in Thai and several other languages and dialects.

9 Released in 2008, *Waltz with Bashir* is a controversial animated film from this nation.

10 One point for each of the 10 minerals in the Mohs scale of mineral hardness (TGCFAOQTCD).

ANSWERS - 1. Green - 2. Platinum - 3. Thailand - 4. Fondue - 5. Mike Tyson - 6. Carolina Hurricanes - 7. *Forrest Gump* - 8. Wat - 9. Israel - 10. Talc, Gypsum, Calcite, Fluorite, Apatite, Orthoclase Feldspar, Quartz, Topaz, Corundum, Diamond

172

Really Big Things

1 The Red River Showdown is an annual football game that sees the rollout of the world's largest version of this state's flag.

2 The world's largest residential palace is the Istana Nurul Iman, the official home of the sultan of this Southeast Asian country.

3 Retailing at $149.99, the world's largest one of these candies for sale weighs 26 pounds, contains 32,000 calories, and features a one-liter bowl for liquids in its tummy.

4 Named Ottavia after the Roman emperor and measuring 1,261 square meters, the world's largest pizza was made with this dietary restriction in mind.

5 Discovered in 2001 in Laos, the 12-inch-long Giant Huntsman replaced the Goliath birdeater as the largest one of these arthropods.

6 At 1,504 feet long and with a draft of 24 feet, the largest ship in history was the oil tanker *Seawise Giant*, a vessel incapable of navigating the Panama Canal, the Suez Canal, and this European channel.

7 This epic story of Krishna and Arjuna is part of the *Mahabharata*, the world's longest poem.

8 At 7,541 pieces—plus 10 minifigures—a model of this fictional spacecraft is one of Lego's largest-ever commercially sold sets.

9 What is Shakespeare's longest play?

10 The largest-yet-discovered star, UY Scuti, would engulf this planet's orbit if placed at the center of our solar system.

> **HEY LEGO!**
>
> The largest Lego set in the world is a 11,695-piece world map, while the largest to represent something real is the 9,036-piece Colosseum.

Before and After

See page 2 if you need a refresher on the rules.

1 These two words have been a rapper's nickname, a villain in the video game *BioShock*, and an Adam Sandler movie AND Little Orphan Annie's father figure.

2 This Scottish-Canadian-American inventor was a founder of the National Geographic Society AND made up of former members of New Edition, this group had a number-three hit with "Do Me."

3 His last role was 1976's *The Shootist* AND he is the only player in NHL history to have more assists than any other player has in total points.

4 This 1984 Alphaville song was sampled in 2009 by Jay-Z and Mr. Hudson AND Gene Wilder is the title character of this 1974 black-and-white comedy.

5 "You go, Glenn Coco" is a quote from this movie AND Duran Duran's 1981 breakthrough top-10 hit.

6 This character's story was published in 1812, but her seven companions were named a century later AND Queen Victoria's 1840 marriage was the first to popularize this kind of event.

HOME VIDEO? WHAT'S THAT?
....
A History of Violence (2005) was the last major Hollywood studio film released in VHS format.

7 This 1987 romantic drama was the first movie to sell 1 million copies on home video AND "Boogaloo" was the working title of this 1976 ABBA hit.

8 The first written reference to this leering figure dates from the mid-18th century, 700 years after the death of Lady Godiva AND individually, he has more Super Bowl rings than any one team.

9 Both the album and film versions of *Get Back* were eventually released under this name AND ET's final two words to Gertie.

10 The subtitle of *Terminator 2* AND a 2004 environmental disaster movie of questionable quality.

Comedy

1. Key and Peele, Weird Al, Snoop Dogg, and Smosh have all appeared as guest hip-hop artists on this YouTube channel.

2. Coming in on Rotten Tomatoes as one of the highest-rated (adjusted score) comedies of all time is this 2017 film written and directed by Greta Gerwig.

3. *I'm a Grown Little Man* was the 2008 debut album of this comedian.

4. A 1969 Lamborghini Miura, a 1964 Aston Martin DB5, and 1970 Ford Mustang Boss 302 are some of the guests on this Jerry Seinfeld show.

5. After learning that their childhood home is on the market, Amy Poehler and Tina Fey throw one last party in this movie.

6. "In football you receive a penalty, in baseball you make an error" is one of the many comparisons in the baseball/football bit by this comic.

7. Employed to critique the nobility and their guests, a jester of this monarch was rebuked by her for not being sufficiently critical of her excesses.

8. Written by Aristophanes in 411 BCE, *Lysistrata* is a comedic play of women withholding sex in order to bring this conflict to an end.

9. This pranking, multi-character satirist idolizes Peter Sellers as his comedic hero.

10. This 1990 film is the highest-grossing, live action, nonanimated comedy movie in US history.

> **WAR—WHAT IS IT GOOD FOR?**
>
> The name of the war in Answer #8 is taken from the Athenian perspective, as it refers to the peninsula on which Sparta is located. If it were named from the Spartan perspective, we would call it the Attican War.

Random Stuff You Should Know

1 A lahar is a deadly, fast-moving mudflow caused by this geologic phenomenon.

2 The 1648 peace of Westphalia ended wars between the Kingdom of France, the Kingdom of Spain, the Swedish Empire, the Dutch Republic, free imperial cities, and this empire.

PRO TIP

Most of the time, the most obvious answer *is* the answer. If you're ever asked, "What is the largest city in X?" chances are it's exactly the city you think is the largest city in "X." But when in doubt, go for the capital!

3 One of the UK and Australia's most watched shows ever was an episode of *Neighbours* in which Scott Robinson married mechanic Charlene Robinson, played by this Australian pop singer.

4 What is the largest city in Poland?

5 Played by Julianna Margulies, this is the name of the lead character of *The Good Wife*.

6 Dalí and Buñuel's *Un Chien Andalou* and the film version of *Silence of the Lambs* both prominently feature the Death's Head species of this insect.

7 This is the word to describe the ownership or possession history of valuable historical objects, such as works of art, automobiles, and musical instruments.

8 This actor appeared in 2005's *The Muppets' Wizard of Oz* as Auntie Em and NBC's *Wiz Live* as the Wizard.

9 The St. John's Ice Caps of the American Hockey League became the top affiliate of this NHL team in 2015.

10 One point each for the 12 highest-selling music acts of all time by records sold, including albums, singles, and digital sales.

ANSWERS - 1. Volcanic Eruption - 2. Holy Roman Empire - 3. Kylie Minogue - 4. Warsaw - 5. Alicia Florrick - 6. Moth - 7. Provenance - 8. Queen Latifah - 9. Montreal Canadiens - 10. Queen, Whitney Houston, AC/DC, Celine Dion, Mariah Carey, Rihanna, Pink Floyd, Led Zeppelin, Elton John, Madonna, Michael Jackson, Elvis, the Beatles

Basketball

1 All Star center Kristaps Porziņģis is from this country.

2 In 1979, the NBA added this ABA-created scoring innovation to their games.

3 This is the most popular type of wood for basketball court floors.

4 After ticket prices rose 670 percent, this company called backsies on a fan's purchase of tickets for Kobe Bryant's last game.

5 On March 2, 1962, Wilt Chamberlain scored this record number for the most points in an NBA game.

6 Who holds the NBA record for the most total playoff points in history?

7 This legendary coach led UCLA to 10 of their 11 NCAA tournament championships.

8 "Roundball Rock" is the name of the NBA on NBC's theme song, written by this former *Entertainment Tonight* host.

9 This team renamed itself to avoid connotations of violence, only to draw unfortunate associations with the Ku Klux Klan.

10 Smashing "A" five times and "right" five times activated NBA Jam's "Super Clean Floors" mode on this home console.

> **BACK IN THE DAY**
> ....
> Dr. James Naismith's original list of rules numbered just 13. Today's NBA rulebook contains just 14 rules, albeit some with up to 17 subsections.

ANSWERS - 1. Latvia **- 2.** Three-Point Shot **- 3.** Maple **- 4.** StubHub **- 5.** 100 **- 6.** LeBron James **- 7.** John Wooden **- 8.** John Tesh **- 9.** Washington Wizards **- 10.** Sega Genesis

177

Before and After

See page 2 if you need a refresher on the rules.

1 Jaegers are giant humanoid robots in this action movie AND Gene Krupa is credited with the invention of this percussion technique.

2 A film character played by Baldwin, Ford, Affleck, Pine, and Krasinski AND a Brewers left fielder who was suspended without pay for the final 65 games of the 2013 season.

3 This Clue character has the game's first roll AND probably Vivien Leigh's most famous role.

4 Jamie Hyneman's partner on *MythBusters* AND "Truly Madly Deeply" duo.

5 The term *up the river* refers to this correctional institution AND four and twenty blackbirds are baked in a pie in this nursery rhyme.

6 In golf, this is the highest-lofting numbered club before the wedges AND the symbol of power in the fictional world of Westeros.

7 *Or the Children's Crusade: A Duty-Dance with Death* is the subtitle of this satirical novel AND American tax code for a nonprofit tax-exempt organization.

FOOD FOR THOUGHT

Royal celebrations— like the marriage between Henry IV of France and Marie de' Medici, for example— would culminate in the unveiling of an oversized pie with a hollow in the crust that, once sliced open, revealed live birds. Seems . . . sanitary.

8 The protagonist of this novel gets a paper cut, tempting a bland, brooding vampire AND the 1962 Academy Award for Best Song, Grammy for Record of the Year, and Grammy for Song of the Year went to this tune.

9 *Out of Sight* and *Get Shorty* author AND Canadian "Hallelujah" songwriter.

10 This actor has played Éomer, Bones, and Judge Dredd AND waking up in a bathtub full of ice with surgical scars and a note saying "call 911" is an example of this modern folklore.

ANSWERS - 1. Pacific Rim Shot **- 2.** Jack Ryan Braun **- 3.** Miss Scarlett O'Hara **- 4.** Adam Savage Garden **- 5.** Sing Sing a Song of Sixpence **- 6.** Nine Iron Throne **- 7.** Slaughterhouse 501(c)(3) **- 8.** New Moon River **- 9.** Elmore Leonard Cohen **- 10.** Karl Urban Legend

More Dogs!

1 Photographer William Wegman is known for his photos of Man Ray and Fay Ray, both of which are dogs of this breed.

2 This hybrid dog breed was created in 1989 by crossing a Standard Poodle and Labrador Retriever.

3 What was the name of the border collie who took the piglet Babe under her protection in the movie of the same name?

4 Although Nana was a Newfoundland in the original 1911 novel *Peter Pan*, she was this breed in the 1953 animated feature.

5 Meryl Streep famously cried, "The dingo's got my baby!" in this movie.

6 Before European contact, Indigenous Americans of the Athabascan cultures developed sled dogs that would become the basis for the Alaskan variant of this breed.

> **TRICKS OF THE TRADE**
>
> At a loss for writing a round? Fictional dogs, cats, birds—they're all ripe for the picking, as the variety of the clues is broad, from film to television and literature to Internet bulldogs skateboarding.

7 The Kintamani is a dog breed native to this Indonesian island.

8 After his owner's death, Hachiko, a dog of this breed, went every day to the Tokyo train station his owner would have returned from.

9 This dog has been spotted in artwork on Egyptian tombs, possibly dispelling its supposed roots on the Croatian coast.

10 Known natively as the Xoloitzcuintli, this Central American dog is bald.

ANSWERS - 1. Weimaraner - 2. Labradoodle - 3. Fly - 4. St. Bernard - 5. *Evil Angels* (also titled *A Cry in the Dark*) - 6. Husky - 7. Bali - 8. Akita - 9. Dalmatian - 10. Mexican Hairless

Random Stuff You Should Know

1 The NFL record for most passing yards in a single game is 554 yards, set by this Los Angeles Rams quarterback on September 28, 1951.

2 Asmara is the capital of this nation in the Horn of Africa.

IN THE RECORD BOOKS

Nonsporting trivia dorks are infamously bad at sports trivia, and football fans have notoriously short memories for records (compared to baseball fans, for example), so picking a record from professional football in 1951 is sure to stump both your typical trivia aficionado AND a self-proclaimed NFL expert.

3 In the United States, the mnemonic *A* for *Ash*, *B* for *Barrel*, *C* for *Current*, *D* for *Dynamite*, and *K* for *Kitchen* refers to usage classifications of these devices.

4 Rochester, Minnesota, is the home city of this world-renowned medical services provider.

5 Besides Washington, this state reports the most sightings of Sasquatch.

6 The site of a failed invasion, ANZAC Cove is in this country.

7 This word can describe an implement used on a tablet or the needle of a record player.

8 In 1993, Exchange Server 5.5 was the first release of this email software.

9 Sixty-nine percent of the residents of Italy's autonomous province of South Tyrol speak this language.

10 One point each for the top-12-selling varieties of cheese in the US by market share.

ANSWERS - 1. Norm Van Brocklin - 2. Eritrea - 3. Fire Extinguishers - 4. Mayo Clinic - 5. California - 6. Turkey - 7. Stylus - 8. Outlook - 9. German - 10. Goat, Cream Cheese, Feta, Ricotta, Provolone, Bleu, American, Swiss, Jack, Parmesan, Cheddar, Mozzarella

Syndicated TV

1. In 2012, *Entertainment Tonight* had its theme song reimagined by this member of the Black Eyed Peas.

2. As the only opponent to appear in all seven seasons of *American Gladiator*, Jim Starr went by this nickname.

3. Aaliyah, Adam Sandler, Alanis Morissette, and Beyoncé were among the literally dozens of now famous celebrities to appear on this syndicated talent contest.

4. Syndicated game shows *Wheel of Fortune* and the current version of *Jeopardy!* were both created by this television producer.

5. Having children take polygraph tests and endorsing quick-weight-loss products are among some of the questionable things that this unaccredited, folksy Texan acolyte of Oprah has done on air.

6. Until the 1980s, this famous Western ran in syndication with the title *Ponderosa*.

7. Criminal convictions probably caused buyers' remorse for those who purchased the syndication rights to this 1980s sitcom for a record $4 million an episode.

8. This 1978 outer-space series gained syndication with the low number of 34 episodes, 41 fewer than its 2003 reimagining.

9. A spin-off of Cartoon Network, this cable network airs only syndicated repeats of Saturday morning cartoons.

10. Deemed a failure because of the inability to acquire many music licensing rights, *Rewind* was the subtitle of the condensed syndicated version of this game show.

ANSWERS - 1. will.i.am - 2. Laser - 3. *Star Search* - 4. Merv Griffin - 5. Dr. Phil - 6. *Bonanza* - 7. *The Cosby Show* - 8. *Battlestar Galactica* - 9. Boomerang - 10. *American Idol*

Fictional Animals

1 After General Woundwort is allegedly slain, his aide Captain Campion becomes Chief Rabbit of Efrafa in this Richard Adams novel.

2 Because of fears of a copyright issue with a famous flying disc, the heroine "Mrs. Frisby" was changed to "Mrs. Brisby" in this 1982 animated adaptation of a 1971 novel.

3 In 2017, John Cena voiced this flower-loving cinematic bull.

FREAKING TERRIFYING

WTF's up with authors terrifying children with animal stories? For real: Answers #1 and #2, alongside *Animal Farm*, are violent AF. They're all basically *Lord of the Flies* with mammals. I mean, *Lord of the Flies* is with mammals, too. But, like, yeah. Blood everywhere in these books!

4 Foxes, lions, mice, dogs, storks, hares, geese, kites, snakes, crabs, cranes, wolves, lambs, tortoises, ants, cats, goats, and cocks are among the animals written about by this fabulist in the seventh and sixth centuries BCE.

5 Bob Dylan turned down the role, so Johnny Cash appeared as this guest character on *The Simpsons*.

6 Actor Luke Cook voices a famous familiar in the episode "Chapter Thirty-Five: The Endless" in this Netflix show.

7 Ninja Turtle nemeses Bebop and Rocksteady are these two animals, respectively.

8 Representing organized religion that only serves those in power, this biblically named raven obeys first Mr. Jones, then Napoleon in George Orwell's *Animal Farm*.

9 Although an alien, this *Men in Black* character appears to the residents of Earth as a smart-aleck pug.

10 When Charlie Weasley discovers that Hagrid's Norwegian ridgeback dragon is actually female in *Harry Potter and the Deathly Hallows*, he renames her this.

Back to the Future

1 President Reagan said, "Where we're going, we don't need roads" during this annual address.

2 Head of Universal Pictures Sid Sheinberg hated the name *Back to the Future* and thought the film should be called *Spaceman from Pluto* until this director passive-aggressively thanked the exec for the joke memo.

3 Michael J. Fox had to shoot almost all of his scenes on weekends or nights because of obligations to this sitcom.

4 In an early draft of the script, the time machine was supposed to be not a DeLorean but this appliance; it was changed because of its risk to children.

5 A physicist polled for research led the filmmakers to believe mistakenly that Doc Brown properly pronounced this word.

6 In the French dub of the movie, Marty is called Pierre Cardin instead of this.

7 In the *Back to the Future* video game, Doc Brown used this famous *Cosmos* scientist's name as an alias.

> **WON'T ANYONE THINK OF THE CHILDREN?**
>
> Apparently, the writers of *Indiana Jones and the Kingdom of the Crystal Skull* didn't have the same regard for child welfare. In that film, Indy uses the appliance in Question #4 to shield himself from a nuclear blast.

8 What was the name of Griff Tannen's hoverboard in *Back to the Future II*?

9 The televisions in *Back to the Future Part II*'s Cafe 80s feature video from Michael J. Fox's sitcom from Question #3 and this 1980s sitcom starring Christopher Lloyd.

10 This actor was asked for permission to use his name as Marty's alias in *Back to the Future III*.

ANSWERS - 1. State of the Union - 2. Spielberg - 3. *Family Ties* - 4. Refrigerator - 5. Gigawatts - 6. Calvin Klein - 7. Carl Sagan - 8. Pit Bull - 9. *Taxi* - 10. Clint Eastwood

Random Stuff You Might *Not* Know

1 Kennedy's PT-109 wreck and the battle of Guadalcanal both occurred in what is today this country.

2 Although New York's 1792 Cadwalader, Wickersham & Taft is the country's oldest law partnership, the oldest law firm in continuous practice is the 1783 firm of Rawle and Henderson from this city.

3 The 2001 documentary *Mind Meld* is about the bond between these two famous sci-fi actors.

4 Wielded by the Zulus, the assegai is a type of this weapon.

5 Kamala Harris succeeded this person as US senator from California.

6 Bauxite is the primary ore source for the mining of this element.

7 Activision is the publisher of this massively successful series of first-person shooters.

8 This demonstration of esophageal skill has been practiced by performers and mystics since 2000 BCE.

9 Frequented by international tourists and previously colonized by Portugal, Vasco da Gama is the largest city in this Indian state.

10 One point each for the 12 longest rivers on Earth.

ANSWERS - 1. Solomon Islands - 2. Philadelphia - 3. Leonard Nimoy and William Shatner - 4. Spear - 5. Barbara Boxer - 6. Aluminum - 7. *Call of Duty* - 8. Sword Swallowing - 9. Goa - 10. Mekong, Lena, Amur-Argun, Congo, Paraná-Rio de la Plata, Ob, Yellow, Yenisei, Mississippi-Missouri, Yangtze, Amazon, Nile

Astronomy and Space Stuff

1 Every second, the sun fuses 600 million tons of hydrogen into this element.

2 This star in Orion's Belt, when spelled differently, is also a Michael Keaton character.

3 The International Space Station's largest module is the Kibo, provided by JAXA, this nation's space agency.

4 In 1846, this planet was discovered by using Newton's theory of gravity to explain irregularities in the movement of Uranus.

5 This electromagnetic radiation consisting of high energy photons turned Bruce Banner into the Hulk.

6 This asterism is known around the world as a wagon, a coffin and mourners, a canoe, seven great wise men, and others.

7 July 13, 1889, at 9:08 p.m. in Arles, France, is the exact date, time, and place of the famous moonrise painting by this artist, as ascertained by astronomers.

> **ASTERISM NEEDED**
>
> *Constellation* refers to a group of stars that form the representation of some sort of figure: swans, crabs, whatever. *Asterism* refers to a subgroup of stars within a constellation that form their own, independent representation.

8 By calculating latitude and longitude in April 1912, Neil deGrasse Tyson notified the director of this movie that the starfield depicted was incorrect, prompting a technical edit for re-release.

9 To the closest minute, how long does it take for light to reach us from the sun?

10 The Schwarzschild metric and Einstein–Rosen bridge are the names of the theory postulating the creation of one of these space-time connecting shortcuts.

ANSWERS - 1. Helium - 2. Betelgeuse - 3. Japan - 4. Neptune - 5. Gamma Rays - 6. The Big Dipper - 7. Van Gogh - 8. *Titanic* - 9. 8 Minutes (8 Minutes, 19 Seconds) - 10. Wormholes

Before and After

See page 2 if you need a refresher on the rules.

1 Aerosmith hit reimagined with Run-DMC AND Chuck Norris's breakout role came in this Bruce Lee martial arts comedy film.

2 Paul Newman's wife AND reporting duo whose source was known pseudonymously as Deep Throat.

3 America Ferrera titular TV role AND World War II pinup known for her million-dollar legs.

ON THE MOUND

On May 17, 1998, the hurler in Question #8 pitched a perfect game, the 15th in MLB history, for the New York Yankees. Three months later, he pitched perfectly into the seventh inning, finishing with a two-hit shutout.

4 Nickname of this Seattle Mariners perfect-game pitcher AND this composer of the *Italian* Symphony is credited with rediscovering the works of J. S. Bach.

5 Icelandic sagas credit this father of Leif Erikson with settling Greenland AND this restaurant chain's 2003 unlimited snow-crab-leg promotion lost $3 million.

6 Jared Leto's band AND Nicholson, Close, Fox, Parker, Brosnan, Black, Portman, and DeVito alien invasion comedy.

7 Wiz Khalifa's Pittsburgh anthem AND in 1900, physician Walter Reed discovered human-to-mosquito transmission of this disease.

8 Known as Boomer, this pitcher is tied with Kenny Lofton for postseason starts with six different teams AND this bank grew with the 1998 merger with Norwest and 2008 acquisition of Wachovia.

9 The singer of "Beer for My Horses" AND with 11 consecutive Gold Gloves, he has the most in baseball history for a first baseman.

10 Miller, Horvath, Caparzo, Wade, and others scour Normandy for a GI in this 1998 movie AND he has two daughters with Eva Mendes.

10. Saving Private Ryan Gosling

7. Black and Yellow Fever - 8. David Wells Fargo - 9. Toby Keith Hernandez -

Grable - 4. King Felix Mendelssohn - 5. Erik the Red Lobster - 6. Thirty Seconds to Mars Attacks! -

ANSWERS - 1. Walk This Way of the Dragon - 2. Joanne Woodward and Bernstein - 3. Ugly Betty

Movie Math

See the explanation on page 7 if you need a refresher on the rules.

1 ____ *First Dates* PLUS ____ *Dresses*

2 ____ *Easy Pieces* TIMES ____ *Degrees of Separation*

3 ____ *Days of Summer* MINUS *The* ____ *Blows*

4 ____ *Things I Hate about You* DIVIDED BY ____ *Mules for Sister Sarah*

5 ____ *Flew over the Cuckoo's Nest* PLUS *Player* ____

6 ____ *: Rise of an Empire* DIVIDED BY ____ *Amigos*

7 *The* ____ *Faces of Eve* TIMES ____ *Days of the Condor*

8 *Slaughterhouse* ____ MINUS *I Am Number* ____

9 *Around the World in* ____ *Days* PLUS ____ *Days of Night*

10 ____ *: The Jackie Robinson Story* MINUS *This Is* ____

> **DID YOU KNOW?**
>
> It seems like no one ever saw *I Am Number* [redacted]. Well, it had a $150 million box office—where are all those people hiding?

ROUND 4 / DIFFICULTY LEVEL 1 **2** 3 4 5 6

Random Stuff You Should Know

1 This state has the first state capital listed alphabetically.

2 The 1898 First United States Volunteer Cavalry was better known by this famous nickname.

3 The 1953 merger of Burton's Ice Cream Shop and Snowbird Ice Cream created this company.

4 In *The Lord of the Rings*, this Lord of Rivendell would be more than 6,000 years old at the time of the Fellowship.

5 This 76ers great last played for Turkey's Beşiktaş basketball team.

6 Mortorq, Pozidriv, and Phillips are all types of these items.

7 Bilbao is the largest city in these people's semiautonomous ethnic enclave.

8 Phil Ken Sebben and Myron Reducto from Cartoon Network's *Harvey Birdman, Attorney at Law* were voiced by this future CBS host.

9 What is the capital of Mongolia?

10 One point each for the 10 highest-grossing movies of all time, adjusted for inflation.

Civil Wars

1 Since World War II, global civil wars have lasted on average just slightly more than this many years.

2 The Contras and the Sandinistas were opposing sides in this country's long civil war.

3 In Marvel's *Civil War* series, Tony Stark and Reed Richards side with the US government, which wants to register superheroes, and are opposed by a side led by this superhero.

4 The First Barons' War began in 1215 after King John of England refused to adhere to this document.

5 The Maori wars were fought between the Indigenous people and Anglo government of this country.

6 In Cyprus, an ongoing conflict has existed for more than a century between factions allied to Greek-descended residents and those allied with this cultural ancestry.

WHAT ABOUT THE SEQUEL?

Like most sequels, the Second Barons' War from 1264 to 1267 was worse than the first installment in the series—mostly because the rebelling Barons used the war as a pretext to massacre thousands of English Jews and destroy all records of their debts.

7 "The Cause," "A Very Bloody Affair," and "War Is All Hell" are episodes of this documentarian's acclaimed series on the US Civil War.

8 Bashar Al-Assad is the president of this country, currently embroiled in a multifaceted civil war.

9 This country's civil war ended in a victory for a group called the Khmer Rouge.

10 An abundance of these ultimately worthless metastable allotropes of carbon helped trigger the Sierra Leone Civil War.

ANSWERS - 1. Four - **2.** Nicaragua - **3.** Captain America - **4.** Magna Carta - **5.** New Zealand - **6.** Turkish - **7.** Ken Burns - **8.** Syria - **9.** Cambodia - **10.** Diamonds

Before and After

See page 2 if you need a refresher on the rules.

1 Former captain of Chelsea Football Club AND Isaiah Mustafa and this *Brooklyn Nine-Nine* TV star were dueling spokesmen for Old Spice.

2 Prince wrote this 1986 hit by the Bangles AND along with the *Hallmark Hall of Fame* and *Walt Disney Presents*, this sports program is one of the longest-running prime-time TV programs.

WHAT'S IN A NAME

Tenacious D's name comes from the NBA play-by-play calls of broadcaster Marv Albert. He would frequently praise a team for their "tenacious defense."

3 This ancient barrier runs from the River Tyne to the Solway Firth AND Phil Spector's production ethos.

4 Tenacious D's "Tribute" was inspired by the music of "Stairway to Heaven" and the concept of this Charlie Daniels Band song AND the state song of the 13th original colony.

5 Ted Stroehmann engages shady P.I. Pat Healy to find his high school love in this movie AND she played Laura Petrie on *The Dick Van Dyke Show*.

6 "Do It Like a Dude," "Price Tag," "Domino," and "Laserlight" are hits by this Londoner AND the author of *The Tales of Beedle the Bard*.

7 White men Freeman Gosden and Charles Correll created this radio and TV duo set in Harlem AND Foreign Man from Caspiar pantomiming the *Mighty Mouse* theme song was a famous bit by this humorist.

8 The leader of Tootles, Nibs, Slightly, and the Twins AND a musical instrument consisting of several closed tubes of different lengths.

9 This holiday is known as Nochebuena in Spain AND Barry McGuire is famous for this 1965 protest song.

10 The femme fatale of *North by Northwest* AND Kendall and Khloe's newest nephew.

ANSWERS - 1. John Terry Crews - 2. Manic Monday Night Football - 3. Hadrian's Wall of Sound - 4. The Devil Went Down to Georgia on My Mind - 5. There's Something about Mary Tyler Moore - 6. Jessie J. K. Rowling - 7. Amos 'n' Andy Kaufman - 8. Peter Pan Flute - 9. Christmas Eve of Destruction - 10. Eva Marie Saint West

Junk Food

1 "We have the meats" is the slogan of this fast-food restaurant.

2 Whereas the ancient mathematician Hero of Alexandria invented a vending machine that dispensed holy water in the first century CE, the first modern vending machine appeared in London in 1615 and dispensed not junk food but this.

3 In 2002, *Time* magazine named this treat number one on its list of Top 10 Iconic Junk Foods.

4 In 2011, the first so-called "fat tax" in the United States assessed a 2 percent tax on all junk food on the 27,000 square miles of this Indigenous nation in Arizona, New Mexico, and Utah.

5 Serving wines, olives, breads, and stews, the popina was a fast-food restaurant for the lower classes of this ancient society.

6 In 1971, franchise owner Al Bernardin invented this more adult McDonald's burger offering.

7 Made with avocado, coconut meat, *cincau,* jackfruit, condensed milk, and sugar, *Es Teler* is a popular snack beverage from this archipelago nation.

> **YOU CAN'T WIN 'EM ALL**
>
> Although Al Bernardin helped create several lasting signature items for McDonald's, he wasn't without his failures. For example, we're not eating the McGobbler turkey burger or McCorn-on-the-Cob right now, are we?

8 Established in 1810, Hindoostane Coffee Shop was London's first ever of these drunken food destinations.

9 Opened in 1990, the world's busiest McDonald's is in this city.

10 Seafood chain Long John Silver's is named after a character invented by this *Treasure Island* author.

ANSWERS - 1. Arby's - 2. Tobacco - 3. Twinkie - 4. Navajo - 5. Roman - 6. Quarter Pounder - 7. Indonesia - 8. Curry House - 9. Moscow - 10. Robert Louis Stevenson

Random Stuff You Should Know

1 Although Groucho, Harpo, Chico, and Zeppo all appeared in movies, this Marx brother did not.

2 Game Show Network's *Skin Wars* is a competition focused on this art.

3 The Midnight Idol, Mr. Las Vegas, and Mr. Entertainment are this performer's nicknames.

4 Native to the Andes, these South American rodents live in colonies called herds.

WELCOME TO PARODIES!

Weird Al's *UHF* parodies the following: *Raiders of the Lost Ark, Close Encounters of the Third Kind, The Treasure of the Sierra Madre, Network, Gandhi, Conan the Barbarian, Wheel of Fortune, Gone with the Wind,* and best of all, Dire Straits' legendary CG music video for "Money for Nothing."

5 This country's name in Old High German translates to "Eastern Empire."

6 Cawker City, Kansas, Darwin, Minnesota, and Branson, Missouri, all lay claim to the world's largest one of these.

7 Fran Drescher, Victoria Jackson, and this famous television actor all starred in Weird Al Yankovic's movie *UHF*.

8 *Musa acuminata* is the scientific name of this large edible berry that we refer to as a fruit.

9 In aviation parlance, what does *UAV* stand for?

10 One point each for the 12 most commonly spoken languages in the United States.

ANSWERS - 1. Gummo - 2. Body Painting - 3. Wayne Newton - 4. Chinchillas - 5. Austria - 6. Ball of Twine - 7. Michael Richards - 8. Banana - 9. Unmanned Aerial Vehicle - 10. Portuguese, Italian, Arabic, Russian, Korean, German, Vietnamese, French, Tagalog, Chinese, Spanish, English

Board Games

49

1 The earliest-known game boards are from the Jiroft culture in present-day Balochistan, which straddles Iran and this neighboring country.

2 An unnamed ancient Egyptian game was nicknamed Hounds and Jackals by this discoverer of King Tut's tomb.

3 In Risk, Mongolia and Kamchatka border this territory.

4 From 1984 until 1990, Chuck Woolery hosted a daytime game show based on this Hasbro word game.

5 Recently discovered in Iraq, the world's oldest dice were made of the bone of this animal.

6 In 1996, Hasbro obtained an injunction against an adult website seeking to use this game's name as its domain.

7 It's no surprise that this board game entered the National Toy Hall of Fame in the hall's inaugural year of 1998.

8 In Stratego, this is the only piece that can capture the Marshal.

9 The ancient Indian game of Pachisi has formed the basis of Parcheesi, Ludo, and this exclamatory game.

10 In Clue, the envelope containing the murderer, the weapon, and the room are kept in this room.

> **GAME TIME**
>
> The Marshal, the highest-ranking piece in Stratego Classic, was numbered as 1. In newer versions, it's ranked number 10. Experts agree that changing the numbers to make the big number superior is stupid. I'm "experts."

ANSWERS - 1. Pakistan - 2. Howard Carter - 3. Japan - 4. Scrabble - 5. Human - 6. Candy Land - 7. Monopoly - 8. Spy - 9. Sorry! - 10. Cellar

Before and After

See page 2 if you need a refresher on the rules.

1 Cloverleaf Industries plots to turn this neighborhood into a freeway in *Who Framed Roger Rabbit* AND an informal public event to openly ask questions of elected officials.

2 Son House, Robert Johnson, and John Lee Hooker all performed this Mississippi-originated music AND Steve Burns hosted this Nickelodeon developmental program for six years.

3 Hype Williams's video for this hip-hop hit was inspired by *Mad Max Beyond Thunderdome* AND Neeson, Thompson, and Knightley rom-com.

THAT'S A REMAKE?

Three's Company = Man about the House
All in the Family = Till Death Do Us Part
Maude = Nobody's Perfect

4 A 1984 Andrew Lloyd Webber musical about trains with actors on roller skates AND this 1987 Madonna music video featured athletic men working in a factory.

5 "Practice, practice, practice" venue AND the singers of "Out of Touch."

6 This 2003 Fountains of Wayne song was one of the first number-one iTunes downloads AND *Saturday Night Live* once ran a sketch parodying these unflattering denim garments.

7 Bill Murray makes an assist on the court in the climactic scene of this movie AND Run DMC's DJ.

8 Despite coming out in 2015, this movie ignored more than a decade of new discoveries in paleontology AND Wrath of the Lich King, Burning Crusade, and Mists of Pandaria are some of the expansion sets for this game.

9 Mysterious "cooler" Dalton moves into a dive bar in this 1989 movie AND Francis Urquhart rises to prime minister in this BBC series.

10 The founder of Tesla Motors AND endemic to North America, this semi-aquatic rodent became a pest when introduced to Europe and Asia.

ANSWERS - 1. Toon Town Hall Meeting - 2. Delta Blues Clues - 3. California Love Actually - 4. Starlight Express Yourself - 5. Carnegie Hall and Oates - 6. Stacy's Mom Jeans - 7. Space Jam Master Jay - 8. Jurassic World of Warcraft - 9. Road House of Cards - 10. Elon Musk Rat

Fairy Tales and Fables

1. After a mouse is spared from being eaten, it gnaws through the nets entrapping this animal in an Aesop fable.

2. Despite popular belief, "Aladdin" and "Ali Baba and the Forty Thieves" are not from this compendium of tales; French translator Antoine Galland added them from Syrian stories.

3. Depicted as bankers in the *Harry Potter* series and cave-dwelling villains in *The Hobbit,* these mythical creatures have a name dating back to 12th-century Normandy.

4. "Little Red Riding Hood," "Cinderella," "Sleeping Beauty," and others were all written by Charles Perrault, whose 1697 book *Tales and Stories of the Past with Morals* was credited to this person.

5. Detective Nick Burkhardt is assailed by modern-day fairy-tale beasts in this NBC show.

6. Inspired by the nickname of opera singer Jenny Lind, fairy-tale author Hans Christian Andersen wrote this bird-named story.

7. This fable of the collapse of the 1917 Russian Revolution into a toxic cult of personality was published by Eric Arthur Blair under a pseudonym in 1945.

8. "The Little Girl and the Wolf" and "The Unicorn in the Garden" are 20th-century fables written by James Thurber and published in this magazine.

9. Written by Charles Perrault, like the book in Question #4, this fairy tale follows a young wife haunted by thoughts of the seven previous wives of her rich husband, the titular character.

10. The music and lyrics of *Into the Woods* were written by this Broadway legend.

THURBER ROAD

James Thurber's eyesight deteriorated throughout his life, so much so that he drew his later cartoons in white chalk on black paper in a giant format. The editors of the magazine in Question #8 photographed the cartoons in the negative and reduced them for publication.

ANSWERS - 1. Lion - **2.** One Thousand and One Nights - **3.** Goblins - **4.** Mother Goose - **5.** Grimm - **6.** "The Nightingale" - **7.** Animal Farm - **8.** The New Yorker - **9.** Bluebeard - **10.** Stephen Sondheim

Random Stuff You Might Know

1 With its size as depicted in a popular movie franchise, this animal should've been called Deinonychus and not named after its medium dog–sized relative.

2 For just over 20 years, Aung San Suu Kyi has been the oft-imprisoned opposition leader of this reclusive nation.

> **FUN FACT**
>
> The *Jurassic Park* franchise is a lie: All raptors were covered in feathers, but this wasn't confirmed by paleontologists until *Jurassic Park III*. They had the opportunity to correct it in *Jurassic World*, but maybe the toys had already hit the assembly line?

3 South Americans call him El Libertador.

4 This compound word can refer to being in intractable opposition to someone or the Caretta Caretta sea turtle.

5 What was Miley Cyrus's first US number-one single?

6 Until the late 19th century, this language was referred to as Bohemian.

7 John Cleese, Douglas Adams, John Oliver, and Emma Thompson were all members of this Cambridge University amateur dramatic club.

8 In what app would you find filters called Clarendon, Gingham, and Lark?

9 Originally derived from the Malay word for "striped," this word now means a cotton fabric dyed in a colored check pattern.

10 One point for each of the 12 most populous capital cities on Earth.

Remakes, Reboots, and Reimaginings **50**

1. *Captains Courageous* and *The Man Who Would Be King* are film adaptations of works by this Victorian and Edwardian author.

2. Marlon Brando and David Niven's *Bedtime Story* was remade as this 1988 Steve Martin and Michael Caine movie.

3. Sting has songwriting credit on this 1997 Puff Daddy hit.

4. Featuring an all-star cast, this 2006 crime drama is a remake of the 2002 Hong Kong movie *Infernal Affairs*.

5. This overly serious 2014 remake completely ignored the humor, satire, and skewering, anti-Reagan, anti-corporate attitude of the 1987 original.

> **BUT WHO'LL REMAKE THE REMAKE?**
>
> Rebel Wilson and Anne Hathaway's *The Hustle* is the remake of the remake in Answer #2. So there.

6. After a copyright issue prevented the use of the original, Nintendo composer Koji Kondo took inspiration from this piece by Maurice Ravel for the theme to *The Legend of Zelda*.

7. *A Fistful of Dollars* was a remake of *Yojimbo*, a film by this acclaimed director.

8. After starring as this famous, reimagined Disney character in 1951, voice actor Kathryn Beaumont played Wendy Darling in Disney's *Peter Pan*.

9. Greer Garson, Celia Bannerman, Jennifer Ehle, and Keira Knightley have all played this Jane Austen character.

10. In *Once Upon a Time*, Ginnifer Goodwin's Mary Margaret Blanchard is better known by this alter ego.

ANSWERS - 1. Rudyard Kipling - 2. *Dirty Rotten Scoundrels* - 3. "I'll Be Missing You" - 4. *The Departed* - 5. *Robocop* - 6. *Bolero* - 7. Akira Kurosawa - 8. Alice - 9. Elizabeth Bennett - 10. Snow White

50 Robots

1 *L'automa cavaliere*, a 1495 "robot" designed and possibly built by Leonardo da Vinci, featured a system of gears and pulleys ensconced in this kind of suit.

2 In the 1870s, Swedish American inventor John Ericsson devised a remote-controlled torpedo; he rose to fame in the prior decade for designing this revolutionary ironclad warship.

3 In 1954, George Devol patented the Unimate, the world's first digitally operated programmable robot; by 1961, Unimates were used in this US corporation's New Jersey plant.

4 Eighties sitcom *Small Wonder* followed the adventures of the Lawson family and their adoptive daughter—a robot girl who went by this name.

5 Some economists and sociologists believe that a fully automated society will necessitate among citizens a UBI, which stands for this.

ZERO STARS

Jean-Marie-Mathias-Philippe-Auguste, comte de Villiers de l'Isle-Adam's *L'Ève future*, or *Tomorrow's Eve*, has been described as staggering in both its foresightedness in science fiction and its flagrant, unrepentant misogyny.

---

6 The dreams of automation are on display in ancient Greece as Homer's *Iliad* depicts golden three-legged, wheeled tables that follow and assist in the workshop of this Greek god of the smiths.

7 In the 1886 novel *Tomorrow's Eve*, a despondent Lord Ewald has built an android replication of his fiancée by a fictionalized version of this inventor.

8 Depicting suburban life where not everything is what it seems, both the 1975 and 2004 film versions of *The Stepford Wives* were unsurprisingly shot on location in this state.

9 Robotics engineer Jamie Paik founded the Reconfigurable Robotics Lab, which specializes in robots that fold akin to this Japanese art.

10 Amusement park android Maeve Millay, the madam of fictional Sweetwater's brothel, is played by this British actor.

ANSWERS - 1. Armor - 2. USS *Monitor* - 3. General Motors - 4. Vicki - 5. Universal Basic Income - 6. Hephaestus - 7. Thomas Edison - 8. Connecticut - 9. Origami - 10. Thandie Newton

Brit Lit

50

1 The BBC named *Middlemarch* by this female author—with a male pen name—as the best British novel of all time.

2 This is the maritime destination in the title of a 1927 Virginia Woolf novel.

3 This William Makepeace Thackeray novel lent its name to a Graydon Carter–helmed publication.

4 Thomas Hardy's obscure stonemason with scholarly ambitions goes by this first name.

5 The name *Canis Lupus Corridor* could be an alternate title to this 2009 Hilary Mantel novel about the court of Henry VIII.

6 Initially poorly reviewed and critiqued for alleged obscenity, *Sons and Lovers* was written in 1913 by this author

WHERE IN THE WORLD?

The sea in Answer #10's title geographically coincides with the eastern Atlantic Ocean off the southern coast of the United States—in essence, the 1,000-by-3,000-km area known as the Bermuda Triangle.

7 This fantasy series first published from 1949 to 1954 was the subject of *Saturday Night Live*'s first-ever Digital Short.

8 The shell of this kind of sea snail calls the boys to assemble in *Lord of the Flies*.

9 The spaceship *Nostromo* in the first *Alien* movie takes its name from a novel by this *Heart of Darkness* author.

10 Jean Rhys's 1966 novel of a terrible arranged marriage is called the *Wide [This] Sea*.

ANSWERS - 1. George Eliot - 2. Lighthouse - 3. Vanity Fair - 4. Jude - 5. Wolf Hall - 6. D. H. Lawrence - 7. The Chronicles of Narnia - 8. Conch - 9. Joseph Conrad - 10. Sargasso

199

Random Stuff You Might *Not* Know

1. Meaning "stomach foot" in Greek, this class of mollusks includes snails and slugs.

2. What is the mascot of the University of Colorado Boulder?

3. From 1757 until 1858, this company ruled British India.

4. This six-word phrase was the slogan of the Dillon Panthers of *Friday Night Lights*.

5. This is the largest and most populous Lusophone nation in the world.

6. His most famous composition is the suite of four violin concerti called *Le Quattro Stagioni*.

7. As the location of its judicial departments, Bloemfontein is one of three capitals of this country.

8. Megan Fox's *Jennifer's Body* was written by this *Juno* screenwriter.

9. In the UK, *Airfix* has become a generic term for anything related to this hobby.

10. One point each for the 12 highest-grossing movies of 1985.

ULTIMATELY, MY DEAR

Natural contrarians, Ultimate Frisbee teams will often have names and even color schemes with little to no relation to their colleges' or universities' official palette and naming conventions. For example, Colorado's D-I men's Ultimate team is known as Mamabird. The Oregon Ducks are the Oregon Ego in Ultimate. Wisconsin Badgers? Nope. Wisconsin Hodags.

ANSWERS - 1. Gastropoda - 2. Buffalo - 3. British East India Company - 4. "Clear eyes, full hearts, can't lose" - 5. Brazil - 6. Antonio Vivaldi - 7. South Africa - 8. Diablo Cody - 9. Model Making - 10. Fletch, Police Academy 2, Spies Like Us, The Goonies, Witness, Jewel of the Nile, Cocoon, Out of Africa, The Color Purple, Rocky IV, Rambo: First Blood Part II, Back to the Future

Crazy Statistics

51

1 There are 10 times more of these organisms in your gut than there are cells in your body.

2 The budget allocated to the US military over 13 hours is equivalent to the amount of money it cost to send and operate this radioactive-powered rover on Mars.

3 Every minute, a typical human emits 14,000 gamma rays because of the radioactivity of this element in our bodies.

4 The first of this quarterback's 6,300 completions was to himself.

5 Excluding Eddie Gaedel and Bob Cain, a 2012 matchup between pitcher Jon Rauch and batter José Altuve holds baseball's record for biggest difference in this.

6 According to Texas A&M, the average American spends a day and a half, or about 38 hours, stuck here per year.

7 Every second, more than an hour of video content is added to this website.

8 More people on Earth own a cellphone than one of these hygiene implements.

9 A study by remote control company Logitech found that 50 percent of lost remotes were found in the couch, 2 percent were later found in the car, and 4–5 percent of lost remotes end up here.

10 With 88.9 guns for every 100 residents, this insane country has more armed citizens per capita than any other country in the world.

DID YOU KNOW?
....

The Second Amendment to the US Constitution is derived from the English Bill of Rights of 1689 that dictated that every Protestant *must* be armed to form militias against the threat of Catholic invasion or insurrection.

51 Before and After

See page 2 if you need a refresher on the rules.

See page 2 if you need a refresher on the rules.

I LOVE IT WHEN A PLAN COMES TOGETHER

Want to kick ass at your local trivia night? Well, you gotta assemble an A-Team. While everyone on your five- or six-person team must be a generalist, recruit members based on specialties. A pop culture ace, a sports nut, a bookworm, a music savant, a bona fide historian. The stakes for winning a trivia night are huge: We're talking FREE BOOZE here. You don't have to like these people, you just have to like them enough to use them.

1. Falkor the Luckdragon is the preferred mode of transport in this movie AND 1999 Bruce Willis and Michelle Pfeiffer movie, or 2010 Taylor Swift song.

2. Popular in the seventies and eighties, this skiing exercise equipment usually just served as a clothes hanger AND the family of running, jumping, and throwing sports.

3. The most widely distributed Scotch whisky in the world AND this Chuck Norris show prominently featured Dodge Ram truck product placements.

4. Robbie Robertson's song about the end of the Civil War AND slang for "take a drink."

5. This demographic cohort comprises those born from 1965 to 1980 AND a pirate's treasure is here.

6. This American author's death has variously been attributed to alcohol, rabies, cholera, TB, drugs, heart disease, suicide, and brain congestion AND Oscar Isaac's heroic resistance pilot.

7. The largest one of these soft-serve restaurants is in Riyadh, Saudi Arabia, AND Natalie Portman's leader of Naboo in *The Phantom Menace*.

8. This 1988 hit was the first a cappella song to reach Billboard's number-one spot AND the most recognized song in the English language.

9. Four-letter abbreviation for Liverpool F.C.'s song AND the creator of Winnie the Pooh.

10. His 1953 funeral was the largest event ever held in Montgomery, Alabama, AND Pottery Barn's parent company.

ANSWERS - 1. The Neverending Story of Us - 2. Nordic Track and Field - 3. Johnnie Walker Texas Ranger - 4. The Night They Drove Old Dixie Down the Hatch - 5. Generation X Marks the Spot - 6. Edgar Allan Poe Dameron - 7. Dairy Queen Padmé Amidala - 8. Don't Worry Be Happy Birthday to You - 9. Y N W A. A. Milne - 10. Hank Williams Sonoma

Game of Thrones

1 Since every other character is either dead or incestuous, an *SNL* "Weekend Update" sketch introduced these two as the sexiest couple on *Game of Thrones*.

2 During the White House Correspondents' Dinner, Keegan-Michael Key referred to this candidate's presidential campaign as "Khaleesi is coming to Westeros."

3 After his conquest of Westeros, this *Game of Thrones* city was founded by Aegon Targaryen the first.

4 This is the last name assigned to bastards of the North.

5 Brothers Robert, Renly, and Stannis all share this last name.

6 Casterly Rock, the home of the Lannisters, is inspired by this Mediterranean landmark.

7 Jaqen H'ghar, a Faceless Man, becomes a mentor to this vengeful Stark daughter.

8 Although we never hear it, the grandmother of this seven-foot-tall character says his real name is Walder.

9 Who are Rhaegal, Drogon, and Viserion?

10 Along with the Lannisters, this institution in Braavos is a primary moneylender to Westeros.

BEHIND THE SCENES

George R. R. Martin took many inspirations for *GoT* from British history. A cursory glance through the Wars of the Roses reveals many similarities: warring families and houses, bizarre executions, accusations of incest. No dragons, unfortunately.

ANSWERS - 1. Samwell and Gilly - 2. Hillary Clinton - 3. King's Landing - 4. Snow - 5. Baratheon - 6. Rock of Gibraltar - 7. Arya - 8. Hodor - 9. Daenerys's Dragons - 10. Iron Bank

Random Stuff You Might *Not* Know

1 In police jargon, the letters *CI* stand for this.

2 Averting a nuclear war, submariner Vasily Arkhipov prevented Captain Savitsky of submarine B59 from launching a nuclear torpedo during this military standoff.

3 This actor played *Gossip Girl*'s Blair Waldorf.

4 At four cubits and a span, this Philistine was the most famous Rephaite of Gath ever.

LET ME AXOLOTL YOU A QUESTION

CDMX was once a city of canals, floating islands, and causeways on a since-filled lake called Texcoco. One neighborhood of Mexico City, Xochimilco, still has hallmarks of the pre-Columbian city, featuring farms and fisheries in canals and artificial islands. It is also the home of the Axolotl, one of the most endangered amphibians on Earth.

5 The BCC Lions, Calabar Rovers, and ACB Lagos are all football clubs from this country.

6 This is King's Cross station's secret platform to access Hogwarts School of whatever.

7 Occupying the Compaq Center, the former home of the Houston Rockets, the 43,000-member congregation of Lakewood Church is led by this pastor.

8 Before 1521, Mexico City was known by this name.

9 Baku, the capital of Azerbaijan, is 92 feet below sea level on the shores of this largest self-contained lake in the world.

10 One point for each of the 12 longest-running musicals (with more than 3,500 performances) in Broadway history.

Books!

1 The central conceit of this book is that if one is crazy enough to fly missions, one will not be grounded, but if one asks to be grounded, one is not crazy and therefore must fly more missions.

2 *Love in the Time of Cholera* is a 1985 novel by this Colombian author.

3 *Divergent*, *Insurgent*, and this novel make up Veronica Roth's Insurgent trilogy.

4 *Dreams of My Father* was followed by this second book by Barack Obama.

5 In Boccaccio's 14th-century book *The Decameron*, seven young women and three men spend two weeks telling stories to pass the time while escaping this demographic disaster.

FUN FACT

Portions of this volume resting in your hands were written under not dissimilar circumstances to those of Boccaccio. Just with more Wi-Fi.

6 This story of a prom gone wrong was the first novel published by Stephen King

7 Loosely based on *Faust*, this 1890 Oscar Wilde novel about a man and a painting scandalized Victorian sensibilities.

8 This creator of characters Haymitch Abernathy, Alma Coin, and Gale Hawthorne is the best-selling Kindle author of all time.

9 Famous for its movie adaptation and beach scene, this James Jones book spent 20 weeks on 1951's *New York Times* best-seller list.

10 The Inklings was a literary discussion group at the University of Oxford that included J. R. R. Tolkien and this fellow English fantasy writer.

ANSWERS - 1. Catch-22 - 2. Gabriel Garcia Márquez - 3. Allegiant - 4. Audacity of Hope - 5. Black Death - 6. Carrie - 7. The Picture of Dorian Gray - 8. Suzanne Collins - 9. From Here to Eternity - 10. C. S. Lewis

Before and After

See page 2 if you need a refresher on the rules.

1 De Saint-Exupéry's 1943 book AND the Pevensies help a young heir overthrow evil king Miraz in this 1951 book.

2 Televangelist Pat Robertson wrote a book with the same title as this 2000 cheerleading movie AND Grace Kelly made *Rear Window* instead of this Eva Marie Saint Academy Award–winning movie.

3 Cordelia is this fictional character's youngest daughter AND the founder of this company said, "They said I'd never build it, that if I built it, it wouldn't fly; that if it flew, I couldn't sell it. Well, I did, and it did, and I could."

FUN FACT

When a fight over a woman named Lucille caused a fire to break out in a smoky Arkansas dance hall in 1949, a young blues guitarist rushed through the flames to recover his prized Gibson guitar. From that day forward, he named all of his guitars "Lucille" "to remind [him] never to do a thing like that again."

4 Gibson guitars nicknamed "Lucille" were the trademark instrument of this bluesman AND the last monarch of England to die in battle.

5 *Modern Sounds in Country and Western Music* is considered this musician's masterpiece AND Scott Baio's au pair show.

6 The Spurs' former French point guard AND this indie actor's first role was a bitchy senior in *Dazed and Confused*.

7 In 1920, author Johnny Gruelle created this fictional doll as a sibling for his main character AND Mr. Brooklyn Decker.

8 From 1997 to 2013, he represented Texas's 14th Congressional District AND a folkloric lumberjack.

9 Billy Wilder said this late-night icon was the "Valium and Nembutal of the nation" AND the author of *The Heart Is a Lonely Hunter*.

10 Number 13 forward for the US Women's National Soccer Team AND this financial services company started in 1935 after the Glass-Steagall Act prevented commercial and investment banks from being a single entity.

ANSWERS - 1. The Little Prince Caspian - 2. Bring it On the Waterfront - 3. King Lear Jet - 4. B. King Richard III - 5. Ray Charles in Charge - 6. Tony Parker Posey - 7. Raggedy Andy Roddick - 8. Ron Paul Bunyan - 9. Johnny Carson McCullers - 10. Alex Morgan Stanley

Computers and Stuff

52

1 The numeric name for this best-ever-selling single model of a computer is slightly misleading; it actually had over 65,000 bytes of RAM.

2 Samsung's Galaxy devices run on this Google-developed operating system.

3 This company, the world's most prolific video game publisher, was founded by Americans based in Japan in 1940 as Service Games.

4 This is a 2014 version of Apple's OS X named after a California national park.

5 Unlike the PC version, which featured a Godzilla-like creature, the Super Nintendo version of this game featured Bowser terrorizing 1961 Tokyo.

6 The Surface 3 is a laptop-tablet hybrid produced by this company.

7 Kraftwerk, ELO, Pink Floyd, Phil Collins, Daft Punk, and the robot voices of *Battlestar Galactica* are among some of those to use this speech synthesizer.

8 Unlike its predecessor technology, accessory cable's type-C iteration can be inserted in any direction.

9 Other than the pilot, made with construction paper cutouts, every episode of this TV show since 1997 has been computer animated.

10 The *SD* in SD memory cards stands for this.

> **YOU HAVE DIED OF DYSENTERY**
>
> ....
>
> In 1984, R. Philip Bouchard designed the wildly successful 1984 educational game *Oregon Trail*, a reimagined version of the original 1971 text-based adventure, made specially for the graphic power of the classroom staple Apple II computer. Expanding on the original, he incorporated five diseases, and said: "Oddly, one of these five has captured the popular imagination and become a huge meme."

Random Stuff You Might Know

1 Featuring the debut of new video games, "Clueless Gamer" is a periodic bit on this late-night host's show.

2 Beethoven was born in this former de facto capital of West Germany.

3 Twitter and teenagers the world over freaked out when he left One Direction.

4 Before starring in her own sitcom at 24 years old, this writer-director became a staff writer and cast member of *The Office*.

5 Platinum, cotton, and wood were originally tested materials until carbonized bamboo was settled on to make this device commercially viable.

IF IT EVER COMES UP

The most viewed "Clueless Gamer" video racked up 19 million views on YouTube and featured Marshawn Lynch and Rob Gronkowski playing *Mortal Kombat X.*

6 Having come to mean "mass destruction" and taken from the Bible, this word comes from the Greek for "revelation."

7 This is the name of the peninsula that, along with Hong Kong Island, forms the territory of Hong Kong.

8 In 1955, two years after he summited Mount Everest, this Kiwi led an expedition across the South Pole.

9 The sennet is a type of this fish, a favorite of the band Heart.

10 One point each for the 10 countries on Earth that produce the most corn.

ANSWERS - 1. Conan O'Brien - 2. Bonn - 3. Zayn Malik - 4. Mindy Kaling - 5. Light Bulb - 6. Apocalypse - 7. Kowloon - 8. Edmund Hillary - 9. Barracuda - 10. Ukraine, South Africa, Argentina, France, India, Indonesia, Mexico, Brazil, China, US

208

Dance

1. Meaning "bent," this is the ballet term for a smooth, continuous bend of the knee.

2. This Hall of Fame running back was the first football player to win *Dancing with the Stars*.

3. Tweet, Jadakiss, and Ginuwine all perform in this 2003 Jessica Alba dance film.

4. Decca Records, unsure how to market new rock and roll records, called this Bill Haley and His Comets hit a foxtrot number.

5. Major American ballet companies generate up to 40 percent of their annual ticket sales from performances of this famous 1892 Tchaikovsky holiday ballet.

> **PRO TIP**
>
> In *Jeopardy!*, anytime ballet and art are mentioned simultaneously, the answer is Answer #9. Duh.

6. Emerging in the 1950s, this is the popular men's dance and music from the Punjab region of India and Pakistan.

7. Becoming a cast member of Stardust Casino's *Goddess* show is the ultimate goal of dancer Nomi in this amazing movie.

8. West Virginia and Norway have both used this Japanese arcade game as part of an aerobic exercise school curriculum.

9. *Rehearsal on Stage*, *The Dance Class*, and *Musicians in the Orchestra* are three of the many ballet subjects painted by this 19th-century French artist.

10. *Dancer in the Dark* is a 2000 Lars von Trier movie starring this Icelandic singer.

Historical Figures

Can you name these six people?

Homophones

A homophone is a word that has the same sound as another word but is spelled differently. (But you knew that.) Provide the two homophones for each clue.

1 Manhattan is one, or a bride's thoroughfare

2 Sandpaper grade, or Econ 101

3 Wall Street panic cry, or a bunch of Al Qaeda operatives

4 On-screen cocaine, or Bambi's fragrant buddy

5 Boat propeller, or conjunction in this sentence

6 Cliff and Newman's duty, or a stag or a bull

7 Still, or office paper

8 168 hours, or diluted cup of joe

9 What Fanny takes a load off, or what Rapunzel did a lot

10 Your sibling's daughter to you, or a city neighboring Monaco

> **BUFFALO TIMES EIGHT**
> ....
> In 1967, linguist Dmitri Borgmann created an English-language nightmare with the sentence "Buffalo buffalo Buffalo buffalo buffalo buffalo Buffalo buffalo," which is grammatically correct for "Buffalo bison that other Buffalo bison bully also bully Buffalo bison." English is ridiculous sometimes.

ANSWERS – 1. Isle Aisle – 2. Coarse Course – 3. Sell Cell – 4. Flour Flower – 5. Oar Or – 6. Mail Male – 7. Stationary Stationery – 8. Week Weak – 9. Weight Wait – 10. Niece Nice

ROUND 4 / DIFFICULTY LEVEL 1 2 3 4 **5** 6

Random Stuff You Might *Not* Know

1. Open Hearts is a collection from Kay Jewelers featuring this *Dr. Quinn* star as spokesperson.

2. *K* is the stock ticker symbol for this Battle Creek, Michigan, food giant.

3. From 1017 until the late 17th century, the Trafford family lived in Trafford Park in this UK city.

HERE'S THE PITCH

In case you find yourself on *Pointless*, *Mastermind*, or any other British quiz show, try to remember the home grounds of a couple of Premier League clubs. Anfield, for example, is the home of Liverpool F.C.

4. Old Dominion University is in this state.

5. This instrument's range is from A0 to C8.

6. Legend has it that in 1833, 10-year-old Barney Flaherty was hired by the *New York Sun*, becoming the first person to ever hold this title.

7. Her breakout role was as Stephanie Zinone in *Grease 2*.

8. De facto enslaved workers had their passports confiscated to prevent them from leaving the building site of the Abu Dhabi campus of this American university.

9. Originating in Trinidad and Tobago, this Afro-Caribbean music shares its name with the nymph who tried to keep Odysseus on her island as her husband.

10. One point each for the 12 number-one singles by Madonna.

ANSWERS - 1. Jane Seymour - 2. Kellogg's - 3. Manchester - 4. Virginia - 5. Piano - 6. Paperboy - 7. Michelle Pfeiffer - 8. New York University - 9. Calypso - 10. "Like a Virgin," "Crazy for You," "Live to Tell," "Papa Don't Preach," "Who's That Girl," "Open Your Heart," "Like a Prayer," "Vogue," "Justify My Love," "This Used to Be My Playground," "Take a Bow," "Music"

Mexico

1. What is the Spanish name of the nation of Mexico?

2. The 1848 Treaty of Guadalupe Hidalgo ended an imperialist war of conquest where this country increased its size by one-third through an invasion of Mexico.

3. Located just south of San Diego, this is Mexico's sixth-most-populous city.

4. The Nahuatl word for "bitter water" later came to refer to this Mexican-originated food.

5. This Mexican baseball superstar returned to his original team in 2003 to become the Spanish-language color commentator for the LA Dodgers.

6. In a unique biological phenomenon, five generations of this insect migrate from the continental United States to wintering sites in central Mexico.

7. Who was the president of Mexico until 2018?

8. Mexican filmmaker Alejandro González Iñárritu won the Best Director Oscar for this movie.

9. The *son mexicano* music of the state of Jalisco later became this popular folk music.

10. La Casa Azul, located in the Coyoacán neighborhood of Mexico City, is the family home of this artist.

> **WHAT'S IN A NAME?**
>
> *Mexico* is a Nahuatl word from at least the 14th century, but experts are torn on whether it means "the place in the navel of the Moon" or "the place in the middle of the agave plant." At least Jimmy Eat World agrees it's in the middle.

Before and After

See page 2 if you need a refresher on the rules.

1 Rebel Wilson played her in *Pitch Perfect* AND this fourth-place *Last Comic Standing* contestant had her own *Inside* show on Comedy Central.

2 "My Dungeon Shook" and "Down at the Cross" are the two essays from this 1963 James Baldwin book AND Miles Davis performed an instrumental cover of this famous Cyndi Lauper hit.

RALLY 'ROUND THE FLAG, BOYS

In airline parlance, *flag carrier* refers to a national airline that has precedence of routes and governmental assistance or outright ownership by a state. Think of Lufthansa, Air France, KLM, and many others.

3 This pitcher won the 1992 World Series with the Blue Jays and the 1996 World Series with the Yankees AND "Obama's Anger Translator" is a sketch on this comedy show.

4 The singer of "Graceland" AND children's game in which these two words dictate players' actions.

5 Robin Williams played an adult version of this J. M. Barrie boy who never grows up AND the largest airline in the US from 1927 until 1991.

6 The nickname of World War I general John Pershing AND one half of Tenacious D and one full *Nacho Libre*.

7 Captain Nemo, Tom Sawyer, and Dr. Jekyll are characters in this terrible Sean Connery movie AND the first four words officially spoken at the Indianapolis 500.

8 This addiction specialist's shows include *On Call* and *Loveline* AND she played Gertie in *E.T.*

9 Jon Krakauer's book about an aspiring outdoorsman in Alaska AND Eliza, Darwin, and Donnie made up this Nickelodeon animated family.

10 The president between William Henry Harrison and James K. Polk AND Edward Norton and/or Brad Pitt.

ANSWERS - 1. Fat Amy Schumer - 2. The Fire Next Time after Time - 3. Jimmy Key and Peele - 4. Paul Simon Says - 5. Peter Pan Am - 6. Black Jack Black - 7. League of Extraordinary Gentlemen Start Your Engines - 8. Dr. Drew Barrymore - 9. Into the Wild Thornberrys - 10. John Tyler Durden

Tom Hanks

1 What is the name of Tom Hanks's wife?

2 Set on a World War II French colonial plantation, this Rodgers and Hammerstein musical was Tom's first high school role.

3 What was Tom's character's name—outside of drag—on *Bosom Buddies*?

4 Tom's back-to-back Academy Awards for Best Actor have been matched only by this actor.

5 *That Thing You Do!* was the first film produced by this Tom Hanks–owned production company.

6 Who was the overly verbose screenwriter of *Charlie Wilson's War*?

7 What was Tom Hanks's highest-grossing box office hit?

8 Tom's son Colin played Lieutenant Henry Jones in this HBO miniseries.

9 When using his Twitter account to document lost items like lone gloves and single flip-flops, Tom will sign off the tweet with these four letters.

10 Tom costarred with John Candy in the role of Lawrence Bourne III in this 1985 movie.

> **IT'S A REMAKE!**
>
> *Love Affair* (1939) was remade into *An Affair to Remember* (1957), which partly inspired Tom's 1993 hit *Sleepless in Seattle*, a film completely unrelated to *Love Affair* (1994), which was inspired by the second, not the first, and was the last film role of Katharine Hepburn, who was in neither. Got all that?

ANSWERS - 1. Rita Wilson - 2. *South Pacific* - 3. Kip Wilson - 4. Spencer Tracy - 5. Playtone - 6. Aaron Sorkin - 7. *Toy Story 3* - 8. *Band of Brothers* - 9. HANX - 10. *Volunteers*

Random Stuff You Should Know

1 He was the second king of the United Kingdom of Israel.

2 What does *GPS* stand for?

3 *Religioso* is the Latin name of this holy insect.

4 In 1988, she became the youngest person to write, produce, and perform a number-one single with "Foolish Beat."

5 The Godwin Austen Peak is better known by this alphanumeric designation.

6 Snoop Dogg and Jared Leto were second-round investors in this Alexis Ohanian–cofounded website.

7 This French word for "a road" originated in the Dutch *bolwerk*, meaning "a bastion of a fort."

8 Known for its wealth and trees, this is the largest county in Florida.

9 This is the name of a 1992 Meryl Streep, Bruce Willis, and Goldie Hawn movie about immortality.

10 One point for each of the 10 sports fielded in the inaugural 1896 Athens Olympic Games.

WAIT, THAT HAPPENED?

In the 1908 London Olympics, dueling, with actual, live gunpowder bang-bang pistols, was fielded as a sport. Literally, people dressed in padding and plate-glassed visors with special handguard-fitted pistols FIRED WAX BULLETS AT EACH OTHER.

ANSWERS - 1. David - 2. Global Positioning System - 3. Praying Mantis - 4. Debbie Gibson - 5. K2 - 6. Reddit - 7. Boulevard - 8. Palm Beach County - 9. *Death Becomes Her* - 10. Swimming, Road Cycling, Track Cycling, Artistic Gymnastics, Greco-Roman Wrestling, Athletics, Fencing, Shooting, Tennis, Weight Lifting

Tourism

1 This sugary company is the official sponsor of the London Eye Ferris wheel.

2 Bergen's Fløibanen incline railway is the most visited tourist attraction in this country.

3 Finnish American architect Eero Saarinen designed this tourist attraction, the tallest monument in the Western Hemisphere.

4 Each year, 30 million people visit the 20 museums and galleries of this national "Institution."

5 Tickets to this world landmark cost 750 rupees for foreigners but only 20 rupees for Indian citizens.

6 International off-roaders flock to the Finke Desert Race, which crosses the Larapinta, or Finke River— believed to be the oldest river in the world—in Alice Springs in this country.

> **WORD OF THE DAY**
> ....
> In the vernacular of Answer #6, *Hoon* means "to recklessly burn out or otherwise irresponsibly drive a car." E.g., "He really hooned the hell out of the Baja buggy at the Finke Desert Race."

7 The disused walls of Fort Wood form the base for this world monument.

8 Port Lockroy on Antarctica's Wienke Island houses a museum and the world's southernmost one of these government customer services.

9 From 1900 until 1986, the building that houses Paris's Musée d'Orsay was used for this purpose.

10 Botticelli's *Birth of Venus* is in this Italian museum, a popular tourist destination.

Before and After

See page 2 if you need a refresher on the rules.

1 The section of a newspaper article between the headline and the body text AND the 1980 movie *Urban Cowboy* popularized this synchronized choreography.

2 The stage name of rapper Adam Yauch AND Gerard Huerta designed this band's iconic lightning bolt logo.

ON A ROLL

When you're just chilling, watching some game shows—perhaps watching the Austin Rogers *Jeopardy!* collection on Netflix—do so with a toilet paper spool. It approximates the size and resistance of the *J!* signaling device. You'll feel like a contestant.

3 He plays Nick Fury AND legend has it that this painter, when told that his art was just random, took a paintbrush and flicked a line of paint precisely on a doorknob across the room.

4 After her husband dies on their wedding night, a young woman joins the army in this 1980 movie AND 1922 F. Scott Fitzgerald character who ages backward.

5 Marie and Frank live across from their daughter-in-law Debra and her husband, the titular character of this sitcom AND the creator of private detective Philip Marlowe.

6 Originating in the 17th century, these words for "candy" translate as "good good" AND in 2013, guitarist Richie Sambora left this band.

7 The titular Rebel without a Cause AND singer known as the "King of Cool."

8 J. Lo's third husband AND the best Hannibal Lecter.

9 Pacino and Penn play a gangster and his lawyer in this 1993 movie AND Mr. Peabody and Sherman's time-travel device.

10 The Duke of Cambridge AND Swiss hero who was a terrible parent when apples and crossbows were around.

ANSWERS - 1. Byline Dancing - 2. MCA/DC - 3. Samuel L. Jackson Pollock - 4. Private Benjamin Button - 5. Everybody Loves Raymond Chandler - 6. Bon Bon Jovi - 7. James Dean Martin - 8. Marc Anthony Hopkins - 9. Carlito's Way Back Machine - 10. Prince William Tell

Famous Ann(e)s

1. This famous Anne's religious views got her both expelled from the Massachusetts Bay Colony and a Westchester County Parkway named after her.

2. Louis de Pointe du Lac, Claudia, and Lestat are characters created by this famous Anne.

3. She played Princess Mia Thermopolis of Genovia and shares a name with Shakespeare's wife.

ON SECOND WATCHING

The shot-for-shot remake of *Psycho* is still bad.

4. She was stabbed in the shower in Gus Van Sant's remake of *Psycho*.

5. Unlike her predecessor, this Anne survived marriage to Henry VIII.

6. Anne was the youngest of the three sisters in this 19th-century literary family.

7. This controversial commentator Ann rose to fame during the Clinton impeachment trial.

8. While Pauline Phillips wrote Dear Abby, her twin sister, Eppie Lederer, wrote under this name.

9. This was the most famous role of Ann B. Davis.

10. Despite making her film debut in 1961, costarring with Elvis, and earning two Oscar nominations, this actor only won her first Emmy nomination in 2010, for an episode of *Law and Order SVU*.

ANSWERS - 1. Anne Hutchinson - **2.** Anne Rice - **3.** Anne Hathaway - **4.** Anne Heche - **5.** Anne of Cleves - **6.** Anne Brontë - **7.** Ann Coulter - **8.** Ann Landers - **9.** Alice Nelson (*The Brady Bunch*) - **10.** Ann-Margret

Random Stuff You Might Know

1 The first private house constructed with a steel frame, the mansion built for this second-richest American of all time is also now the Cooper Hewitt Museum in New York City.

2 This Lauren Weisberger novel was adapted into a hit movie and a Broadway musical.

3 Scarface, Willie D, and Bushwick Bill were original members of this influential Houston rap group.

4 He was senior senator of Delaware from 1973 to 2009.

5 Name two out of three of King Lear's daughters.

6 This is the Greek word for "panting."

7 How many players are on a curling team?

8 This Cuban American and his wife are credited with the invention of the concept of reruns.

9 What is the capital of Senegal?

10 One point each for the 13 pilot call signs from *Top Gun*.

ANSWERS - 1. Andrew Carnegie - 2. *The Devil Wears Prada* - 3. Geto Boys - 4. Joe Biden - 5. Regan, Cordelia, Goneril - 6. Asthma - 7. Four - 8. Desi Arnaz - 9. Dakar - 10. Goose, Hollywood, Iceman, Jester, Merlin, Slider, Viper, Chipper, Cougar, Sundown, Stinger, Wolfman, Maverick (Charlie didn't fly).

Advertising Stuff

1. From 1981 until 2001, this six-word sentence was the recruitment motto of the US Army.

2. Get the door, it's this pizza chain.

3. Until a 1999 merger, "Put a tiger in your tank" was the slogan for this gasoline company.

4. In 1896, an ad in *Leslie's Weekly* magazine was the first to feature this landmark as the logo for Prudential Insurance.

5. Spearheaded by the 1959 "Think Small" ad, *Advertising Age* in 1999 called this automaker's advertisements the number-one ad campaign of all time.

6. "Raise your hand, raise your hand" if you're wearing this deodorant.

7. Narrated in different versions by both Steve Jobs and Richard Dreyfus, "The Crazy Ones" was a TV commercial for this two-word Apple ad campaign.

8. In 1973, this soda went by the nickname the Uncola.

9. "Labour isn't working" was a 1978 slogan that helped this iron-fisted woman become prime minister.

10. In 1896, this slogan was first placed on the masthead of the *New York Times*.

FREE AD SPACE

Nirvana's "Smells Like Teen Spirit" came from a friend insulting Kurt Cobain, saying he "smells like" the deodorant brand. He didn't know that at the time and inadvertently juiced the product's sales.

ANSWERS - 1. "Be all that you can be." - 2. Domino's - 3. Esso (now Exxon) - 4. Rock of Gibraltar - 5. Volkswagen - 6. Sure - 7. Think Different - 8. 7UP - 9. Margaret Thatcher - 10. "All the News That's Fit to Print"

Before and After

See page 2 if you need a refresher on the rules.

1 Disney XD revived this popular eighties cartoon in 2017 AND nearly every actor you can think of appeared on this HBO horror series.

2 This ghostwritten novel series followed the family and love lives of Liz and Jess Wakefield AND Troy, Gabriella, and Sharpay sing and dance their way through this Disney TV movie.

FROM THE DEPTHS OF IMDb

Here's a partial list of the alumni in the HBO horror show in Answer #1: Patricia Arquette, Demi Moore, Kirk Douglas, Whoopi Goldberg, Jon Lovitz, Timothy Dalton, Blythe Danner, Roger Daltrey, Steve Coogan, Katey Sagal, Rita Wilson, John Stamos, Priscilla Presley, Iggy Pop, Benicio Del Toro, Isabella Rossellini, and Ben Stein. WTF is happening with this show?

3 The lead singer of Culture Club AND the director of *The Ides of March* and *Good Night, and Good Luck.*

4 This nineties R&B hip-hop star was childhood friends with Nate Dogg and Snoop Dogg and stepbrother to Dr. Dre AND the hot hatch versions of the Peugeot 205 or Volkswagen Golf.

5 This indie band rose to fame with 2004's "Float On" AND in *Parks and Recreation,* Andy Dwyer's oft-renamed band retained this name for the longest period.

6 This console is the successor to the Wii U AND Cool Papa Bell and Mickey Mantle, to name two.

7 This Scot wrote *The Wealth of Nations* AND Dirty Harry carries a .44 magnum by this company.

8 Gallifrey is the home planet to this fictional character AND this song by The Who is the theme to *CSI.*

9 This system, abbreviated, directly relies on the theory of relativity to calculate coordinates AND in 1967, this author wrote *The Outsiders* as a college freshman.

10 The 21 Club, Harry's New York Bar in Paris, and the Ritz Paris all claim to have invented this spicy cocktail AND the author of *Frankenstein.*

ANSWERS - 1. Duck Tales from the Crypt - 2. Sweet Valley High School Musical - 3. Boy George Clooney - 4. Warren GTI - 5. Modest Mouse Rat - 6. Nintendo Switch Hitters - 7. Adam Smith and Wesson - 8. Doctor Who Are You - 9. GPS E Hinton - 10. Bloody Mary Shelley

Soap Operas

1 *Neighbours* is a popular, long-running soap opera from this country.

2 Debuting in 1999 and canceled in 2008, this NBC show featuring supernatural story lines was the last new soap opera created for a major network.

3 New wife Krystle Carrington is shocked in season two when her husband Blake's supposedly deceased wife, Alexis, is revealed to be alive in this 1980s soap.

4 Lee Daniels and Danny Strong, the creators of *Empire*, have cited this Shakespeare play about unfaithful daughters as inspiration.

5 It wasn't until the mid-1970s that *General Hospital* revealed this fictional town where it takes place.

6 The Newmans, Winters, and Baldwin-Fishers are relative newcomers to this CBS soap opera, which originally centered on the wealthy Brooks and poor Foster families.

7 In *The O.C.*, this was the name of Summer Roberts's toy pony.

8 Helen Wagner, Don Hastings, and Eileen Fulton all acted for 50 years until the 2010 cancellation of this CBS soap opera.

9 This soap veteran has played Brenda Barrett on *General Hospital*, Gina Kincaid on *Beverly Hills, 90210*, and Sam Marquez on *Las Vegas*.

10 In *Melrose Place*, Alison Parker is a young receptionist at D&D Advertising under the domineering control of this Heather Locklear character.

> **CALIFORRRNYAHHH**
>
> Some of *The O.C.*'s notable appearances: Daniel Craig, Corey Feldman, Reginald VelJohnson, Sam Waterston . . . It's the *Law & Order* of LA.

ANSWERS - 1. **Australia** - 2. **Passions** - 3. **Dynasty** - 4. **King Lear** - 5. **Port Charles, New York** - 6. **The Young and the Restless** - 7. **Princess Sparkle** - 8. **As the World Turns** - 9. **Vanessa Marcil** - 10. **Amanda Woodward**

Random Stuff You Might Know

1 SUR and Villa Blanca are two restaurants owned by this Bravo TV personality.

2 What is the capital of Bangladesh?

3 Despite challenges from AT&T and Comcast, this Tennessee city has instituted citywide fiber-optic broadband that has attracted business from Volkswagen and Amazon.

4 Born January 12, 1992, the heuristically programmed algorithmic computer model 9000 is the villain of this 1968 sci-fi movie.

5 "Du Hast" is a 1997 industrial metal song by this German band.

6 In the central European standard or "German" keyboard, the Y of QWERTY is replaced with this letter.

7 Both the concept of self-service and the turnstile were invented by Clarence Saunders for this southern grocery store chain.

8 In cricket, how many balls are delivered by the bowler per over?

9 Referred to by residents simply as La Piazza, this is the main public square in Venice, Italy.

10 One point each for the top 12 career home-run hitters in MLB history.

URBAN LEGEND ALERT

The "QWERTY" keyboard layout was not designed to alleviate early typewriter's proclivity toward jamming when neighboring keys were pressed in quick succession. While the jamming problem was definitely real, the QWERTY layout was originally Q W E. T Y. The Remington company eventually replaced the period with *R*, creating a more modern layout.

ANSWERS - 1. Lisa Vanderpump - 2. Dhaka - 3. Chattanooga - 4. *2001: A Space Odyssey* - 5. Rammstein - 6. Z - 7. Piggly Wiggly - 8. Six - 9. San Marco (St. Mark's) - 10. Harmon Killebrew, Mark McGwire, Frank Robinson, Sammy Sosa, Jim Thome, Ken Griffey Jr, Willie Mays, Albert Pujols, Alex Rodriguez, Babe Ruth, Hank Aaron, Barry Bonds

Engineering Things

57

1. The Catskill, the Delaware, and the Croton aqueducts are the three systems that provide water to this American city.

2. In 1843, engineer Isambard Kingdom Brunel designed the SS *Great Britain*, the first iron ship propelled by one of these thrust generators.

3. This world's first recorded engineer, the designer of the pyramid of Djoser in 2600 BCE, later lent his name to the villain in the movie *The Mummy*.

4. This engineer with South African, Canadian, and US citizenship founded the company Space X, the largest private producer of rocket engines in the world.

5. Made popular by M. C. Escher, the impossible "Penrose stairs" are one of the many engineering paradoxes featured in this 2010 Christopher Nolan movie.

6. Appia, Aurelia, Flaminia, and Cassia are all names of these Roman engineering projects.

7. Cost overruns and impractical design issues plagued Zaha Hadid's design for this nation's 2020 National Olympic Stadium.

8. This structure surpassed the Washington Monument in height, and was eventually beat by the Chrysler Building for the title of world's tallest in 1930.

9. In 1944, General Erwin Rommel was assigned to reinforce this series of fortifications running from Norway to Spain.

10. This was the world's first multisport domed stadium.

WONDERS OF THE WORLD

The Seven Wonders of the Ancient World are well known. If you're a quiz dork worth your weight in whatever you're supposed to be weighed in, you know them. But there are also the New7Wonders, chosen online in 2001: Great Wall of China, Petra, the Colosseum, Chichén Itzá, Machu Picchu, the Taj Mahal, and *Christ the Redeemer*.

ANSWERS - 1. New York City - 2. Propeller - 3. Imhotep - 4. Elon Musk - 5. *Inception* - 6. Roads - 7. Japan - 8. Eiffel Tower - 9. The Atlantic Wall - 10. Astrodome

American Women

1 Recent feminist rallying cry "Nevertheless, she persisted" originated in Senate Majority Leader Mitch McConnell's attempt to silence this senator's objections to the nomination of Jeff Sessions to attorney general.

2 First delivered in 1851, Sojourner Truth's "Ain't I a Woman?" speech was later rewritten in a southern dialect even though Truth was a native New Yorker whose first language was this—not English.

SNOWCLONES

The series title *Orange Is the New Black* features a "snowclone." Stemming from the premise that the Inuit and Yupik languages have many words for *snow*, a snowclone is a phrase that can be retasked to meet the speaker's needs while maintaining instant recognition. Some other examples are "To [blank] or not to [blank]" and "[blank]-gate."

3 *Orange Is the New Black* episodes "Lesbian Request Denied" and "Thirsty Bird" were directed by this two-time Academy Award for Best Actress winner.

4 Revolutionary War fighters Margaret Corbin and Mary Ludwig Hays are both said to be the inspiration for this perhaps apocryphal heroine.

5 This economist is the first woman to serve as Federal Reserve chair and secretary of the treasury.

6 President Obama's first official act was to sign the Fair Pay Act of 2009, named after this former Goodyear employee and women's labor-rights advocate.

7 Sisters Ashley, Brittany, and Courtney are current and former drag racing drivers—and reality TV stars—with this surname.

8 This Long Island native raps, stars in her own show, was part of an *Ocean*'s crew, and played a "Crazy Rich Asian."

9 In 2019, she was the recipient of both the Women's Ballon d'Or and the Best FIFA Women's Player award.

10 Writer, critic, theoretician, and academic who studies slavery Saidiya Hartman was a 2019 recipient of this "genius" grant.

ANSWERS - 1. Elizabeth Warren - 2. Dutch - 3. Jodie Foster - 4. Molly Pitcher - 5. Janet Yellen - 6. Lilly Ledbetter - 7. Force - 8. Awkwafina - 9. Megan Rapinoe - 10. MacArthur Fellows Program

Kanye and the Kardashians

1 In 2019, this periodical declared Kylie Jenner the world's youngest billionaire at age 21; the discovery of forged tax documents forced a retraction one year later.

2 Sampling the Jackson 5, Kanye West produced this song, Jay-Z's first top-10 single.

3 This is the name of Kourtney, Kim, and Khloe's fashion boutique.

4 Kanye's 2002 mixtape *Get Well Soon* was the first to feature this breakthrough solo hit.

5 This TV personality said that *Keeping Up with the Kardashians* is, despite the catfights, about a family that "truly loves and supports one another."

6 Kanye's 2007 "Stronger" hit samples this French duo.

7 In what seems like a century in Kardashian years, this former Laker actually lasted four years in marriage to one of the Kardashian clan.

8 Kanye's *808s and Heartbreak* album is named after the Roland TR808, one of these devices.

9 This is the first name of Brandon Jenner's ex-wife, his partner in their former self-named indie band.

10 Kanye and Jay-Z's "[Expletive] in Paris" features an audio sample from this Will Ferrell movie.

> **TIME WASTER/ BRO DEFLECTOR**
>
> Got a couple sports bros who think they're freaking geniuses? Drop this one on them: Only five colleges or universities have produced both a US president and a Super Bowl–winning quarterback. One university has produced TWO QBs.

Random Stuff You Might *Not* Know

1 Patrick Kane, Patrick Sharp, and Jonathan Toews (TAZE!) are forwards who played together on this hockey team.

2 This famous banker's bulbous nose was so heavily pockmarked that nearly no untouched photos of him exist.

3 He is known as the Man in Black.

FUN FACT

....

Like many bankers,
Answer #2 was a
malignant narcissist.

4 Deadmau5, David Guetta, and Calvin Harris have all headlined the Electric Zoo festival on this New York City island.

5 This star of *The Hitchhiker's Guide to the Galaxy* and *Be Kind Rewind* was born Dante Terrell Smith.

6 Invented in 1996, this Canadian mixture of malt liquor and natural citrus flavors entered the American beverage market in 1999.

7 Known to his people as Shōwa, he was emperor of Japan from 1926 to 1989.

8 German for "to roll," this Austrian triple-meter dance is the oldest extant ballroom dance.

9 John Cho and Karen Gillan starred in this 2014 short-lived ABC sitcom.

10 One point each for the 12 systems of the human body.

Excretory (Urinary), Reproductive, Digestive, Immune
Skeletal, Nervous, Cardiovascular (Circulation), Endocrine, Muscular, Lymphatic, Respiratory,
5. Mos Def - 6. Mike's Hard Lemonade - 7. Hirohito - 8. Waltz - 9. *Selfie* - 10. Integumentary (Skin),
ANSWERS - 1. Chicago Blackhawks - 2. J. P. Morgan - 3. Johnny Cash - 4. Randall's Island -

World War I

58

1 This was the name for the alliance between the United Kingdom, the Third French Republic, and the Russian Empire.

2 A Canadian soldier and doctor, John McCrae wrote the celebrated poem "In Flanders Fields," which immortalized this flower as the symbol of remembrance for those who died in war.

3 Archduke Franz Ferdinand was assassinated in this city.

4 What is a Fokker Dr.1 (Dreidecker)?

5 The disastrous Gallipoli Campaign occurred when British Empire forces attempted to invade what today is this country.

6 In April 1917, to further destabilize the provisional government of Russia, Germany financially and diplomatically engineered this man's return to Russia.

DID YOU KNOW?

Running 12 minutes, the longest animated film at the time of release in 1918— and first animated documentary of all time—was made by cartoonist Winsor McCay about the sinking of Answer #7.

7 Before his death on January 11, 2011, Audrey Warren Lawson-Johnston of Bedfordshire was the last survivor of the sinking of this ship.

8 James Reese Europe of the 369th New York Infantry Regiment—known as the Harlem Hellfighters—is credited with introducing this American art form to France and England.

9 Germany sent 20,000 rifles to this country to assist in their 1916 Easter Uprising against British colonial rule.

10 British soldiers, having difficulty with the French language, referred to this Belgian city and center of major conflicts as Wipers.

7. Lusitania - 8. Jazz - 9. Ireland - 10. Ypres

ANSWERS - 1. Triple Entente - 2. Poppy - 3. Sarajevo - 4. Triplane - 5. Turkey - 6. Vladimir Lenin -

Before and After

See page 2 if you need a refresher on the rules.

1 Most historians place the lifetime of this ruler of Israel and Judah around 1000 BCE AND the Thin White Duke, Aladdin Sane, or Ziggy Stardust.

2 Album containing "Everybody Hurts" and "Man on the Moon" AND the acronym PETA stands for this.

3 First published in Dutch, this author's sole book is a chronicle of the period between June 12, 1942 and August 1, 1944, AND in *Old School* Dean Pritchard fights with Mitch, Bernard, and this nicknamed character.

4 This company owns Rolls-Royce and Mini, abbreviated AND Orson Welles got his start performing plays for this New Deal agency, abbreviated.

5 He pities the fool AND Pan Am rival, abbreviated.

6 UK prime minister at the 1919 Paris Peace Conference AND Dr. Doug Ross actor.

7 The sheik of Abu Dhabi and the New York Yankees own this MLS franchise, abbreviated AND neither the cable industry nor Congress have any control over this nonprofit channel.

YOU WANT ANSWERS?

BTW, here's the answer to that school, prez, and QB question from page 227:

- Miami of Ohio: Benjamin Harrison and Ben Roethlisberger
- Stanford: Herbert Hoover and Jim Plunkett/John Elway
- Navy: Jimmy Carter and Roger Staubach
- Michigan: Gerald Ford and Tom Brady
- University of Delaware: Joe Biden and Joe Flacco

8 "Shaking the tree over here, boss" is a famous line from this movie AND this actor played Dylan McKay.

9 Controversial US ambassador to the UN from 2005 to 2006 AND perpetually relegated, this League One football club are known as the Trotters.

10 In this movie with revolutionary CGI, Linda Hamilton confronts a doppelgänger played by her identical twin sister, Leslie AND rapper whose song "I'm Different" just keeps repeating the title.

ANSWERS - 1. King David Bowie - 2. Automatic for the People for the Ethical Treatment of Animals - 3. Anne Frank the Tank - 4. BMWPA - 5. Mr. TWA - 6. David Lloyd George Clooney - 7. NYC FC SPAN - 8. Cool Hand Luke Perry - 9. John Bolton Wanderers - 10. Terminator 2 Chainz

Anagrams

In this round, each question has three clues. The answer to each clue is an anagram for the other two clues' answers. (For example: Jim's *Office* wife; cartographer's paper; Hendrix's plug-in. Answer: Pam, Map, Amp.)

1 Admiral Akbar warns about this; used for a makeshift tent; enthralled.

2 Keeps 1980s and '90s kids off drugs; honey; to understand written symbols.

3 Created; honey liquor; Judi Dench.

4 Angela Merkel; Jesus's birthplace; create a memory.

5 Grizzlies, plural; takes it all off; curved sword.

6 Jagger and Richards, for short; diabetes begins; shorthand for people who write shorthand.

7 Boone's first name; lying to yourself; Jesus's limbs

8 English country houses; kidnap money; Da Vinci Airport gets them home.

9 Barry Bonds; 2.47 acres; Aristotle, to Alexander the Great.

10 Home city of pizza; Comic Con attractions; Boeing's products

ANSWERS - 1. Trap, Tarp, Rapt - **2.** DARE, Dear, Read - **3.** Made, Mead, Dame - **4.** German, Manger, Engram - **5.** Bears, Bares, Sabre - **6.** Stones, Onsets, Stenos - **7.** Daniel, Denial, Nailed - **8.** Manors, Ransom, Romans - **9.** Cheater, Hectare, Teacher - **10.** Naples, Panels, Planes

Random Stuff You Might *Not* Know

1 Rome's ancient enemy Carthage is within this modern North African nation.

2 The Bhartiya Sansad is the bicameral legislative body of this country.

3 What is Thomas Edison's middle name?

4 More astronauts come from this state than any other in the country.

IT'S AN HONOR

In addition to James Brudenell, some other people who are immortalized with garment namesakes are Arthur Wellesley, 1st Duke of Wellington, and his rubber boots called Wellingtons, and Charles Macintosh and his rubber coat, the Mackintosh.

5 James Brudenell, the major general in command of the Charge of the Light Brigade, is best known today for this sweater that bears the name of his peerage.

6 This musician and his late wife appeared on *The Simpsons* only on the condition that the character of Lisa remained a vegetarian forever.

7 The blackbuck, Tibetan, oryx, and Dorcas gazelle are all species of this animal.

8 This patriot's most famous victory was at the 1297 Battle of Stirling Bridge.

9 *Punto banco*, *chemmy*, and *à deux tableaux* are three varieties of this high-class casino card game.

10 One point each for the 10 artists or groups with the most singles ever in the Billboard Hot 100.

Friends

1 Matthew Perry shares his name with a US Navy commodore who, in 1853, by show of force, opened this nation up to Western trade.

2 In *17 Again*, Matthew Perry's Mike O'Donnell gets a second chance at high school by becoming a student played by this actor.

3 In "The One with the Prom Video," Ross is humiliated and dejected when this date of Rachel eventually shows up.

4 This was the only *Suite Life of Zack and Cody* twin to play Ross's son, Ben.

5 Anna Faris plays this surrogate mother to Chandler and Monica.

6 In *Band of Brothers*, David Schwimmer's despised Lieutenant Sobel attempted to motivate Easy Company with this cheesy Lone Ranger cry.

7 In a 1985 Tampax ad, Courteney Cox became the first person to ever say this word—in this context— on US television.

8 After receiving three nominations for *Friends*, Matt LeBlanc finally won a Golden Globe for best actor in a comedy in 2012 for playing this *Episodes* character.

9 Jennifer Aniston attended a high school bearing this man's name, much like the nearby airport.

10 Actor Maggie Wheeler auditioned for the role of Monica but instead ended up cast as this recurring strident on-again-off-again character.

WHY SO EASY?

Here's the thing with shows like *Friends*: Everyone knows it . . . except hardcore trivia geeks because they probably think it's beneath them. So in a round like this, Dilbert McBrainiac will definitely have no idea, but like, Madison and like, Taylor (no, boy-Taylor, not girl-Taylor) will nail this round. As a populist, I give it a Difficultly Level 1.

Before and After

See page 2 if you need a refresher on the rules.

1 This actor is a Mac guy AND Paul McCartney cited Phil Spector's production of this 1970 hit as a reason for the Beatles' breakup.

2 With eight batting titles, he is tied with Tony Gwynn for the most in National League history AND this Staten Island institution's mascot is the Seahawks.

3 James Bond's employer AND Revelation 13:18 mentions this number.

4 The Trammps' "Disco Inferno" is the last song on this movie's soundtrack album AND this Jimmy Fallon romantic comedy was released as *Perfect Catch* outside the United States.

5 The musician born Christopher Wallace AND a 1930 book about Al Capone is cited as the first printed reference to this slang term for FBI agents.

6 This film features the quote "The horror . . . the horror" AND Janet Jackson's "Together Again" is the very first track on the very first US version of this long-running compilation series.

DID YOU KNOW?

The Hershey's candy in Question #8 was so named because it was initially a failure. The chocolate candy was supposed to be molded into perfect spheres, but that proved impossible with the technology of 1928, so the failure-based name stuck.

7 Ana Steele's BDSM-enthusiast millionaire boyfriend AND a dilapidated Easthampton mansion featured in a beloved 1975 documentary.

8 This famed city supervisor was called the Mayor of Castro Street AND this Hershey's product is perpetually on top-10 lists of worst Halloween candy.

9 This actor starred in two Paul Verhoeven films in the 1990s AND Jimi Hendrix's "Hey Joe" B-side.

10 Beatles album featuring "In My Life" AND after winning a $100 million settlement, Nashawn Wade founds an airline in this 2004 movie.

ANSWERS - 1. Justin Long and Winding Road - **2.** Honus Wagner College - **3.** MI666 - **4.** Saturday Night Fever Pitch - **5.** Notorious B. I. G. Men - **6.** Apocalypse Now That's What I Call Music - **7.** Christian Grey Gardens - **8.** Harvey Milk Duds - **9.** Sharon Stone Free - **10.** Rubber Soul Plane

Things about *Star Wars*

1 George Lucas and producer Gary Kurtz turned to the concept of *Star Wars* after trying to purchase the rights to this comic title, later made famous by a Queen soundtrack.

2 After a child psychiatrist suggested that Luke Skywalker needed outside confirmation about Darth Vader's villainy, George Lucas added this character to the script of *The Empire Strikes Back*.

3 In the US, this toy company created an action figure for every single background character—regardless of the fact that they didn't yet have names.

NERD ALERT

In 2018, an Obi-Wan Kenobi toy with double telescoping lightsaber sold for $76,000. Take that, sensible investment in T-bills!

4 Expressing nervous doubt, Luke, Leia, Han, C3PO, Obi-Wan, and Annakin have all said variations of this seven-word sentence at least once in every *Star Wars* movie.

5 *The Empire Strikes Out*, *The Han Solo Affair*, and *Revenge of the Brick* are all *Star Wars* animated short films featuring characters from this line of toys.

6 After *Return of the Jedi*, this Shirley MacLaine, Jack Nicholson, and Debra Winger film was 1983's second-highest box office gross.

7 What color was Luke Skywalker's second lightsaber?

8 In search of a new college mascot in 2010, the University of Mississippi's student body attempted to vote in this Mon Calamari, "It's a trap!" character.

9 The Max Rebo Band is the house band for this gangster's palace.

10 Released on December 16, 2016, this *Star Wars* film followed the daring attempt to steal the plans for the first Death Star.

ANSWERS - 1. *Flash Gordon* **- 2.** Yoda **- 3.** Kenner **- 4.** "I have a bad feeling about this." **- 5.** Lego **- 6.** *Terms of Endearment* **- 7.** Green **- 8.** Admiral Ackbar **- 9.** Jabba the Hutt **- 10.** *Rogue One*

Random Stuff You Might *Not* Know

1 The destruction of forests and habitats made up of these saline coastal trees increases the wave power and destructive force of hurricanes.

2 Duncan, Malcolm, and Banquo are all characters in this Shakespeare play.

3 This longtime Utah Jazz power forward is second on the NBA's all-time points list.

VERY SUPERSTITIOUS
·············
Theater dorks say you can't say Answer #2 in a theater, or disaster will strike. They instead use the euphemisms "the Bard's play" or "the Scottish play."

4 In World War II, British propaganda spread the rumor that carrots enhance night vision to obscure from the Germans that they had invented this device.

5 Also known as tone color or tone quality, this word describes the unique acoustic qualities of different instruments and voices.

6 This music artist's long-running feud with her former songwriter and producer, Dr. Luke, included several lawsuits and prevented her from releasing a new album for five years.

7 Podgorica is the capital of this country.

8 Irish author Eoin Colfer has described this children's fantasy character of his creation as "*Die Hard* with fairies."

9 According to Alexa, this was the most visited website in the world in 2015.

10 One point each for the 10 countries the Danube River borders or runs through.

ANSWERS - 1. Mangrove - 2. *Macbeth* - 3. Karl Malone - 4. Radar - 5. Timbre - 6. Kesha - 7. Montenegro - 8. Artemis Fowl - 9. Google - 10. Germany, Austria, Slovakia, Hungary, Croatia, Serbia, Romania, Bulgaria, Moldova, Ukraine

Domestic Animals

1 With a partitioned glass cargo area labeled with a "No Dogs" sticker for the animals' safety, the Cullinan is a $480,000 SUV by this marque.

2 Although it finally went extinct in 1627, the wild aurochs was domesticated millennia earlier and became this farm animal.

3 As the temperature drops, a shivering and rotating motion creates an 81-to-93-degree winter cluster, thus allowing these domesticated animals to survive the winter.

4 Also a star sign, this is the species name for sheep.

5 In 1828, this presidential candidate chose as his symbol the steadfast and reliable donkey, eventually begetting the Democratic donkey of today.

> **FACT**
>
> Answer #5 is on American currency. He shouldn't be. He's the worst.

6 The domesticated Amur carp is known by this three-letter name.

7 Domesticated in the 1980s as pets, these spiny Internet cuties are humankind's most recent mammal domestication.

8 The domestic canary comes from this locale.

9 Fossil records show that obviously the dog was our first domestic animal, and the pig was the third, but this barnyard animal was humankind's second domestication.

10 Which was domesticated first, the guinea pig or the horse?

ANSWERS - 1. Rolls-Royce - **2.** Cow - **3.** Honeybees - **4.** Aries - **5.** Andrew Jackson - **6.** Koi - **7.** Hedgehog - **8.** Canary Islands - **9.** Goat - **10.** Guinea Pig (5000 BCE vs. 3500 BCE)

ROUND 2 / DIFFICULTY LEVEL 1 2 3 **4** 5 6

Billy Billy Shakespeare

1 In the accepted chronology of Shakespeare's works, both the first and last plays contain this number in their titles.

2 Making Shakespeare an early proponent of the prequel, the *Part 1* of this play franchise was written after *Part 2* and *Part 3*.

3 The earliest surviving American feature-length film is a 55-minute adaptation featuring actor Frederick Warde as this battle-fallen English king.

4 A Tunisian city, "blackness" in Romani, "vile dog" in Arabic, and—most likely—an anagram of a Carib word, have all been speculated as the origins of this Shakespearean character's name.

5 Although records of its performances and publications exist, copies of the sequel to this Shakespearean play have been "lost."

6 *Much Ado about Nothing* features "a kind of merry war betwixt Signor Benedick" and this sharp-witted Messinan.

PRO TIP

You don't have to read every single Shakespeare play, because there's only a couple things that *Jeopardy!* or any quiz master will ask you about. For example, Benedick is always paired with Answer #6; Answer #4 is always referenced as a potential anagram.

7 In *As You Like It*, Jacques's "All the world's a stage" soliloquy is a reference to "*Totus mundus agit histrionem*," or "all the world is a playground," the Latin motto of this 1599 building.

8 Captain William Keeling's journal of 1607 indicates that his ship, *Red Dragon*, while moored off of what is today Sierra Leone, was the location of the first recorded staging of this longest Shakespeare play.

9 The 12th-century pseudohistory *The History of the Kings of Britain* by Geoffrey of Monmouth first recorded this Shakespearean king.

10 Alluding to the newly crowned King James, the three witches in *Macbeth* tell this character that he will not be king but his descendants will.

9. King Lear - 10. Banquo

3. Richard III - 4. Caliban - 5. Love's Labour's Lost - 6. Beatrice - 7. The Globe Theatre - 8. Hamlet -

ANSWERS - 1. Two (*The Two Gentlemen of Verona; The Two Noble Kinsmen*) - 2. Henry VI -

Winter Sports

1 Played on skates like hockey, but with 11 per side, two 45-minute halves, a ball and stick similar to that of field hockey, and on an ice rink the size of a football pitch, this is the world's second-most-participated-in team ice sport.

2 The Patrouille des Glaciers, a 53-kilometer and 4,000-meter-altitude-change skiing and mountaineering race, takes place every two years between Zermatt and Verbier in this country.

3 Originating in Hokkaido, Yukigassen is a competitive game of capture the flag inspired by this winter activity.

4 Based on a summer motorcycle racing format, Minnesota's Duluth Nationals kicks off the season of this X-Games-featured snowmobile racing sport.

5 Snowboard pioneer Tom Sims was Roger Moore's stunt double in this 1985 Bond film, Moore's last.

6 Jimmy Cliff's version of "I Can See Clearly" was a top-40 hit from this 1993 winter sports comedy film.

> **FUN FACT, WELL, NOT ACTUALLY FUN**
>
> At the rate we're going, there won't be snow in a couple of years, so have fun skiing inside a refrigerated box in Dubai!

7 In 2017, Mitch Seavey set a new Iditarod record when he and his dog team crossed the finish line in this Alaskan city after 8 days, 3 hours, 40 minutes, and 13 seconds.

8 The USA Warriors are a team of wounded veterans who compete in both stand-up and sledge versions of this sport.

9 Named after its inventor, this figure-skating jump, beginning on the back inside edge of one foot and ending on the back outside edge of the opposite foot, was first performed in 1909.

10 With 132 gold, 125 silver, and 111 bronze—368 medals total over 23 different Winter Olympics—this is the most successful nation at the Winter Games ever.

ANSWERS - 1. Bandy - 2. Switzerland - 3. Snowball Fight - 4. Snocross - 5. *A View to a Kill* - 6. *Cool Runnings* - 7. Nome, Alaska - 8. Sledge Hockey (Para Ice Hockey) - 9. Salchow Jump - 10. Norway

Random Stuff You Might *Not* Know

1 Although Netflix doesn't release viewership data, it did claim, somewhat dubiously, that at least 76 million households watched at least two minutes of this Henry Cavill fantasy series.

2 Between 1940 and 1949, this duo starred in 25 movies, including *Buck Privates* and *Mexican Hayride*.

3 The Jacob Leinenkugel Brewing Company is based in Chippewa Falls in this state.

BEHIND THE STICKS

Leinenkugel's Summer Shandy is an excellent seller, especially on draft. I find it too sweet to have as a full glass, but cutting it with a pilsner like Radeberger is great. Get it on draft around May and sell a ton of it until everyone gets sick of it around July or so.

4 Fifty-eight percent of the world's supply of this Mexican orchid–derived flavoring—Spanish for "little pod"—is cultivated in Indonesia.

5 Darfur is in this country.

6 Now owned by Japanese company Korg, this company famously supplied amplifiers, organs, and wah-wah pedals to the Beatles, the Rolling Stones, the Kinks, Jimi Hendrix, and more.

7 In the 2019 season, he passed Barry Sanders to hold the third-most NFL rushing yards of all time.

8 This was the pseudonym that Hamilton, Madison, and Jay used to write *The Federalist Papers*.

9 In 2002's *Mattel v. MCA Records*, Mattel's lawsuit claiming a 1997 song by this Europop group infringed on its trademarks was ultimately dismissed.

10 One point each for the 17 brands that have their eyewear manufactured by eyewear monopoly Luxottica.

ANSWERS - 1. *The Witcher* - 2. Abbott and Costello - 3. Wisconsin - 4. Vanilla - 5. Sudan - 6. Vox - 7. Frank Gore - 8. Publius - 9. Aqua - 10. Armani, Brooks Brothers, Bulgari, Burberry, Chanel, Coach, D&G, Michael Kors, Miu Miu, Polo, Prada, Ralph Lauren, Starck Eyes, Tiffany & Co., Tory Burch, Valentino, Versace

Drinks Glasses

Name the cocktail/drink/beer glass. Yep, they've all got names.

Monsters

1 *The Jewel of Seven Stars* by Bram Stoker is one of fiction's first examples of one of these monsters cursing someone.

2 The 1962 novelty hit "Monster Mash" was performed by Bobby "Boris" Pickett and this backing band.

3 This movie studio created both Bela Lugosi's *Dracula* and Boris Karloff's *Frankenstein*.

HARD TRUTH
....
In many stories, the real monster was man.

4 Dr. Henry Jekyll and monster hunter Abraham Van Helsing are depicted as friends of Dr. Victor Frankenstein in this Showtime TV show.

5 This actor voices James P. "Sulley" Sullivan in *Monsters, Inc.*

6 All people of Hrothgar's kingdom fear the monster Grendel, except for this hero.

7 Featured in the *Mahabharata* and *Ramayana*, the Timingila is a giant sea monster capable of swallowing whales whole in stories from this religion.

8 If the NFL were in ancient Greece, then Hyperion, Cronus, Crius, and Iapetus could be players for this team.

9 Although the word *zombie* isn't uttered in *The Night of the Living Dead*, this ghost synonym, a word for an Arabic demon—not an undead person—is.

10 Often used in the names of multiple monsters, this four-letter prefix is Old English for "man."

ANSWERS - 1. Mummy - 2. The Crypt-kickers - 3. Universal Studios - 4. *Penny Dreadful* - 5. John Goodman - 6. Beowulf - 7. Hinduism - 8. Tennessee Titans - 9. Ghoul - 10. Were

Lesser-Known Works

1 "The Signal Man" was a rare horror mystery story by this author, based on his survival of the deadly June 9, 1865, Staplehurst rail crash.

2 Thought to be positioned on a wall opposite Michelangelo's *David* in Florence's city hall, *The Battle of Anghiari* was a 1505 mural supposedly painted over by this artist.

3 The B-side to "Paperback Writer," this 1966 Beatles song was considered by Ringo Starr his greatest drumming track while with the band.

4 *The Cuckoo's Calling, The Silkworm, Career of Evil,* and *Lethal White* are all crime novels written under a pseudonym by this best-selling living British author.

5 Better known for her thrillers and mysteries, this author published six novels under the pen name Mary Westmacott.

6 Although he has lesser-known sculptures of Lincoln in the White House and Teddy Roosevelt in the Capitol building, Gutzon Borglum is best known for this massive sculpture.

> **DID YOU KNOW?**
>
> Had Answer #8 kept pitching, he definitely would've been a Hall of Famer as a pitcher. His nine-shutout 1916 season wouldn't be matched until Ron Guidry in 1978. For non-baseball nerds: This is amazing.

7 Holding the record for eight consecutive number-one singles, this pop singer was also the first Black woman ever on the cover of *Seventeen* magazine.

8 Although most associated with the number 714, he could also be linked to the numbers 94–46 and 2.28.

9 In addition to his other major scientific discoveries, this scientist theorized on the speed of sound in 1687.

10 In 2006, NBC Universal sold *Oswald the Lucky Rabbit*, an early work of this man, to the company that bears his name in exchange for Al Michaels's services on football broadcasts.

ANSWERS - 1. Charles Dickens - 2. Leonardo da Vinci - 3. "Rain" - 4. J. K. Rowling - 5. Agatha Christie - 6. Mount Rushmore - 7. Whitney Houston - 8. Babe Ruth - 9. Isaac Newton - 10. Walt Disney

ROUND 4 / DIFFICULTY LEVEL 1 | 2 | 3 | **4** | 5 | 6

Random Stuff You Might Know

1 Where are the Strangers', Scholars', Hunters', and Warriors' Gates?

2 Since 1882, England and Australia have competed for this storied cricket test match trophy.

NOT THE BEST OF FRIENDS
....
Like their cartoon namesakes, Hobbes must obviously be imaginary to Calvin. John Calvin died in Switzerland in 1564 having never visited England, 24 years before Thomas Hobbes was even born in Wiltshire.

3 Born Sonny John Moore, this EDM artist got his start as lead singer of hard-core punk band From First to Last.

4 He is the only person on Earth to have been awarded both the Nobel Peace Prize and Medal of Honor.

5 This city is the capital of the German state of North Rhine Westphalia.

6 Before *Leviathan*, Thomas Hobbes became famous for the first English translation of this ancient Athenian author's *History of the Peloponnesian War*.

7 This Czech American tennis great is Andy Murray's coach.

8 From 1970 to 1990, the Swedish fighter plane Viggen was manufactured by this company.

9 This correctional institution was the subject of a 1968 number-one country single by Johnny Cash.

10 One point for each of the eight characters to die in *Hamlet*.

Chemistry

1 This word describes a variety of compounds and/or elements that can be separated through mechanical—and not chemical—processes.

2 Whereas an acid is a substance that creates hydronium ions when dissolved in water, a base is a substance that creates this diatomic anion.

3 This chemical substance holds the top spot on the Mohs scale of mineral hardness.

4 "For his research into the nature of the chemical bond and its application in the elucidation of the structure of complex substances," this chemist was awarded the 1954 Nobel Prize in Chemistry.

5 John Goodenough, M. Stanley Whittingham, and Akira Yoshino received the 2019 Nobel Prize in Chemistry for development in this kind of battery.

WOKE BOND

John Goodenough sounds like a postfeminist male assistant to James Bond.

6 J. J. Thomson taught and employed Ernest Rutherford, who in turn taught and employed James Chadwick, and the three of them, in order, discovered these three subatomic particles.

7 The Van der Waals force, a force other than ionic or chemical bonds that attracts atoms to one another, was once thought to be behind the ability of this animal to cling to glass and Teflon by one toe.

8 The most prominent feature of the location formerly known as Bedloes Island is clad in this chemical element, with an atomic number of 29.

9 The letters *FRS* after someone's name indicates they are a fellow at this institution, the world's oldest scientific academy in continuous existence.

10 First publicly demonstrated by Lee Marek's Kid Scientists in 1999 on *The Late Show with David Letterman*, these two ingredients in a popular backyard experiment do not actually cause a chemical reaction.

Before and After

See page 2 if you need a refresher on the rules.

1 Leo and Kate's 2008 reunion film AND Tom Hanks takes a rare turn as a cold-blooded murderer in this gangster movie.

2 Fourth son of King George III, now part of a Canadian province's name AND environmentalist author of *The Monkey Wrench Gang*.

3 Jeff Goldblum's character in *Jurassic Park* AND author of *The Tipping Point* and *Outliers*.

4 The leader of Public Enemy AND Kathy Griffin's Emmy-winning reality show followed her life on this.

5 In 1929, US Army Air Corps colonel John Macready worked with Bausch and Lomb to create the first of this brand's sunglasses AND the founder and first president of baseball's American League.

6 It was formerly known as Saigon AND a favela in Rio is the setting for this 2002 Brazilian crime movie.

7 The author of *Uncle Tom's Cabin* AND the Trapp Family Lodge is in this New England ski town.

8 British-English notation uses these two prefixes before *semiquaver* to describe a 64th note AND this singer played Mitchie Torres in *Camp Rock* and *Camp Rock 2*.

9 He has not recorded a studio album since 1993's *River of Dreams* AND Jeff Winger on NBC's *Community*.

10 *Dear White People*, *Selma*, and *Thor: Ragnarok* star AND "Hold Me Now" and "Doctor! Doctor!" eighties Brit-Pop band.

THE CALLBACK

When a comedian late in a set makes a reference to a previously mentioned joke, it's called a "callback." Don't be afraid to put callbacks in your trivia rounds. Mentioning something in later rounds that you alluded to earlier gives clever and attentive players a great extra-point opportunity.

ANSWERS - 1. Revolutionary Road to Perdition - 2. Prince Edward Abbey - 3. Ian Malcolm Gladwell - 4. Chuck D-List - 5. Ray-Ban Johnson - 6. Ho Chi Minh City of God - 7. Harriet Beecher Stowe Vermont - 8. Hemi Demi Lovato - 9. Billy Joel McHale - 10. Tessa Thompson Twins

Cameos

1 Elon Musk and this chairman and cofounder of Oracle both appeared as themselves in *Iron Man 2*.

2 The real Jordan Belfort appeared as an emcee introducing Leonardo DiCaprio's character in this 2013 movie.

3 Featuring brief appearances by stars such as Frank Sinatra, Marlene Dietrich, Peter Lorre, Buster Keaton, and Noël Coward in posters with small oval photos, reminiscent of cameo brooches, this 1956 Best Picture winner brought the term *cameo* to a wider, nonentertainment public.

4 He made cameo appearances in *Taxi Driver, After Hours, Gangs of New York*, and *The Aviator*.

5 On a 2012 episode of *iCarly*, this immensely famous woman says—tongue in cheek—that the correct way to address her is "Your Excellency."

6 This former child star and current pop singer appeared on *Grey's Anatomy* as Hayley May, a 16-year-old girl who attempted to claw her own eyes out.

7 In "The One with Rachel's Big Kiss," this *Heathers* star not-so-shockingly kisses Jennifer Aniston's character on *Friends*.

> **FUN FACT**
>
> Answer #8 can rest easy—a Kardashian never appeared on *New Girl*.

8 This music megastar agreed to a cameo on *New Girl* so long as the Kardashians would never appear on the show.

9 This English pop singer played Mia Grey, Christian Grey's adopted sister, in *Fifty Shades of Grey*.

10 Jim and Marilyn Lovell had cameos alongside Tom Hanks and Kathleen Quinlan, the actors playing them, in this 1995 movie.

Random Stuff You Might *Not* Know

1 Although animals have been building these structures for 10 million years, the earliest known instance of humans building one dates from the fourth millennium BCE in Jawa, Jordan.

2 The Academy of Science Fiction, Fantasy, and Horror Films awards were originally called Golden Scrolls; they're now called this.

3 According to the World Health Organization, 2 to 15 percent of those infected with HIV also contract the coinfection of HIV/HCV, in which the second *H* stands for this disease.

4 YouTube channel CinemaSins tallies faults of movies in this popular series.

5 Known as the Pink City, this is the capital of the Indian state of Rajasthan.

6 Hosting both the first-ever outdoor NBA game in 1972 and the opening day of the 2001 baseball season, Hiram Bithorn Stadium in this city is named for a baseball pioneer.

IUCN RED LIST

The International Union for Conservation of Nature's Red List ranges from Least Concern (like dogs) to Extinct. (The latter refers to 99 percent of everything that's ever lived. Also, the passenger pigeon.)

7 Located in northwest Russia, this is the most populous city north of the Arctic Circle.

8 She plays Betty Cooper in *Riverdale*.

9 The second-most-severe classification of the IUCN Red List species threat chart is EW, which stands for this.

10 One point for each of the 10 movies with soundtracks that have more than 1 billion streams.

ANSWERS - 1. Dam - 2. Saturn Awards - 3. Hepatitis - 4. *Everything Wrong With* - 5. Jaipur - 6. San Juan, Puerto Rico - 7. Murmansk - 8. Lili Reinhart - 9. Extinct in the Wild - 10. *Bohemian Rhapsody, Tiger Zinda Hai, Trolls, A Star Is Born, Fifty Shades of Grey, Suicide Squad, Moana, Frozen, The Greatest Showman, Furious 7*

Corporate Parents

Name the corporate parent for each question's group of subsidiaries.

1 Skoda, SEAT, and Ducati

2 Dollar Shave Club, Ben & Jerry's, and Tazo Tea Company

3 Ring, Twitch, and IMDb

4 Gatorade, Tropicana, and SodaStream

5 The Weather Company, Redbooks, and Watson

6 Thums Up, Barq's, and Honest Tea

7 7UP, Canada Dry, and Mott's

8 Bazooka, Ring Pop, and Push Pop

9 DK, Knopf Doubleday, and Crown

10 Extremely large hedge fund and tax avoidance vehicle Braeburn Capital

> **VARIATIONS ON A THEME**
>
> You can reverse this round. Name the corporate parent and award multiple points for multiple subsidiaries named, or one point for three out of four, and so on. Switch it up.

ROUND 2 / DIFFICULTY LEVEL 1 2 **3** 4 5 6

Before and After

See page 2 if you need a refresher on the rules.

1 According to the Bible, this is humankind's preexisting condition AND Las Vegas nickname.

2 Architect of UVA AND Airplane band's successor.

3 *The Lion King*'s "Be Prepared" lyricist AND the San Francisco Treat.

4 E. M. Forster's novel about the British Raj AND singer of the 2002 R&B hit "Video."

5 Led Zeppelin guitarist AND three words after a website's 404.

FUN FACT

Chapters 1 and 2 of the novel in Question #7 dropped in February 1837 in *Bentley's Miscellany*. The final installment, chapters 52 and 53, wouldn't be released until April 1839.

6 Michael Kittredge melted crayons into a scented gift called *Christmas 1969* for his mother, thus beginning this Massachusetts-based company AND song written for Marilyn, then Diana.

7 *The Parish Boy's Progress* is the subtitle to this 1839 novel AND John Lennon's voice famously cracks in this hit, the last song recorded in a 13-hour recording session.

8 The third book of The Hitchhiker's Guide series AND 1995's "Missing" duo.

9 Clara Peller's 1984 advertising slogan AND Russian dish named after a family of wealthy merchants.

10 Series documenting Jimmy McGill's transformation into a calculating criminal AND Pulitzer Prize winner for *Humboldt's Gift*.

ANSWERS - 1. Original Sin City - 2. Thomas Jefferson Starship - 3. Tim Rice A Roni - 4. A Passage to India Arie - 5. Jimmy Page Not Found - 6. Yankee Candle in the Wind - 7. Oliver Twist and Shout - 8. Life, the Universe, and Everything but the Girl - 9. Where's the Beef Stroganoff - 10. Better Call Saul Bellow

Who Voiced This Character?

Each clue describes a film or TV character. Figure out the voice actor—you know, like the name of the round suggests. Here's an easy example: "Andy's Lawman best friend" is obviously *Toy Story* character "Woody," thus the answer is voice actor Tom Hanks.

1 An anterograde, amnesiac, regal blue tang.

2 Originally Mrs. Chamomile, a cursed castle cook.

3 Immune to the panic caused by the mention of Fossas, the self-proclaimed lord of the lemurs.

4 Both of Highland High School's metalhead delinquents.

5 Cinema's Space Ranger of Star Command.

6 Television's Space Ranger of Star Command.

7 Daughter of King Harold and Queen Lillian of Far Far Away.

8 The owner of Whale Wash and sometimes loan shark to Don Lino.

9 A 10,000-year prisoner in the Cave of Wonders.

10 Basically Claudius but animated.

> **PRO TIP**
>
> Rounds that leave out the middle step, like this, are super challenging. Notoriously good at this kind of logic is Ken Jennings, who can do that Clue to Initials to Roman Numeral to Saying a Number thing really, really well.

Random Stuff You Might *Not* Know

LUCK O' THE IRISH

Roughly, the four provinces of Ireland are Ulster in the north, Leinster in the east, Answer #2 in the south, and Connacht in the west.

1 He was the first US president to attend a G8 Summit, then called the G6.

2 Clare, Cork, Kerry, Limerick, Tipperary, and Waterford are collectively known as this.

3 This is the only state capital that shares no common letters with its state.

4 With nine, this island country has hosted more seasons of *Survivor* than any other locale.

5 Christian allegory *The Pilgrim's Progress* was written by an author who shares this last name with a mythical oxen's friend.

6 In 2019, the capital of Kazakhstan was renamed Nur-Sultan from this name.

7 *Rubico* refers to a green clay sometimes found as the surface material of one of these.

8 In the Carboniferous period, Euramerica merged with this supercontinent to form Pangaea.

9 In addition to writing *Cars*, *Tangled*, and *Crazy, Stupid, Love*, Dan Fogelman created this NBC tearjerker.

10 One point for each of *The Atlantic*'s top 12 greatest breakthroughs since the wheel. (For example, number 32 is the cotton gin; number 33 is pasteurization.)

ANSWERS - 1. Gerald Ford - 2. Munster Province - 3. Pierre, South Dakota - 4. Fiji - 5. Bunyan (John & Paul) - 6. Astana - 7. Tennis Court - 8. Gondwana - 9. *This is Us* - 10. Sanitation Systems, Nitrogen Fixation, Steam Engine, Internet, Vaccination, Internal Combustion Engine, Paper, Optical Lenses, Semiconductor Electronics, Penicillin, Electricity, Printing Press

American Revolution

1 The Third Amendment of the Constitution was written to prevent this onerous practice, one of the causes of the Revolution.

2 Benjamin Rush, Paul Revere, and John Hancock were all primary members of this secret society.

3 This victorious commander of the Battle of Saratoga is commemorated by a nameless memorial that depicts just a boot.

4 On Benjamin Franklin's famous "Join or Die" political cartoon, this state is the tail of the snake of the 13 colonies.

5 Because the British sent infected enslaved people behind continental lines, George Washington instituted the first military variolation, or vaccination against this disease.

> **FUN FACT**
>
> George Washington was a leader who understood that his fledgling nation could not operate if all of its citizens—and their enslaved people—were sick and spreading disease.

6 On the night of August 29, 1776, a surrounded George Washington, with the help of a dense fog, evacuated the entire Continental army across this river.

7 Known as the Coercive Acts in Great Britain, the Intolerable Acts were the 1774 punitive measures against this colonial protest.

8 In 1775, after Virginia colonial governor Lord Dunmore abandoned his mansion, a cache of weapons was seized by William & Mary students, who were led by this 17-year-old future president.

9 Spain, allied with France and thus the US, gained this future state as part of the spoils of war at the conclusion of the conflict.

10 A little-known engagement related to the American Revolution occurred in May 1781, when the US ally Spain besieged this West Florida settlement, known today as the "Cradle of Naval Aviation."

5. Smallpox - 6. East River - 7. Boston Tea Party - 8. James Monroe - 9. Florida - 10. Pensacola
- South Carolina - 3. Benedict Arnold - 4. South Carolina -
ANSWERS - 1. Quartering - 2. Sons of Liberty - 3. Benedict Arnold - 4. South Carolina -

ROUND 2 / DIFFICULTY LEVEL `1` `2` `3` `4` **5** `6`

City by Team

1 The 1899 contraction of baseball's National League eliminated this city's Colonels; today's NCAA fans root for its Cardinals.

2 Club Independiente de Santa Fe and Millonarios Fútbol Club play at 8,675-foot elevation at Estadio El Campín in this South American capital city.

3 Winning 13 USSR Championships, 9 USSR Cups, and 3 USSR Super Cups, this city's Dynamo was the most successful soccer club ever in the Soviet Top League.

4 From 1979 until 2006, this city's Clippers were the top minor league affiliate of the New York Yankees.

5 Founded in 2012, the Fuego play in the Pecos League of Professional Baseball Clubs, and are exactly 402 years younger than their home city, this state capital.

BEHIND THE STICKS

The Slingers are named after a drink. Originally just describing any drink with sweetened water and liquor, it came later to describe specifically gin, sweet vermouth, simple syrup, bitters, soda water, and lemon juice. *Sling* comes from the German *Schlingen* for "to swallow," but I think it might mean diabetes, with all that sugar in it.

6 In 2014, the Armor relocated to Grand Rapids, ironically leaving this New England city without a basketball team.

7 Wydad Athletic Club and Raja Club Athletic are two soccer teams in this North African city; sadly, neither is sponsored by Rick's Café.

8 This city's Blue Bombers are the current holders of the Grey Cup.

9 FC Dallas plays not in Dallas but at Toyota Field in this Texas suburb.

10 For the 2006–07 season, Australia's National Basketball League allowed its first and only Asian team to compete: the Slingers, from this city.

ANSWERS - 1. Louisville, Kentucky - **2.** Bogotá - **3.** Kyiv - **4.** Columbus, Ohio - **5.** Santa Fe, New Mexico - **6.** Springfield, Massachusetts - **7.** Casablanca - **8.** Winnipeg - **9.** Frisco - **10.** Singapore

Cars

1 Tata Motors owns Land Rover and this other storied British marque.

2 In a front-engine, rear-wheel-drive car, this component connects the power train with the axle.

3 David Carradine and a very young Sylvester Stallone star in this cult classic film about a transcontinental automotive slaughter.

4 In Stephen King's *Christine*, the villain car is a 1957 Fury made by this automaker.

5 With nine consecutive driver's titles, Sébastien Loeb is the World Rally Championship's most successful driver of all time for this French marque.

6 World War II's Willys MB or Ford GPW are better known by this name.

7 A maker of million-dollar supercars, Koenigsegg Automotive AB is from this country.

8 Producer Philip D'Antoni became known for movies with car chases, including *Bullitt* and this 1971 Gene Hackman crime thriller.

9 This means "engine hood" in British English.

10 This tire manufacturer releases a famous glamour photography calendar each year.

> **PRO TIP**
>
> Most people in a typical cross section of New York City, where I live, know nothing of automobiles, so apologies if this round seems excessively simplistic. This is not what I would ask of a so-called petrol-head.

ANSWERS - 1. Jaguar - 2. Driveshaft - 3. *Death Race 2000* - 4. Plymouth - 5. Citroën - 6. Jeep - 7. Sweden - 8. *The French Connection* - 9. Bonnet - 10. Pirelli

64 Random Stuff You Might *Not* Know

1 Mitch and Gail Leery are the parents of this fictional TV character.

2 In 1946, in San Bernadino, California, 23-year-old Glen Bell founded this restaurant.

3 The larva of the geometer moth is better known by this measured nickname.

4 This famous Italian tourist locale name translates to "five lands."

BY ANY OTHER NAME

A British article during WWII noted "Quislings Everywhere." The name later became synonymous with "traitor." After the war, Quisling was executed by firing squad. His widow lived in a mansion until 1980; the residence would eventually become a Holocaust museum.

5 *Wired* and *The Atlantic* have both accused this popular website of plagiarizing their content.

6 Billy Joel's "We Didn't Start the Fire" mentions this Robert Heinlein book about a man from Mars.

7 "She's a witch of trouble in electric blue" is the first line of the first verse of this Cream single.

8 Vidkun Quisling was the Nazi-collaborating leader of this country during World War II.

9 This iconic yellow-stitched British footwear company was founded by a German Army medic.

10 One point for each of the 15 instrument parts utilized by Beethoven in his Symphony No. 5 in C minor, Opus 67.

ANSWERS - 1. Dawson - **2.** Taco Bell - **3.** Inchworm - **4.** Cinque Terre - **5.** BuzzFeed - **6.** *Stranger in a Strange Land* - **7.** "Strange Brew" - **8.** Norway - **9.** Dr. Martens - **10.** Piccolo, Flute, Oboe, Clarinet, Bassoon, Contrabassoon, Horn, Trumpet, Trombone, Timpani, First Violin, Second Violin, Viola, Cello, Double Bass

Other Characters in Bond Movies

I'm going to name a character from a non–James Bond entertainment property (either television or film). You're going to think of the actor, then tell me the only James Bond movie in which that actor appeared. Here's an example: "Drax the Destroyer" would make you think of actor Dave Bautista, so the answer is the Bond film *Spectre*.

1. The chronometer-hiding Captain Koons appeared in this Bond film.

2. Dr. Quinn also got an introducing credit for this Bond movie.

3. Jean Grey was a femme fatale in this Bond installment.

4. Before witch hunting, Gretel was featured in this entry of the Bond franchise.

5. Salty Quint also hunted James Bond in this movie.

6. A comedic parody that Vesper Lynd also starred in after this official Bond movie.

7. Best Actress Oscar–winning character Leticia Musgrove appeared on-screen a year before this Bond movie.

8. Freddie Mercury appears in this Bond installment.

9. Fred Fenster was marginally more intelligible while antagonizing Bond in this movie.

10. Olenna Tyrell romanced Bond in this film.

> **ABSOLUTELY FABULOUS**
>
> Joanna Lumley, Patsy of *AbFab* fame, also appeared in *On Her Majesty's Secret Service* as one of Blofeld's Angels of Death. She was 23 at the time.

ANSWERS - 1. *A View to a Kill* (Christopher Walken, *Pulp Fiction*) - **2.** *Live and Let Die* (Jane Seymour, *Dr. Quinn, Medicine Woman*) - **3.** *GoldenEye* (Famke Janssen, *X-Men*) - **4.** *Quantum of Solace* (Gemma Arterton, *Hansel & Gretel*) - **5.** *From Russia with Love* (Robert Shaw, *Jaws*) - **6.** *Dr. No* (Ursula Andress, *Casino Royale*) - **7.** *Die Another Day* (Halle Berry, *Monster's Ball*) - **8.** *No Time to Die* (Rami Malek, *Bohemian Rhapsody*) - **9.** *License to Kill* (Benicio Del Toro, *The Usual Suspects*) - **10.** *On Her Majesty's Secret Service* (Diana Rigg, *Game of Thrones*)

Before and After

See page 2 if you need a
refresher on the rules.

1 "The Bad Touch" band AND Jiang Qing was a member of this radical Cultural Revolution leadership group.

2 Brendon Urie's band AND Yakky Doodle, but not Donald, was the inspiration for this Rick Dees novelty hit.

3 Coldplay's front man AND in a trilogy, he played Detective Sergeant and then Detective Lieutenant Marcus Burnett.

4 Collective term for chapters four, five, and six of the Gospel according to Matthew AND where Moses got his tablets.

5 Cookie Masterson is a fictional host of this pop culture trivia franchise AND selections by Maya Angelou and John Steinbeck adorn the pavement of a San Francisco alley named for this author.

6 The Childlike Empress rules Fantastica in this book AND Smash Mouth, Loretta Lynn, Social Distortion, Bon Jovi, Neil Diamond, and One Direction all recorded songs with this title.

7 Awarded for this musical in 2004, the first T of Robert Lopez's double-EGOT AND British English for automotive sleepers.

8 His résumé includes *The Little Rascals*, *Baretta*, and wrongful death suits AND Adaline in *The Age of Adaline*.

DID YOU KNOW?

The organization in Question #9 is probably the most valuable—and perhaps most monstrous and exploitative—company in the history of humankind.

9 In Spanish, it's *pagar a la catalana*, and in English, this slang means to "pay your own share" AND valued at $7.9 trillion in today's dollars, this was the world's first publicly listed organization.

10 Danny and Wendy have domestic problems in this fictional Colorado retreat AND 2012 Sandler, Samberg, and Gomez animated films.

ANSWERS - 1. Bloodhound Gang of Four - **2.** Panic! at the Disco Duck - **3.** Chris Martin Lawrence - **4.** Sermon on the Mount Sinai - **5.** You Don't Know Jack Kerouac - **6.** The Neverending Story of My Life - **7.** Avenue Q Car - **8.** Robert Blake Lively - **9.** Going Dutch East India Company - **10.** The Overlook Hotel Transylvania

Animals

1. A backward-facing pouch that keeps its young safe from dirt disturbed during burrow-digging and cubic feces are two of the oddities of this marsupial.

2. Whereas most falcons hunt through active patrol flights, birds of this clade spot their prey by hovering over open country and then dive in for the kill.

3. Every year, more than 300 species of birds return to their northern European breeding grounds by flying over this strait separating Sicily from Calabria.

4. The diademed sifaka is a species of this Malagasy primate.

5. Kazooie is a bird, and Banjo is this kind of animal.

6. Built in 1912, Navin Field was renamed Briggs Stadium in 1938, and then went by this name from 1961 until 1999.

7. Animal-abusing showman Isaac A. Van Amburgh thrilled 19th-century audiences by inviting a child to sit in a cage with these two animals in his re-creation of biblical symbolism.

8. Japanese amberjack is better known to sushi eaters by this name.

9. The unicorn horns used in the construction of the throne chair of the Kingdom of Denmark more than likely belong to this animal.

10. Yellow mongoose and ground squirrels will often cohabit with these African animals in their extensive network of tunnels and burrows.

> **FISH FRAUD**
>
> According to a UCLA/ Loyola Marymount University study, 47 percent of LA's sushi is mislabeled. Genetic testing revealed that nearly half the fish were advertised as a different species altogether. In reality, the fish were usually cheaper or threatened or endangered species.

ANSWERS - 1. Wombat - 2. Kestrel - 3. Strait of Messina - 4. Lemur - 5. Bear - 6. Tiger Stadium - 7. Lion and Lamb - 8. Yellowtail - 9. Narwhal - 10. Meerkat

Random Stuff You Should Know

1 The Amazonas Filarmônica is based in this city of 2 million residents.

2 By winning 2000's DirecTV 500 at Texas Motor Speedway, he broke a record set by his father and became the driver with the fewest starts to win his first race.

3 In 1967, two industrialist-founded institutes merged to create this institution.

BIGGER IS BETTER
....

Released in 1970, *Tiger Child* was the first film shot in the format that is Answer #7. I never saw it, but I assume it's about some sort of striped kid.

4 Name any of the four producers—other than Mariah Carey herself—of 1997's number-one hit "Honey."

5 Reed Hastings is cofounder and CEO of this company.

6 This term was coined for a 1952 study describing the severe weather patterns of a band from Texas to South Dakota.

7 This is the proprietary name for horizontally running 70 mm film cameras and projectors.

8 The 1895 schism between two versions of this sport resulted in, among other rule variations, one version having 13 players per team and the other fielding 15 players per team.

9 In ballet, this word describes a dancer's appearance of being lightweight or floating in the air.

10 One point for each of the 12 most populous US state capitals (proper cities, not their metro areas).

Musical Geography

1 "Riders on the Storm" and "Love Her Madly" appear on this album titled partly after a West Coast city.

2 Haydn's 93rd to 104th symphonies, including Symphony no. 104 itself, are collectively named after this city.

3 In 1942, Dizzy Gillespie wrote a tune about a night in this North African country.

4 In 1986, Shane MacGowan wrote about a rainy night in this neighborhood—London's, not New York's.

5 Despite recording the album *The Richest Man in Babylon*, electronica group Thievery Corporation hails from a city on this river, not the Euphrates.

> **COVER ME**
>
> Spotify estimates 100 covers of the Rolling Stones' "(I Can't Get No) Satisfaction," 150 covers of Answer #7, and 2,200 covers of "Yesterday," so there's that.

6 "The Future's So Bright, I Gotta Wear Shades" was written by a band whose name is a play on the name of this ancient cultural center of the Mali Empire.

7 After the Beatles' "Yesterday," this beach song is believed to be the second-most-covered song of all time.

8 Indie band Of Montreal is not from Montreal; instead they're from this home city of REM, the B-52s, and Neutral Milk Hotel.

9 Although Bob Marley wrote "No Woman, No Cry," he gave songwriter credit to his friend Vincent Ford so that royalty payments could fund his soup kitchen in this Kingston, Jamaica, neighborhood.

10 In a 2003 album title, cellist Yo-Yo Ma said "obrigado" to this country.

ANSWERS - 1. *L.A. Woman* **- 2.** London Symphonies **- 3.** Tunisia **- 4.** Soho **- 5.** Potomac River **- 6.** Timbuktu (Timbuk 3) **- 7.** "The Girl from Ipanema" **- 8.** Athens, Georgia **- 9.** Trenchtown **- 10.** Brazil

Before and After

See page 2 if you need a refresher on the rules.

1 Kenan Thompson voices Tiny Diamond in this animated sequel AND literally "feat of strength," this French term now means "feat of brilliance."

2 Nickname for Lisa Lopes of TLC fame AND song used for a 1982 sports sequel and a 1986 Gary Busey movie of the same name.

3 Sports organization that went defunct in 2001 and 2020 AND "The Chart" catalogs sexual encounters in this six-season Showtime show.

4 The 1935 French film *Fanfare of Love* became 1951's West German *Fanfares of Love* and this 1959 comedy AND Nestlé has had to confirm that it has no influence over Jim Gaffigan's reference to this product.

5 Art director Marvin Potts's young son drew smiley faces on frosted windows, thus inspiring this corporate mascot AND this nickname for a battleship inspired the nickname for a jellyfish.

6 Sarah Palin coined this dubious term AND a delivery vehicle smaller than a van with no windows aft of the front doors.

7 This band's 1999 album *14:59* alluded to their 15 minutes of fame AND this 1998 music video could generously be classified as an homage to *Koyaanisqatsi*.

8 The universe's most famous Corellian light freighter AND 1980s soap described as *Dallas* with grapes.

9 "Video Games" singer AND he brought high-flying lucha libre–style wrestling to the WCW, and then in 2002, the WWE.

10 A public health care system that cared for its own PM, abbreviated AND Spice Girls manager Simon Fuller assembled this coed pop group.

Kings and Queens

1. Established in the 11th century, this country is the world's oldest continuous kingdom.

2. The Queen of Hearts is the antagonist of *Alice's Adventures in Wonderland*, but this character is the villain of the sequel.

3. The creator of Candy Crush, King Digital Entertainment, was founded in Sweden but is headquartered in this island nation.

4. This county is the most linguistically diverse place on Earth.

5. In two passages of the New Testament, Jesus refers to this biblical character as the queen of the South.

6. Released in 1985, this was Run DMC's second studio album.

7. This children's game is now synonymous with competitive, zero-sum outcomes.

8. Both Raven Symone and Halle Berry starred as the titular character of 1993's *Queen*, a miniseries based on a novel about this author's grandmother, who was enslaved on a plantation.

9. On May 7, 2016, members of this club raised the Premier League Trophy at King Power Stadium.

10. Although all bees feed on this substance during their larval stage, it is the volume of the secretion that turns some larvae into queen bees.

> **SEMANTICS**
>
> The Japanese monarchy is the oldest in the world, dating back to around 660 BCE, but Japan is no longer a kingdom or empire. It's only the institution of monarchy that's old, not the type of state government.

ANSWERS - 1. Norway - 2. Red Queen - 3. Malta - 4. Queens County, New York - 5. Sheba - 6. King of Rock - 7. King of the Hill - 8. Alex Haley - 9. Leicester City - 10. Royal Jelly

Random Stuff You Might *Not* Know

1 Cab Calloway's 1932 dance that featured toe stands and side walks was initially called the Buzz, and later, the backslide; it finally settled on this name in 1983.

2 At 13,671 feet in height, Toubkal, located in this mountain range, is the highest peak in the Arab world.

IT'S COMPLICATED

Emily Dickinson only published a handful of her poems during her lifetime. Upon her death, her younger sister, Lavinia, found 1,800 poems and gave them to Mabel Loomis Todd to edit. Mabel was in a relationship with Emily's brother, Austin. Like I said: It's complicated.

3 Selling more than 3.6 million units since 2002, a model based on the manga *Fist of the North Star* is the best-selling one of these arcade gambling devices ever made.

4 The series *Dickinson* and *For All Mankind* both air on this streaming service.

5 This poet, scientist, statesman, artist, and novelist had the privilege of seeing both Mozart at 7 years old and Mendelssohn at 12 years old.

6 *Greebling*, *SNOT (Studs Not on Top)*, and *Parts Monkey* are terms created by fans of this toy hobby.

7 Jennifer Lopez, Derek Hough, and this "So Sick" singer judge *World of Dance*.

8 Bluegill, crappies, and largemouth bass are all members of the centrarchid family, better known by this bright name.

9 Used from the late medieval period until about 1800, this rectangular keyboard instrument's name is from the Latin for "key" and the Greek for "string."

10 One point for each of the 12 clubs—as of 2020—playing in professional football leagues located in London.

ANSWERS - 1. Moonwalk - **2.** Atlas Mountains - **3.** Pachinko - **4.** Apple TV+ - **5.** Johann von Goethe - **6.** Lego - **7.** Ne-Yo - **8.** Sunfish - **9.** Clavichord - **10.** Brentford, A.F.C. Wimbledon, QPR, Fulham, Chelsea, Arsenal, Crystal Palace, Tottenham, Millwall, West Ham United, Leyton Orient, Charlton Athletic

Asian Food

1 Related to mochi, these Japanese rice paste balls are served three to five per skewer and eaten year-round with tea.

2 Meaning "turning pig," *babi guling* is a roast dish eaten by the locals of this Indonesian island.

3 "Of all the fruit, the mango's the best; of all the meat, the pork's the best; and of all the leaves, lahpet's the best" is the translation of a rhyme describing the favored cuisine of this reclusive Asian nation.

4 In the Japanese written language, rice crackers known as *senbei* share the same Chinese characters as this Chinese breakfast pancake.

5 On January 31, 2019, Google's home page Google Doodle featured this national dish of Malaysia.

6 This massive Japanese company—known in the US for automobiles—is a cofounder and majority shareholder of KFC Japan.

7 Until the mid-19th century, countless wars of conquest were fought over the Banda Islands in Indonesia, then the world's only source of this seed-derived ground spice.

8 Reflecting its origins as Mesopotamia, this nation's cuisine has for 5,000 years been split between Assyrian cuisine in the north and Babylonian in the south.

9 The Bonchon Chicken chain restaurant and a popular fishcake variety both hail from this second-most-populous South Korean city.

10 Symbolic in TV and film of working late, this food container was originally named and patented as "oyster pail."

> **WE WISH YOU KENTUCKY CHRISTMAS**
>
> Five percent of KFC Japan's annual revenue is accrued on Christmas, stemming from KFC store manager Takeshi Okawara's Christmas Chicken Party Barrel campaign of 1970. In 1974, it went national and has since become a Japanese cultural tradition.

ANSWERS - 1. Dango - 2. Bali - 3. Myanmar - 4. Jianbing - 5. Nasi Lemak - 6. Mitsubishi - 7. Nutmeg - 8. Iraq - 9. Busan - 10. Chinese Takeout Container

Nineties Sitcoms

1. Gary and Dorothy constantly break up and Tony sleeps around while still pursuing Deborah in this nineties sitcom.

2. In 1997, *Klubnichka*, or "Strawberry," was this country's first sitcom ever.

3. Created by and starring Nick Giannopoulos and George Kapiniaris, nineties sitcom *Acropolis Now* satirized the Greek immigrant experience in this country.

4. In *Friends*, Ross gains a professorship at NYU, and to impress his new students, he affects this.

RECAST THEM
....
Nineties sitcom characters Becky Connor (*Roseanne*) and Vivian Banks (*The Fresh Prince of Bel-Air*) were famously recast.

5. To celebrate his radio show's 1,000th episode, Dr. Frasier Crane plans a celebration at this landmark.

6. Played by Tisha Campbell-Martin, she is Martin's long-suffering girlfriend on *Martin*.

7. In 1998's *The Hughleys*, D. L. Hughley played a character with this first name—the same as his own.

8. Sold more than 1,000 times, this sitcom that aired from 1990 to 1995 is BBC Worldwide's most exported TV show.

9. This is NBC's only nineties sitcom to share its title with a Best Picture Academy Award–winning film.

10. Referred to later in 1997's "The Betrayal" episode, this was Kramer's original name in the pilot episode of *Seinfeld*.

ANSWERS - 1. *Men Behaving Badly* - 2. Russia - 3. Australia - 4. An English Accent - 5. Seattle Space Needle - 6. Gina Waters - 7. Darryl - 8. *Keeping Up Appearances* - 9. *Wings* - 10. Kessler

Board Games

67

1 "A game for those who seek to find a way to leave their world behind" reads the box of this 1995 Milton Bradley board game.

2 The house of correction, the whipping post, and this stocks-related *P* punishment were some of the penalties incurred by players of the 19th-century game The Mansion of Happiness.

3 This was Settlers of Catan's first language of publication.

4 The ancient Hindu game called *gyan chauper* became the Victorian Virtue Rewarded and Vice Punished, which became this 1940s Milton Bradley game.

5 This first railroad square in the UK version of Monopoly still costs 200 pounds, not 9.

6 *Seki*, meaning "mutual life," refers to a group of game pieces in benign stasis in this ancient game.

7 Although not exactly a board game, Jumbling Tower is an off-brand version of this game.

8 Setup for this other game-inspired board game included painstakingly positioning 75 white and 4 yellow marbles on the game board.

9 It's Scrabble, but 3D.

10 Cones of Dunshire, originally a fictional game from this show, was realized by Mayfair Games, the American distributor of Catan.

> **BANNED ON THE WEST SIDE**
>
> Austin Rogers is banned from playing Trivial Pursuit at the pub Gaf West. (The last time I played, in like 2005, there were six players. I went third. Three other people never got a turn.)

Random Stuff You Might *Not* Know

1 While Cloud Strife is the protagonist, he is the antagonist of *Final Fantasy VII*.

2 Hollies, Byrds, and Buffalo Springfield members formed this supergroup in 1968.

3 As US representative, Jeannette Rankin was the first woman to hold federal office and hailed from this second-most-populous Montana city.

FUN FACT

Jeannette Rankin became a representative in 1916, before women were granted the right to vote. She was one of 50 to vote against the American declaration of war in World War I, and was the only member of Congress to vote against the declaration of war on Japan in World War II.

4 Reflecting its clingy proclivity, Bindwood and Lovestone are archaic English names for this plant.

5 These five horribly appropriate words open T. S. Eliot's *The Waste Land*.

6 In the 1960s, the automotive application of DC dynamo generators was largely replaced by this engine accessory.

7 This team won the inaugural College Football Playoff National Championship game.

8 The name of this region of Italy is derived from the name of the ancient language of its capital city, Rome.

9 She originated the term—later the title of one of her songs—"Hot Girl Summer."

10 One point for each of the 10 non-American cities to have at least one season of an official international installment of the *Real Housewives* series.

ANSWERS - 1. Sephiroth - 2. Crosby, Stills & Nash - 3. Missoula - 4. Ivy - 5. "April is the cruelest month." - 6. Alternator - 7. Ohio State Buckeyes - 8. Lazio (Latium) - 9. Megan Thee Stallion - 10. Athens, Vancouver, Melbourne, Cheshire (UK), Auckland, Sydney, Toronto, Budapest, Johannesburg, Naples

It's Baseball Season

1 Founded in 1883, this baseball team is the oldest franchise in American professional sports to continuously remain in one city and retain its name.

2 This nation boasted one of the earliest professional baseball leagues, created in 1878 but abolished in 1961.

3 Two early sets of baseball rules were created in 1837 and 1845 by two separate New York clubs with these two Washington Irving–inspired names.

4 He was the second Black player to break Major League Baseball's color barrier and the first Black player in the American League.

5 American and National League owners brought this Teddy Roosevelt judicial appointee into the newly created commissioner's position to restore public faith in baseball after the Black Sox scandal.

6 OPS+ is a stat that adjusts on-base plus slugging percentage and normalizes it per ballpark; from 2016 to 2019, he led the majors in OPS+.

7 Racking up 18, this Washington National led the NL in wins for 2019.

8 Gibson, Pujols, Hornsby, and Musial are stars in this storied franchise's firmament.

9 With 10 total, he is second all-time to Barry Bonds's 12 in Silver Slugger Awards; he's number one as catcher.

10 With two major-league clubs over more than 130 years, this city's name has never appeared in full on a major-league jersey, home or away.

BEHIND THE STICKS

An arsenal of tricky sports questions, like #10 for example, is necessary to have as a pub trivia host. It can render even a know-it-all or blowhard speechless. Because silence is golden, sports questions are worth their weight in gold.

ANSWERS - 1. Phillies - 2. Cuba - 3. Gotham and Knickerbocker Base Ball Clubs - 4. Larry Doby - 5. Judge Kenesaw Mountain Landis - 6. Mike Trout - 7. Stephen Strasburg - 8. St. Louis Cardinals - 9. Mike Piazza - 10. Philadelphia

Before and After

See page 2 if you need a refresher on the rules.

1 Subtitle to the second of Cate Blanchett's *Elizabeth* films AND subtitle to the second *Avengers* film.

2 Richard Hendricks's on-screen data compression algorithm company AND named after a chapter in *The Wind in the Willows*, this was Pink Floyd's debut album.

3 Manga and anime series about underground street racing AND a cargo load's lashing or tie-down point.

BEFORE THEY WERE FAMOUS

The Bowie-affiliated musician in Question #8 had a small role as "Himself" in the eighth episode of season two of *Tales From the Crypt*.

4 Bravo series following the Indian American community of Miami AND Culture Club's only US number-one hit.

5 Fictional rebel Takeshi Kovacs's "stack" is re-sleeved into a body portrayed by Anthony Mackie in this Netflix sci-fi show AND short for "high strength to weight ratio reinforced polymer."

6 Rapping alien duo from an eponymous 1991 Sega Genesis game AND "Pitching, Defense, and the Three-Run Homer" was the unofficial slogan of this longtime Orioles manager.

7 Part of a Dylan song title, or nominally Seymour and Grey AND the first edition of this seminal 1847 first-person narrative novel was published under the pen name Currer Bell.

8 To kick their drug habits, this musician moved with David Bowie to West Berlin in 1976 AND 3rd Bass's 1991 hip-hop hit, or jack-in-the-box theme.

9 Singers of "Pumped Up Kicks" AND Disneyland term for small-scale automated guideway transit system.

10 Bob Dylan's late-career 17-minute narrative of the Kennedy assassination AND hit outside the baselines.

ANSWERS - 1. The Golden Age of Ultron - 2. Pied Piper at the Gates of Dawn - 3. Initial D Ring - 4. Family Karma Chameleon - 5. Altered Carbon Fiber - 6. ToeJam & Earl Weaver - 7. Queen Jane Eyre - 8. Iggy Pop Goes the Weasel - 9. Foster the People Mover - 10. Murder Most Foul Balls

Movie Math

68

See the explanation on page 7 if you need a refresher on the rules.

1 _____ *Heads in a Duffel Bag* TIMES *The Adventures of Buckaroo Banzai across the* _____ *th Dimension*

2 _____ *Ninjas Kick Back* PLUS _____ *Going on 30*

3 *The* _____ *Commandments* MINUS _____ *Cloverfield Lane*

4 _____ *First Dates* DIVIDED BY _____ *Fingers of Death*

5 *The* _____ *Steps* MINUS *The* _____ *th Chamber of Shaolin*

6 *Miracle on* _____ *th Street* PLUS _____ *Short Films about Glenn Gould*

7 _____ *Pick Up* TIMES *The* _____ *Jakes*

8 _____ *Weeks Later* DIVIDED BY _____ *Weddings and a Funeral*

9 _____ *The Year We Make Contact* MINUS _____ *Things I Hate about You*

10 _____ *Jump Street* PLUS _____ *Jump Street*

> **THE SHORT AND LONG OF IT**
>
> At 1 hour, 28 minutes, *Marty* (1955) is the shortest Academy Award for Best Picture winner. The 3-hour, 54-minute *Gone with the Wind* (1939) is the longest.

ANSWERS - 1. 64 (8 × 8 = 64) - **2. 16** (3 + 13 = 16) - **3. 0** (10 − 10 = 0) - **4. 10** (50 ÷ 5 = 10) - **5. 3** (39 − 36 = 3) - **6. 66** (34 + 32 = 66) - **7. 104** (52 × 2 = 104) - **8. 7** (28 ÷ 4 = 7) - **9. 2000** (2010 − 10 = 2000) - **10. 43** (21 + 22 = 43)

Random Stuff You Might *Not* Know

1 Truvada is an example of a combination of drugs in one pill and a strategy for HIV prevention known by this four-letter acronym.

2 What is the capital of Papua New Guinea?

3 The Garibaldi, Old Dutch, Royale, and Verdi are all styles of this.

4 In addition to designing stackable and waterproof luggage at a time when chests were all rounded, this designer invented the world's first unpickable lock.

GET THAT ICE

Valued at $1.65 billion in 2020, the most valuable NHL franchise is the New York Rangers.

5 This franchise is currently the least valuable one of the NHL's Original Six.

6 Adapted into an HBO limited series, this was Gillian Flynn's first novel.

7 Completed in 1871, *Arrangement in Grey and Black No. 1* is better known by this name.

8 Mathematician Ludolph van Ceulen has this number engraved on his tombstone.

9 Jo, Sam, and Matt are the parents and brother, respectively, of this Disney character.

10 One point for each of the 15 member states of the United Nations whose names, in the common English usage, begin with the letter C.

Food and Stuff

1. Prepared much like coleslaw, only using ketchup instead of mayonnaise, Lexington-style barbecue slaw is native to this US state.

2. Arabic for "to grind," this is the name for a Middle Eastern ground sesame seed paste.

3. Made with cucumber and mint in a yogurt base, this is the name of the popular sauce or dip from South Asia.

4. In *Animal House*, this is the food expelled to the line "I'm a zit, get it?!"

5. This food is on the cover of the album *The Velvet Underground & Nico*.

6. This is the word for "eggplant" in British English.

7. Adam Richman was the host of this Travel Channel culinary show.

8. In *Quantum of Solace*, James Bond is accompanied through La Paz by this MI6 agent with a Beatles-inspired name.

9. In an episode of *Family Guy*, Peter Griffin continuously sings this song by the B52s.

10. The town of LaPlace, Louisiana, calls itself the world capital for this Cajun sausage.

> **IT'S COMPLICATED**
>
> Though *Kê-chiap*, a Chinese pickled fish brine, made it to Malaysia as *kicap* when the British picked it up, the condiment retained little apart from its name. Tomato catsup wasn't invented until the early 19th century. Describing the sauce as "catchup" dates from 1690, though, so your dad joke is over three centuries old.

ANSWERS - 1. North Carolina - 2. Tahini - 3. Raita - 4. Mashed Potatoes - 5. Banana - 6. Aubergine - 7. Man v. Food - 8. Strawberry Fields - 9. "Rock Lobster" - 10. Andouille

ROUND 2 / DIFFICULTY LEVEL 1 2 3 **4** 5 6

Before and After

See page 2 if you need a refresher on the rules.

1 The author of *Journey to the Center of the Earth* AND the actor who played Mini-Me.

2 The author of *The Invisible Man* AND the home arena of the Flyers and 76ers.

3 This multinational investment bank was founded in 1865 as an opium dealer to China, abbreviated AND the first modern demonstration of this birthing procedure, abbreviated, was in 1826.

4 This famous athletic shoe has had more than 30 iterations AND in 2015, he won two majors and in 2017, the Open.

5 This NHL team plays in St. Paul's Xcel Energy Center AND the mound entrance music to *Major League*'s fictional pitcher Ricky Vaughn.

6 With more than 686 million YouTube views, this is the highest-charting Norwegian song since "Take On Me" AND smitten teen Lloyd Dobler attempts to get with Diane Court in this 1989 romantic comedy.

WRITER'S BLOCK

Having trouble writing categories? Need new inspiration? Try your local PBS station. *Nature, Nova, American Experience*—these shows are so chock-full of content that a single episode on the Alps or Mars exploration or the history of the circus can jump-start a flagging round.

7 In 1959, this man's forces ousted President Fulgencio Batista AND neighborhood with the largest LGBTQ+ community in the United States.

8 This is the name of the cherry-flavored version of Mountain Dew AND Josh Klinghoffer, Dave Navarro, and John Frusciante have all served as guitarists for this band.

9 This admiral won the Battle of Trafalgar AND serving 27 years in Robben Island, this leader's prison cell is now a tourist attraction.

10 Channing Tatum and Jonah Hill produced this buddy cop movie AND this video game was the debut of E. Honda, Dhalsim, and Chun-Li.

ANSWERS - 1. Jules Verne Troyer - 2. H. G. Wells Fargo Center - 3. HSBC Section - 4. Air Jordan Spieth - 5. Minnesota Wild Thing - 6. What Does the Fox Say Anything - 7. Fidel Castro District - 8. Code Red Hot Chili Peppers - 9. Horatio Nelson Mandela - 10. 21 Jump Street Fighter II

Slogans

1 Fill in the blank: "Blockbuster Video: Wow, what a _____!"

2 Convicted murderer Gary Gilmore's final words before execution by firing squad inspired ad man Dan Wieden's 1988 creation, this famous three-word slogan.

3 "Some people change your life forever" was the tagline to this 2015 Cate Blanchett film.

4 "Growing up is tough. Period." was the tagline to this 1970 Judy Blume novel.

5 Until 2014, "Move fast and break things" was the internal motto of this social media giant.

6 German company Stihl claims that they're "a _____ above the rest."

7 According to the PR department, humanoid robot ASIMO embodies the "Power of Dreams," this company's ethos.

8 This cleaner claims it's "stronger than dirt," unlike its namesake, a legendary Greek warrior who kills himself in grief when Odysseus is awarded Achilles's magical armor.

9 Jimmy Fallon, Jennifer Garner, and Samuel L. Jackson have all asked the viewing audience this four-word question slogan.

10 Fill in the blank: "Silly rabbit, _____ ."

> **PRO TIP**
>
> If you make it onto *Jeopardy!*, learn the major touch points of Homer and Virgil. Odysseus vs. Aeneas; their differences and similarities; the main folks in the *Iliad*, like Hector, Agamemnon, and Menelaus and his red hair. *Jeopardy!* questions on classics have waned in recent years, but when these clues *do* come up, they're gonna be big-dollar-value.

ANSWERS - 1. Difference - 2. Just Do It - 3. *Carol* - 4. *Are You There God? It's Me, Margaret.* - 5. Facebook - 6. Cut - 7. Honda - 8. Ajax - 9. What's in your wallet? - 10. Trix are for kids!

Random Stuff You Might *Not* Know

1 These are the first and last letters of the Greek alphabet.

2 This is the southern half of the northernmost state in Germany or, in the United States, the most prominent and highest-producing dairy cow.

THAT'S THE DOUBLE-TRUTH, RUTH

All cable providers are terrible.

3 The 1956 autumn uprising in this country was the first threat to Soviet control of Eastern Europe after the solidification of power following World War II.

4 After declining an upgrade, Lisa Brown of Spokane, Washington, was renamed A**hole Brown on her next bill from this cable company.

5 Originating with a Persian term, this word meaning "marketplace" has been adopted in Arabic, Urdu, Kurdish, and eventually English.

6 Automobiles by Russia's AutoVAZ company are better known by this four-letter brand name.

7 This 1969 song was written by Merle Haggard and Roy Edward Burns as a reaction to people protesting the Vietnam War.

8 She became the spokesperson for Miss Dior perfume in 2010.

9 The Acropolis, ancient Babylon, Kings Landing from *Game of Thrones*, and Minas Tirith from *Lord of the Rings* are some of the massive builds in this popular sandbox video game.

10 One point for each of the eight women to play in the ensemble of *Ocean's Eight*.

ANSWERS - 1. Alpha and Omega - 2. Holstein - 3. Hungary - 4. Comcast - 5. Bazaar - 6. Lada - 7. "Okie from Muskogee" - 8. Natalie Portman - 9. *Minecraft* - 10. Awkwafina, Cate Blanchett, Helena Bonham-Carter, Sandra Bullock, Anne Hathaway, Mindy Kaling, Sarah Paulson, Rihanna

Racing

1 At the funeral games for Patroclus organized by Achilles, Diomedes—with the help of Athena—bests Menelaus, Antilochus, and others in this epic poem.

2 Although they famously earned a Did Not Finish (DNF) in Calgary, racers from this country stunned the world with a 14th-place Olympic finish—beating the US, Russia, and France—six years later in Lillehammer.

3 Hailing from this nation, Jacobus Johannes "Jaap" Eden is the only person to ever hold world championships in both cycling and speed skating.

4 The iconic theme to 1981's *Chariots of Fire* was written by this Greek composer.

5 For the 2019 season, Chorizo's 19 wins landed it in second place to the Polish's 21 wins in a mascot sausage race series held in this city.

6 Historians argue whether this race effectively concluded or merely peaked on July 20, 1969.

> **TIME MARCHES, ER, SKATES ON**
>
> Jaap's 1893 world record for the men's 1,500 meter in speed skating was 2:35.0. Today, his countryman Kjeld Nuis holds the world record, set in 2019, of 1:40.17. That's serious improvement.

7 Sega's 1976 arcade racing game *Moto Cross*—rebranded in the US as *Fonz*—was the first video game to include this kind of interactive feedback.

8 Powering racing cars like the Jaguar XJR-12, the Ferrari 250 Testarossa 58/59, and the McLaren F1 GTR, this engine format has propelled more cars—20 to be exact—to victory in the 24 Hours of Le Mans than any other.

9 This term describes the family of sports that use maps and compasses to navigate through checkpoints over unfamiliar land.

10 The three-lap world records in shortcut and non-shortcut races on this longest track of *Mario Kart 64* are 3'15"33 and 4'52"71, respectively.

ANSWERS - 1. *The Iliad* **- 2.** Jamaica **- 3.** The Netherlands **- 4.** Vangelis **- 5.** Milwaukee **- 6.** Space Race **- 7.** Haptic Feedback **- 8.** V12 **- 9.** Orienteering **- 10.** Rainbow Road

Before and After

See page 2 if you need a refresher on the rules.

1 An explorer's shout from the crow's nest AND shout heard from an airborne sleigh.

2 Simon and Garfunkel's "animated" original name AND he voiced the character Barry B. Benson in a 2007 animated film.

OLD FAITHFUL

That original name of Simon and Garfunkel is a trivia standby. Keep it in mind.

3 "To Be with You" band AND title of the 2020 sequel to the 2014 adventures of Hiro and Baymax.

4 The first skirmish between the Qing dynasty and the British Empire fought in 1839 AND Paul Dano and Lily James starred in the 2016 BBC adaptation of this Russian epic.

5 The Treblemakers are finally defeated by the Bellas at the conclusion of this movie AND Bronson Pinchot's role as an art dealer in *Beverly Hills Cop* led to this eighties sitcom's creation.

6 The youngest position player to ever take part in an MLB All-Star Game AND Catherine Keener and Sandra Bullock both portrayed this famous Alabaman author.

7 In Charles Mingus's elegy to jazz great Lester Young, he says "Goodbye" to this head covering AND originally, three wickets in three consecutive deliveries.

8 City 100 miles north of LA and 325 miles south of San Francisco AND Gilda Radner's impersonation target.

9 Joseph Gordon-Levitt was set to star in a canceled film adaptation of this Jim Henson series AND this seminal Bill Haley and His Comets record was the B-side to a song called "Thirteen Women (and Only One Man in Town)."

10 Feigned grief AND "Shout" band.

ANSWERS - 1. Land Ho Ho Ho - **2.** Tom and Jerry Seinfeld - **3.** *Mr. Big Hero 7* - **4.** Opium War and Peace - **5.** Pitch Perfect Strangers - **6.** Bryce Harper Lee - **7.** Pork Pie Hat Trick - **8.** Santa Barbara Walters - **9.** Fraggle Rock around the Clock - **10.** Crocodile Tears for Fears

278

Pop Princesses

1 Kyary Pamyu Pamyu is known as the pop princess of this neighborhood, shorthand for Japanese youth culture.

2 This former Fifth Harmony member is a paid spokesperson for Skechers footwear.

3 This 2012 track was Taylor Swift's first Billboard Hot 100 chart number one.

4 This "Habits (Stay High)" Swede has been dubbed the dark-pop queen.

5 Since Whitney Houston's *The Bodyguard* album is classified as a soundtrack, this country-pop album by Shania Twain is the best selling album by a solo female artist of all time.

> **PRO TIP**
>
> Pop artists' #1 hits are low-hanging fruit. Get your Rihannas and Mariahs and Britneys down pat for some extra pub quiz points!

6 Michael and Madonna are King and Queen, and there are many lowercase "pop princesses," but she's the true, capital-letters Princess of Pop.

7 With the most YouTube subscribers of any music group, Jisoo, Jennie, Rosé, and Lisa are the members of this girl group.

8 An homage to a group 30 years their senior, this pop group was called the Fab Five.

9 Hal David and Burt Bacharach's "Wishin' and Hopin'" was a 1964 hit for British pop-and-soul icon Dusty Springfield, who recorded it two years after this American pop-and-soul icon.

10 This former pop princess was nominated for a 2017 Best Supporting Actress in Television Golden Globe and a 2019 Best Lead Actress in a Drama Primetime Emmy.

ANSWERS - 1. Harajuku - 2. Camila Cabello - 3. "We Are Never Ever Getting Back Together" - 4. Tove Lo - 5. *Come On Over* - 6. Britney Spears - 7. Blackpink - 8. Spice Girls - 9. Dionne Warwick - 10. Mandy Moore

279

ROUND 4 / DIFFICULTY LEVEL 1 2 3 4 **5** 6

Random Stuff You Might *Not* Know

1 Cursed by Apollo, she kept her divine gift of seeing the future, but her visions were never believed.

2 This metropolis bears the name of a chief of the Duwamish and Suquamish tribes.

3 Van Eyck's 1434 *Arnolfini Portrait* hung in Philip IV of Spain's palace and likely inspired Velázquez's 1656 *Las Meninas* painting, as both artists put one of these objects on the farthest wall of their compositions.

4 Both named after a Swedish village, elements number 39 and 70 are the only elements on the periodic table that begin with this letter.

> **BEHIND THE STICKS**
>
> A poinsettia is Answer #5 with cranberry juice. A soleil is that drink with pineapple juice.

5 This brunch cocktail is named after the plant *Acacia dealbata*.

6 This original song from *Moulin Rouge!* was ineligible for an Academy Award because it had been written for Baz Luhrmann's earlier film, William Shakespeare's *Romeo + Juliet*.

7 He was both the first NFL player to complete a touchdown pass to himself and the QB for the Super Bowl XXXVII–winning Tampa Bay Buccaneers.

8 This term was first used in a 1935 article pertaining to athletics; it has nothing to do with the roman numeral for four.

9 In 2012, the law library of the University of Mississippi School of Law was renamed in honor of this author.

10 One point each for naming up to 12 of the 32 states in Estados Unidos Mexicanos.

I'll Have Seconds

1 Cy Young is first with 511 wins; this pitcher's 417 puts him in second.

2 He was the second person in space and the fifth person to walk the surface of the moon.

3 While private label or generics are the highest selling, this is the second-highest-selling brand of paper towel in the United States.

4 Although it was the third single, this is the second track off 1999's . . . *Baby One More Time*.

5 *Foundation and Empire* is the second installment of the Foundation series by this author.

6 She was the second person to fly solo and nonstop across the Atlantic Ocean.

7 He handily defeated Alf Landon to win his second term as US president.

8 This was the subtitle of the second season of *American Horror Story*.

9 This is the world's second-most-populous capital city.

10 He had the second-shortest US presidency.

> **PRO TIP**
>
> US presidents are a finite list. There are only so many of them, and only a bunch of them had anything remotely memorable happen to them. Since all the "second this" or "third that" are already known, you won't have to memorize that much, and it'll give you a distinct leg up on your opponents.

ANSWERS - 1. Walter Johnson - 2. Alan Shepard - 3. Bounty - 4. "(You Drive Me) Crazy" - 5. Isaac Asimov - 6. Amelia Earhart - 7. Franklin Roosevelt - 8. Asylum - 9. New Delhi - 10. James Garfield

State's Signs

Each US state has their own official route marker for state roads. Some signs are iconic; others are generic. Name the state for each of these 12 route markers.

1

2

3

4

5

6

7

8

9

Different Words for the Same Thing

1 The rock dove is more commonly called this name.

2 The *pilomotor reflex* or *piloerection* is the technical term for this R. L. Stine skin reaction.

3 The Snellen chart is the real name for this doctor's office staple.

4 A *muselet* keeps this from popping.

5 *Pandiculation* is this morning reflex, familiar to anyone who watches their cat or dog wake up.

6 *Paresthesia* is when this happens to your hands or feet

7 This symbol, also known as the *lemniscate*, goes on and on and on . . .

8 *Runcation* is another word for this gardening task.

9 Where would you find a *tittle*?

10 And to flip it, what's everyone's favorite word for the act of throwing something or someone out a window?

> **DID YOU KNOW?**
>
> Prague has a rich tradition of throwing its leaders out of windows. In the Third [Answer #10] of Prague, in 1618, Protestant lords tossed three Catholic lords from the windows of Prague Castle, which led to the first battle of the 30 Years' War.

ANSWERS - 1. Pigeon - 2. Goose Bumps - 3. Eye Exam Chart - 4. Champagne Cork - 5. Stretching - 6. Fall Asleep - 7. Infinity - 8. Pulling Weeds - 9. The Dot Atop an *i* or *j* - 10. Defenestration

Random Stuff You Might Know

1 Exhibition Road in South Kensington, London, is home to many academic and scientific institutions, including its "big three" museums: Science Museum, Natural History Museum London, and this.

2 On October 29, 2019, he put up 40 points and 20 rebounds—the most by a Laker since 2003—in an NBA-record time of less than 30 minutes of play.

3 This WWII battle atoll is the capital of Kiribati.

AND NOW YOU KNOW

Ti in the Gilbertese language is pronounced "s"; thus the nation of Kiribati's pronunciation is "Kiribaas." Gotta say, this is one of my all-time favorite facts.

4 In feudalism, this surname—that of an American Founding Father—indicated a status above serf but below even the pettiest of nobility.

5 En route to Vienna and an affair, Isadora Wing boards a plane with 117 psychoanalysts—including her husband—in this 1972 Erica Jong novel.

6 Before creating and executive producing hit shows for ABC, she wrote Britney Spears's *Crossroads* and Anne Hathaway's *The Princess Diaries 2*.

7 In 2015, President Goodluck Jonathan became the first president to peacefully relinquish power in this nation's history.

8 Pantone 488 C, dubbed "the ugliest color in the world," has been used the world over in packaging for these products.

9 Germanic-speaking spa towns have this three-letter governmental official designation, German for "bath."

10 One point each for up to 12 of the 24 prime ministers of the United Kingdom since 1900.

ANSWERS - 1. The Victoria and Albert Museum - 2. Anthony Davis - 3. Tarawa - 4. Franklin - 5. *Fear of Flying* - 6. Shonda Rhimes - 7. Nigeria - 8. Tobacco Products - 9. Bad - 10. Robert Cecil, Arthur James Balfour, Henry Campbell-Bannerman, H. H. Asquith, David Lloyd George, Bonar Law, Stanley Baldwin, Ramsay MacDonald, Neville Chamberlain, Winston Churchill, Clement Attlee, Anthony Eden, Harold Macmillan, Alec Douglas-Home, Harold Wilson, Edward Heath, James Callaghan, Margaret Thatcher, John Major, Tony Blair, Gordon Brown, David Cameron, Theresa May, Boris Johnson

It's Electric

1 The choreographed dance called the Electric—better known as the Electric Slide—is set to this Marcia Griffiths and Bunny Wailer song.

2 Also called the Parthian Battery, an ancient device—theorized to be a galvanic cell—was named after this Middle Eastern capital city.

3 "Danger! High Voltage" and "Gay Bar" are songs by this Royal Oak, Michigan, group.

4 On the nine-volt battery, is the smaller (male) snap terminal positive or negative?

> **THE WOOOORRRRRRSSST**
>
> Scientific fact: Answer #10 fanboys are the absolute worst.

5 Italian electricity pioneer Alessandro Volta demonstrated his battery in person for this soon-to-be emperor.

6 This was the final studio album recorded by the Jimi Hendrix Experience.

7 This word can refer to either the gas emitted by the mechanical power that converts 80 percent of the world's electricity or Valve's computer gaming distribution service.

8 Discharging 30 kiloamperes and 100 megavolts while emitting radio, light, X , and gamma rays, this is the most prevalent manifestation of plasma on Earth.

9 "Bedlam in Belgium," "Badlands," and "Brain Shake" are the final three tracks on *Flick of the Switch*, a 1983 album by this band.

10 "Signs" band or Model Y manufacturer.

ANSWERS - 1. "Electric Boogie" - 2. Baghdad - 3. Electric Six - 4. Positive - 5. Napoleon - 6. *Electric Ladyland* - 7. Steam - 8. Lightning - 9. AC/DC - 10. Tesla

Before and After

See page 2 if you need a refresher on the rules.

1 A round red sign with a white horizontal bar indicates this traffic direction AND Mariano's entrance song.

2 The national flag of the United Kingdom AND Lee Child's former army MP.

3 Nickname for the Athletic-then-Yankee who was arguably the Deadball Era's best power hitter AND he won the 2017 Heisman Trophy, Walter Camp Award, and unanimous All-America team honors.

> **MAYBE NOT THE MOST ACCURATE**
>
> Despite his nickname, the first half of Question #3 hit only 93 of his nickname. This is convoluted.

4 *L.A. Candy* and *The Fame Game* author AND his son married Elizabeth Taylor, and he married Zsa Zsa Gabor.

5 For the 1931–32 ceremony, this film won the fifth-ever Best Picture Academy Award AND Don Cheadle's 2004 humanitarian film.

6 Home fries, macaroni salad, baked beans, and/or french fries, topped with meats, spicy mustard, and Nick Tahou's hot sauce AND observable seafloor spreading validated this geologic theory.

7 News reports callously omitted AIDS as cause of death for this sportswear designer's 1986 passing AND per the US Supreme Court, 83 percent of this landmark is in New Jersey, not New York.

8 In *It's Always Sunny in Philadelphia*, The Nightman must pay this to get into a boy's soul or maybe hole AND in 1938, Ruth Graves Wakefield invented this treat, named for her inn.

9 Diddy's clothing line AND the author of *The Pelican Brief*.

10 Enslaved by Thomas Jefferson, James Hemings was the first man to prepare this dish in the United States AND Groundskeeper Willie's four-word description of the French.

ANSWERS - 1. Do Not Enter Sandman - 2. Union Jack Reacher - 3. Frank "Home Run" Baker Mayfield - 4. Lauren Conrad Hilton - 5. Grand Hotel Rwanda - 6. Garbage Plate Tectonics - 7. Perry Ellis Island - 8. Troll Toll House Cookies - 9. Sean John Grisham - 10. Macaroni and Cheese Eating Surrender Monkeys

Sports Championships

1 Hosting World Championships since 1982 in 17 states and Toronto, the PDGA is the sanctioning body for a version of golf; the *D* in its name indicates its use of this sporting equipment.

2 Since 1987, this country has won 5 of the 11 World Polo Championships.

3 This Tennessee university won the 2019 College World Series.

4 Although one team owner has overseen six as well, three different owners with this last name have seen their team win a combined six Super Bowls.

5 OWL is the acronym for the championship league of this video game.

6 La Liga was created in 1929, and two years later, this club won the first of its 33 championships.

7 The first World Series took place in this year.

8 This is the most populous constituent nation represented in the two-time International Cricket Council's T20 World Cup–winning West Indies team.

9 During his sole Formula One World Drivers' Championship season in 1997, Jacques Villeneuve crashed on lap two in the race at the track named for his father, Circuit Gilles Villeneuve, in this city.

10 In 1903, Maurice Garin became the first winner of this storied race.

> **IT'S A FAMILY AFFAIR**
>
> Question #4's answer owns the Steelers. Erotic massage enthusiast Bob Kraft is the owner of the six-time Super Bowl–winning Patriots, who cheat.

Random Stuff You Might Know

1 Thousands have signed a petition to remove the name of racist KKK member Edmund Pettus from a bridge in Selma, Alabama, and rename the structure after this civil rights leader and congressman.

2 West Valley City is the second-most-populous municipality in this state.

WHAT'S MY NAME AGAIN

Some surprising brands are named after their founders. Birds Eye frozen foods is not symbolic; it's named for Clarence Birdseye. Oldsmobile isn't an allusion to antique status; it's the "mobile" of founder Ransom E. Olds. Microphone maker Shure doesn't claim that their product is steadfast in a clever way; Sidney Shure was sure of that.

3 With a fortune currently valued at $182 billion, Jeff Bezos is richer than the GDP PPP of Tunisia but poorer than the GDP PPP of this Nahuatl-named nation.

4 Satellite surveys have discovered that between the 11th and 13th centuries CE, this capital of the Khmer Empire was the largest city on Earth.

5 In what may be an early example of product placement, Édouard Manet's *A Bar at the Folies-Bergére* features bottles of this English beer.

6 The 1970 Superbird had a horn that mimicked the iconic "beep beep" of the Road Runner and was manufactured by this marque.

7 In 1963, a man named Harvey Ball designed this round icon of 1960s and '70s culture.

8 Her signature song is 1981's "I Was Country When Country Wasn't Cool."

9 Although genetically identical, a variation in gene MYB25 is thought to remove this feature from the skin of one fruit, creating a differently named variety.

10 One point for each of the 14 Billboard number-one hits by Rihanna.

ANSWERS - 1. John Lewis - 2. Utah - 3. Guatemala - 4. Angkor - 5. Bass - 6. Plymouth - 7. Smiley - 8. Barbara Mandrell - 9. Fuzz - 10. "We Found Love," "Disturbia," "Work," "Umbrella," "Love the Way You Lie," "The Monster," "Live Your Life," "S.O.S.," "Take a Bow," "Only Girl (in the World)," "S&M," "Diamonds," "Rude Boy," "What's My Name?"

Colors

1. This is the only daily newspaper in Cambridge, Massachusetts.

2. The word for this fruit was transferred, in chronological order, from Sanskrit to Tamil to Persian to Arabic to Italian to French and then finally, in the 13th century, to English; the color came two centuries later.

3. An 1895 cartoon lent its name to this particularly sensationalist brand of reportage.

4. A lush, green countryside could be described with this *V*-word.

5. This is a 10th century Danish monarch or your headphones.

6. Their first top-10 hit was a song about the reincarnation of an Italian astronomer.

7. Victorious Roman generals, Byzantine emperors, and Carolingian kings were among those historically allowed to wear this color.

8. This was originally matte gray with white stripes; only when it didn't "pop" on TV did creator George Barris repaint it in gloss black with orange stripes.

9. In 2014, 13 years after an eponymous movie, this "red mill" celebrated its 125th anniversary.

10. In color printing, CMYK stands for Cyan, Magenta, Yellow, and Key, which signifies this color.

> **GALILEO GALILEO**
>
> Answer #6 called Galileo the king of night vision, which made my dorky mid-1990s mind think of the $1,000 night-vision goggles, not of Galileo's astonishing accomplishments with the then-new invention of the telescope. He literally stared at the night sky, into the darkness, and discovered how the damned universe works. Duh.

ROUND 2 / DIFFICULTY LEVEL   1 2 3 **4** 5 6

Before and After

See page 2 if you need a refresher on the rules.

1 A shoeless high school dance AND Dr. Seuss included a rhyme containing the word *contraceptive* in this 1963 book to ensure his publisher was reading it.

2 The United Kingdom's diabetes awareness foundation, Diabetes UK, was founded by this early sci-fi author AND this bank's Wikipedia page has more than 20 separate subsections on lawsuits, fines, and controversies.

3 In 1991, Wilson Phillips's "You're in Love" was bumped from the top of the Billboard chart by this Amy Grant song AND the Mandalorian's youngish charge.

I'M NACRED

Nacre is especially prized as a material to make caviar spoons. Nacre will not impart the metallic taste that a metal spoon does and will thus give you the lushest, most opulent fish egg–eating experience, you plutocrat, you!

4 Nacre is known by this term AND this naval base was attacked on December 7, 1941.

5 George and Lennie novella AND "Down Under" band.

6 A self-loading firearm AND this torque converter is a fluid coupling within this automotive component.

7 Home city of the Arkansas Symphony Orchestra AND massive 1954 Bill Haley and His Comets hit.

8 *Ropin' the Wind* country artist AND the oldest clothing retailer in the United States.

9 Kate Chastain has six and Lee Rosbach has seven seasons on this reality TV show AND although written in 1862, the fa la las and melody of this carol may have medieval Welsh origins.

10 Jim Gaffigan and Zendaya voiced a straight-to-Netflix Chinese animated movie with this children's game title AND seven times did this nicknamed pitcher record the final out in a division, playoff, or World Series win.

ANSWERS - 1. Sock Hop on Pop - 2. H. G. Wells Fargo - 3. Baby Baby Yoda - 4. Mother of Pearl Harbor - 5. Of Mice and Men at Work - 6. Semiautomatic Transmission - 7. Little Rock Around the Clock - 8. Garth Brooks Brothers - 9. Below Deck the Halls - 10. Duck Duck Goose Gossage

Amusement Parks

1 Commonly called Bakken, or "the Hill," and founded in 1583, the world's oldest amusement park, Dyrehavsbakken, is in this country, only 17 km from Tivoli, the world's second-oldest.

2 Winning the Golden Ticket for Best Amusement Park in the World for 16 consecutive years, this Ohio attraction is home to the Blue Streak, Gemini, Raptor, and Steel Vengeance roller coasters, among others.

3 Legoland Malaysia is not in the capital Kuala Lumpur; instead, it is in the city of Johor Bahru bordering this country.

4 Disneyland's original ticketing system featured "A," "B," and "C" and then "D" tickets, indicating higher-priced rides; an "E" ticket was added in 1977 for this attraction.

5 According to travel site Travegeo, this amusement-less country is the world's largest country without an amusement park.

6 This word refers to the measurement of the distance between the inward facing, load-bearing edges of railway—or, in this round, roller coaster—tracks.

7 Pleasure Beach amusement park, located in this English resort town, features the world's only Wallace & Gromit ride.

8 Only three roller coasters on Earth are designed using this German mathematician–named band, which describes a nonorientable surface with only one boundary curve.

9 In the self-directed music video for 1995's "Fantasy," she Rollerblades into New York's Rye Playland and rides its iconic Dragon Coaster.

10 It was originally scheduled for May 1, but a disaster on April 26 forever stalled the grand opening of the Pripyat Amusement Park in this year.

> **ALSO, ALSO**
>
> *Big, The Muppets Take Manhattan,* and *Fatal Attraction* were also filmed at Playland.

Random Stuff You Might *Not* Know

1 The media nicknamed this clarinetist the King of Swing.

2 The $10,000 Escada Couture Swarovski Crystal line holds the Guinness World Record for the most expensive one of these garments.

3 Although established in 1890, this dairy company didn't open its first store (in Folsom, Pennsylvania) until 1964.

> **THEY'RE LISTENING**
>
> · · · · · · · · · · · · · · · · ·
>
> Four of the answers to Question #10 are owned by Mark Zuckerberg, who never does anything unethical with personal data, ever.

4 Bordering both Nevada and Arizona, this is the largest county in the United States.

5 The largest—and second-most-expensive—house in the world is located in this city and owned by Mukesh Ambani.

6 Spiritually following the steps of Jesus Christ, the Way of the Cross has this number of images or stations.

7 After Thanksgiving, this is the second-largest day in the United States for food consumption.

8 Filmmaker and cyclist Bryan Fogel explores the world of sports doping in this 2017 Academy Award–winning documentary.

9 Shawn Mendes rose to fame by performing Justin Bieber covers and winning a Ryan Seacrest cover song contest with this A Great Big World song.

10 One point for each of the 12 most downloaded mobile apps worldwide for 2019 on both the Google Play Store and the Apple App Store.

ANSWERS - 1. Benny Goodman - 2. Jeans - 3. Wawa - 4. San Bernardino - 5. Mumbai - 6. 14 - 7. Super Bowl Sunday - 8. *Icarus* - 9. "Say Something" - 10. Spotify, UC Browser, Netflix, Snapchat, YouTube, Sharex, Likee, Instagram, Facebook, Messenger, TikTok, WhatsApp

Taglines

1. MOVIE TAGLINE—"In space no one can hear you scream."

2. PRODUCT TAGLINE—"The Ultimate Driving Machine"

3. COMPANY TAGLINE—"Better Living through Chemistry"

4. MOVIE TAGLINE—"Can two friends sleep together and still love each other in the morning?"

5. TV SHOW TAGLINE—"His mind is the ultimate weapon."

6. COMPANY TAGLINE—"You can trust your car to the men who wear the star."

7. PRODUCT TAGLINE—"Lifts and separates"

8. MOVIE TAGLINE—"Paul Sheldon used to write for a living. Now he's writing to stay alive."

9. MOVIE TAGLINE—"Off the record, on the Q.T., and very *hush-hush*"

10. TV TAGLINE—"Genius has side effects."

WHAT'S THE WORD?

Describing a tagline or motto, the word *slogan* derives from the Scottish and Irish words *sluagh-ghairm*, literally meaning "army cry." It meant a rallying call to unify a force or a password to tell friend from foe.

ANSWERS - 1. *Alien* - 2. BMW - 3. DuPont - 4. *When Harry Met Sally* - 5. *MacGyver* - 6. Texaco - 7. Playtex Cross Your Heart Bra - 8. *Misery* - 9. *L.A. Confidential* - 10. House

293

Abbreviations, Acronyms, and Initialisms

1 USATT is the United States' governing body for this indoor sport; they couldn't be called USAPP because it would've infringed on a Parker Brothers trademark.

2 In aviation, the *V* in VTOL means this.

3 In finance, the *I* in IRA means this.

4 In Derry, the *R* in IRA means this.

BEHIND THE LETTERS

....

If anyone says, "Oh, you know this [really, really old word] is actually an acronym for [completely modern language]?" they are ALWAYS INCORRECT. Notwithstanding the answer to #7, which was clever wordplay applied to a preexisting word, acronyms are a thoroughly modern invention.

5 Second- and third-century CE Christian catacombs reveal that the Greek words for "Jesus Christ, God's Son, Savior" create an acronym that spells out the Greek name of this kind of animal.

6 ExxonMobil's non-American filling stations go by this name, the pronunciation of the abbreviation of its predecessor company.

7 One of the earliest English-language acronyms came in 1668, when the first letters of the surnames or titles of five ministers of King Charles II were arranged to form this word describing an influential, often secretive, political clique.

8 Whereas NATO can be pronounced in full, K.G.B. is pronounced as individual letters, thus there should be no periods in the former and periods in the latter—at least according to this newspaper's style guide.

9 When used in healthcare and science, the *m* of the mixed-case acronym "mRNA" stands for this word.

10 This letter is the System of Units (SI) symbol for 1,000.

ANSWERS - 1. Table Tennis - 2. Vertical - 3. Individual - 4. Republican - 5. Fish (*ichthys;* ΙΧΘΥΣ) - 6. Esso - 7. Cabal - 8. *The New York Times* - 9. Messenger - 10. k

Sports

1. Eddie Cicotte, Happy Felsch, Chick Gandil, and Buck Weaver were all members of this infamously nicknamed baseball team.

2. In December 1891, this Canadian phys-ed student and instructor invented basketball in Springfield, Massachusetts.

3. Wayne Gretzky was part owner and head coach of which NHL franchise?

4. The three sports venues to host two teams in the same league are MetLife Stadium, SoFi Stadium, and this California arena.

5. On September 15, 2007, this World Rally champion and video game namesake died in a helicopter crash on his estate in Scotland.

> **GROWING PAINS**
>
> I played Answer #9 in college. I was a handler and in charge of the club's funds until I blew them on keg parties. Worth it.

6. The Dunlop Curve, Ford Chicane, and Mulsanne Straight are all famed landmarks on the Circuit de la Sarthe, the locale of this world-famous endurance race.

7. What sport are you watching if the *rikishi* are attempting to push one another out of the *dohyō*?

8. Coveted by professional climbers as one of Seven Summits, Vinson Massif in the Ellsworth Mountains is the tallest mountain on which continent?

9. The Scoober, Hammer, Flick, and Backhand are all throws used in this "sport," popular with the collegiate set.

10. The construction of this new neighboring stadium temporarily gave Cincinnati's Cinergy Field a taller wall than Fenway's Green Monster.

ANSWERS - 1. 1919 Chicago Black Sox - 2. Dr. James Naismith - 3. Phoenix Coyotes - 4. Staples Center - 5. Colin McRae - 6. 24 Heures du Mans - 7. Sumo - 8. Antarctica - 9. Ultimate Frisbee - 10. The Great American Ballpark

Random Stuff You Might *Not* Know

1 This fifth-most-common Hispanic surname means "son of the wolf," not "1990s Braves catcher."

2 Allowing a soloist to demonstrate their virtuosity, this is the name for the largely improvised solo passage toward the end of a concerto movement.

3 This music artist wrote and recorded the single "Speed" for the 1994 movie of the same name.

IT'S ALL IN THE NAME

Answer #6 was known in his pro career as "The Admiral" because of his time at the US Naval Academy in Annapolis, Maryland.

4 Jinnah International Airport serves this city.

5 New York's Hell Gate Bridge inspired both the iconic Sydney Harbour Bridge and a bridge across the River Tyne in this city.

6 The NCAA Division I Men's Basketball record for blocks in a season is 207 and was set by this Navy Midshipman.

7 "And then I thought I would never speak again, because my voice would kill anyone," says the author of this 1969 autobiography.

8 Unable to find footage of the infamous Janet Jackson/Justin Timberlake Super Bowl halftime performance, three men were motivated to found this website.

9 Tony Leung, Dennis To, and most famously, Donnie Yen, have all played this teacher of Bruce Lee.

10 One point for each of the 15 countries with capital cities at or above 5,000 feet in elevation.

ANSWERS - 1. López - 2. Cadenza - 3. Billy Idol - 4. Karachi - 5. Newcastle upon Tyne - 6. David Robinson - 7. *I Know Why the Caged Bird Sings* - 8. YouTube - 9. Ip Man - 10. Guatemala City, Guatemala; Kigali, Rwanda; Maseru, Lesotho; Windhoek, Namibia; Kabul, Afghanistan; Nairobi, Kenya; Tehran, Iran; Mexico City, Mexico; Sana'a, Yemen; Asmara, Eritrea; Thimphu, Bhutan; Addis Ababa, Ethiopia; Bogotá, Colombia; Quito, Ecuador; La Paz, Bolivia

Philosophy

1 The masterpiece fresco *The School of Athens* features portraits of contemporaries like Da Vinci and Michelangelo as philosophers and—staring at the audience—a self-portrait of this artist himself.

2 Ataraxia, the freedom from fear, and aponia, the absence of bodily pain, are the core tenets of this ancient Greek philosophy.

3 To squelch University College London student pranks, the mummified head of this founder of utilitarianism had to be moved out of permanent public display.

4 In Monty Python's "Philosophers' Football Match" sketch, Greek playwright Sophocles went by this nickname.

5 "Entities should not be multiplied without necessity," or, simpler solutions are more likely, is a 17th-century statement by John Punch attributed to this 14th-century Franciscan.

6 In Hinduism, this word refers to "the right way of living"; in Buddhism, it's the "cosmic law and order."

7 Legendarily written during the Warring States period, the *Analects*—a collection of sayings and teachings by this philosopher—was finalized during the Han dynasty.

8 "On the seeker's path, wise men and fools are one," says this Sufi poet.

9 *The Origins of Totalitarianism*, *The Human Condition*, and *On Revolution* are 20th-century works by this philosopher.

> **PRO TIP**
> "Sufi poet" is always Answer #8. (Trivia writers need to branch out more.) Learn that one.

10 Former Federal Reserve chairman Alan Greenspan attended weekend philosophy salons organized by and at the apartment of this completely overrated objectivist.

Before and After

See page 2 if you need a refresher on the rules.

1 *Taxi*'s Reverend Iggy Ignatowski or *Modern Family* creator AND Beau and Jeff's dad.

2 A 1970 documentary about an album of the same name, which includes a song of the same name AND US Army slogan from 1980 to 2001.

3 By financing the Edison Electric Illuminating Company, this banker enjoyed New York's first electrically lit private home AND this comedian got 300,000 likes after pointing out that Elon Musk stole her Twitter joke.

4 Ben & Jerry's banana-flavored offering AND a plumber's accessory or Foo Fighters' song.

5 Host of his own children's show from 1953 to 1966, this comic estimates he was hit by more than 20,000 pies in his career AND Marc Benioff's cloud-based CRM juggernaut.

6 *Star Wars* character named by its creator with letters and numbers resembling its shape AND slang for 3.5 grams of cocaine.

7 Wilderness settings tie the installments of this video game series together AND Timbaland-produced Justin Timberlake single.

8 Maurice Sendak's masterpiece AND Terry Crews starred in the sitcom based on this Ice Cube movie of the same name.

HINT

Charlemagne's dad is NOT Charles Martel—that's his grandfather, nicknamed "The Hammer." Which in French is, uh, Martel.

9 His last major role was as The Inventor in *Edward Scissorhands* AND this Schenectady-based grocery chain has 132 stores throughout Massachusetts, New York, and Pennsylvania.

10 Charlemagne's dad AND Nova Laboratories' SAINT Number 5 is struck by lightning and becomes sentient in this movie.

ANSWERS - 1. Christopher Lloyd Bridges - 2. Let It Be All You Can Be - 3. J. P. Morgan Murphy - 4. Chunky Monkey Wrench - 5. Soupy Salesforce - 6. BB-8 Ball - 7. Far Cry Me a River - 8. Where the Wild Things Are We There Yet? - 9. Vincent Price Chopper - 10. Pepin (or Pippin) the Short Circuit

Shoes

75

1. Probably won't be the first time you'll hear that this four-letter word describes the wooden or plastic mold around which a shoe is constructed.

2. Combining elements of all the models Michael Jordan wore during his championship seasons, a special model Air Jordan was released in 2008 and called this many "Rings."

3. After reading of a Manchester City supporter arrested for looking up women's skirts, John Lennon wrote about a man with mirrors upon his boots in this "joyful" Beatles song.

4. This word refers to either an accent or a type of shoe.

5. In 1992, shoe mogul Robert Greenberg stepped down as CEO of sneaker brand LA Gear to found this third-largest athletic footwear brand in the US.

6. After Bob Lange–designed footwear ended up on the feet of Nancy Greene, who won the 1967 inaugural World Championship, plastic—instead of leather—boots became de rigueur in this sport.

7. This is the name of the metal plate attached to the bottom of a tap shoe.

8. *Voyageurs*, or French Canadian traders, called the lameness developed from extensive use of this footwear *mal de raquette*.

9. In 1966, California resident Margot Fraser returned to her native Germany, where she discovered this footwear company, founded in 1774; she came back to California and soon sold the brand in health food stores.

10. "At just 5'1", the petite star uses supersize heels to literally elevate her looks," wrote *Vogue*'s Janelle Okwodu on this pop star.

> ### FANTASTIC VOYAGEUR
>
> While plying the waterways of Canada in search of furs or laden with goods, *voyageurs* would measure time in "pipes," as in how many smoke breaks they'd taken in a given day. Which is pretty much how many bartenders measure time to this day. "It's been seven vapes since I opened." Don't smoke, kids!

ANSWERS - 1. Last - 2. Six - 3. "Happiness Is a Warm Gun" - 4. Brogue - 5. Skechers - 6. Skiing - 7. Tap - 8. Snowshoes - 9. Birkenstock - 10. Lady Gaga

Random Stuff You Might *Not* Know

1. Grozny is the capital of this federal republic of the Russian Federation.

2. An unbranded Starbucks store, the Herald Square Café, resides on the second floor of this department store's flagship location.

3. In mathematics, *R* represents real numbers, its subset rational numbers are represented by *Q*, and its subset integers are represented by this letter.

4. Now known as Magna PT, the world's largest supplier of automotive and commercial transmissions was known by this name until 2018.

5. In 1997, he was briefly dismissed from his role as host of *Gospel America* for appearing in a black leather outfit to promote his album *In a Metal Mood: No More Mr. Nice Guy*.

PRO TIP

Learn as many British-English to American-English translations as you can: *Lorry* is "truck"; *aubergine* is "eggplant." They're useful. Well, not in real life, but in the context of trivia, they're useful. Or if you want to impress a British date.

6. Anthropologists speculate that in addition to its usage as sun protection, this cosmetic was also used as protection from the evil eye.

7. The Hungarian, Finnish, and Estonian languages are collectively named after this Russian mountain range, their hypothesized homeland.

8. This actor plays the Madam Secretary of *Madam Secretary*.

9. Arugula is known by this name in British English.

10. One point for each of the 14 least populous state capitals (city proper; not metro area).

ANSWERS - 1. Chechnya - 2. Macy's - 3. *Z* - 4. Getrag - 5. Pat Boone - 6. Eyeliner - 7. Ural Mountains - 8. Téa Leoni - 9. Rocket - 10. Carson City, Nevada (55,916); Harrisburg, Pennsylvania; Charleston, West Virginia; Olympia, Washington; Concord, New Hampshire; Jefferson City, Missouri; Annapolis, Maryland; Dover, Delaware; Helena, Montana; Juneau, Alaska; Frankfort, Kentucky; Augusta, Maine; Pierre, South Dakota; Montpelier, Vermont (7,855)

The Bathroom

76

1 The first recorded indoor toilet dates from 3200 BCE in the Mesopotamian city of Uruk during the time of this early civilization.

2 Contrary to popular belief, the alcohol content in this bathroom product is not to kill germs; it is instead a carrier agent for active antimicrobial ingredients.

3 This "American" manufacturer of bathroom fixtures, sinks, toilets, and more brands their products with an iconic cursive-script logo.

YOU MIGHT BE THERE RIGHT NOW

Here are some other synonyms for *bathroom*: the head, bog, latrine, lavatory, john, jacks (for our Irish readers), and many more.

4 The Japanese communal bathhouses called *sentō* heat their facilities via a boiler, whereas their more prestigious cousins, *onsen*, heat their baths via this geothermal source.

5 Napoleon's defeat, the French word for "water," and the French word for "place" have all been suggested as possible origins for this three-letter British-English euphemism for "toilet."

6 In *Pulp Fiction*, hitman Vincent Vega is gunned down in the bathroom by this prizefighter played by Bruce Willis.

7 In 1977, Johnson & Johnson introduced this brand of toothbrushes with angled heads.

8 Zvezda and Tranquility are the locations of the only two toilets in this multinational project.

9 This joint-sealing material comes in the most common acrylic latex, long-lasting vinyl latex, mildew-resistant silicone, and tough-to-shape polyurethane varieties.

10 *Scientific American* reports that 15 million trees could be saved yearly if every American abandoned toilet paper for this fixture.

ANSWERS - 1. Sumer - 2. Mouthwash - 3. American Standard - 4. Hot Springs - 5. Loo - 6. Butch Coolidge - 7. Reach - 8. International Space Station - 9. Caulk - 10. Bidet.

Before and After

See page 2 if you need a refresher on the rules.

1 Giselle's pigskin-tossing husband AND from 1994 to 2009, this legislation denied 1.9 million attempted firearm purchases.

2 No. 48 Lowe's Chevrolet driver AND Acuvue, Neutrogena, and Clean & Clear are brands from this company.

3 A jingle that went "Whatever it is I think I see, becomes [this candy] to me" AND the manufacturer of the supercharged V12 engine that powered the famed Supermarine Spitfire airplane.

INTO THE WILD BLUE YONDER

The Spitfire's Merlin engine was built under license by Packard Automobiles and transformed a mediocre World War II aircraft called the P-51 Mustang from a passable plane to a world-beater. Take that, Allison V-1710!

4 The sitarist on "Norwegian Wood (This Bird Has Flown)" AND in 1993, he played the character Dr. Richard Kimble.

5 First postmaster general in 1775 AND "Happy Days Are Here Again" was this president's campaign theme song.

6 Pop singer born Katheryn Elizabeth Hudson AND rock star, bandleader, and festival founder born Peretz Bernstein.

7 A flamboyant Van Halen frontman AND created in 1997, this retirement plan allows for tax-free withdrawals.

8 This maker of athletic shoes has two factories in Massachusetts and three in Maine AND two dance elements, a full turn on one foot, and a dismount are mandatory parts of the routine on this athletic apparatus.

9 "Second place is first loser" was a famous slogan of this lifestyle brand AND *A Savage Journey to the Heart of the American Dream* was the subtitle of this book.

10 Henry James novel named for a Greenwich Village landmark AND 9's relation to 81.

ANSWERS - 1. Tom Brady Bill - 2. Jimmie Johnson & Johnson - 3. Tootsie Rolls-Royce - 4. George Harrison Ford - 5. Benjamin Franklin Roosevelt - 6. Katy Perry Farrell - 7. David Lee Roth IRA - 8. New Balance Beam - 9. No Fear and Loathing in Las Vegas - 10. Washington Square Root

Rhyme Time

The answer to each clue is two words that rhyme. A quick example: A Disney chipmunk's water buckets = "Dale's Pails." Get it?

1 Giving Hydra's formal greeting to the wrong person

2 Stretch to grab a *Prunus persica*

3 A wastewater exit in Batman's manor

4 A cooper's product filled with noels

5 A Quattro owned by the designer of Sagrada Família

6 A smug smile in Ankara

7 A very small Irving-created Owen

8 *Tommy Boy* lead's vinyl dance performance floor

9 A sienna coronet

10 A Stockholm herringbone

PRO TIP

Learn the taxonomic names of the most common fruits, vegetables, and animals. Should you make the big show, you'll be the *Malus domestica* of your mother's eye.

ANSWERS - 1. Hail Fail - 2. Peach Reach - 3. Wayne Drain - 4. Carol Barrel - 5. Gaudí Audi - 6. Turk Smirk - 7. Teeny Meany - 8. Farley Marley - 9. Brown Crown - 10. Swede Tweed

303

Random Stuff You Might Know

1 Waste Weir #1, the remains of the gravity dam that was once the terminus of the Chesapeake and Ohio Canal, became the namesake of this now-infamous building complex.

2 Featuring pop figures with X'ed-out eyes, the art of Brian Donnelly is signed with this four-lettered name.

READ BETWEEN THE LINES

Overly wordy questions rife with terminology, like #4 here, are great ways to get your audience thinking. Basically all the words there are superfluous except for one or two indicators toward the intent of the question. To translate, Question #4 could be read as, "where's Anatolia?"

3 Besides the band themselves, Dion DiMucci and Bob Dylan are the only two fellow rock musicians featured on the cover art of this album.

4 The Osmanoğlu dynasty of the Kayi tribe had by the 15th century conquered all neighboring Anatolian *beylics*, thus founding this empire.

5 This Yukon capital has been lauded by the *Guinness Book of World Records* as the city with the least polluted air on Earth.

6 This is the name for the hearth within a smithy.

7 What is the capital of Latvia?

8 In the transliteration of Mandarin to Latin characters, this three-letter suffix means "gate," notably used in the name of a famous Beijing site.

9 The Billboard Hot Country chart's longest tenure at number one is held by "Meant to Be," a collaboration between Bebe Rexha and this state-named duo.

10 One point each for up to 13 of the 23 men who served in the 19th century as vice president of the United States.

ANSWERS - 1. Watergate - 2. KAWS - 3. *Sgt. Pepper's Lonely Hearts Club Band* - 4. Ottoman Empire - 5. Whitehorse - 6. Forge - 7. Riga - 8. -men - 9. Florida Georgia Line - 10. Thomas Jefferson, Aaron Burr, George Clinton, Elbridge Gerry, Daniel Tompkins, John C. Calhoun, Martin Van Buren, Richard Mentor Johnson, John Tyler, George M. Dallas, Millard Fillmore, William R. King, John C. Breckinridge, Hannibal Hamlin, Andrew Johnson, Schuyler Colfax, Henry Wilson, William A. Wheeler, Chester A. Arthur, Thomas A. Hendricks, Levi P. Morton, Adlai Stevenson I, Garret Hobart

Firsts

1. The first film in the Marvel Cinematic Universe was *Iron Man* in 2008, but the first film to ever star a Marvel character was a 1944 serial featuring this character.

2. In 1789, she became the first Second Lady of the United States; she was also the second First Lady.

3. He starred as the first man on the moon in 2018's *First Man*.

4. On April 18, 1923, Babe Ruth hit the first home run on the opening day of Yankee Stadium, just hours after this "March King" conducted "The Star-Spangled Banner."

5. In 1877, during the Romanian War of Independence, the NMS *Rândunica* became the first device of its kind to sink a ship, the Ottoman Empire's *Seyfi*, without also sinking itself.

> **THAT SINKING FEELING**
>
> One of the world's first submarines was the *H. L. Hunley*, designed by a man of the same name, for the losers in the Confederacy during the American Civil War. It sank three times, killing 21 secessionists, and managed to down the Union warship *USS Housatonic*.

6. "The 1" is, unsurprisingly, the first track of this 2020 Taylor Swift album.

7. Maud Watson was the first woman to win this tennis tournament in 1884; she defended her title in 1885 but lost in 1886, and her opponent, Blanche Bingley, became the first recipient of the Venus Rosewater Dish trophy.

8. Sound of Music, Richard Schulze's hi-fi shop established in 1966 in St. Paul, Minnesota, was this retail giant's first store.

9. In 2006, a Democratic member of the Alabama House of Representatives initiated a bill to pardon Lillie Mae Bradford, who in 1951 became the first—albeit less recognized—Black woman to protest this city's segregationist transit laws.

10. In the 1912 Stockholm Olympics, this First Nations and American athlete won both the first-ever decathlon and first-ever pentathlon.

ANSWERS: 1. Captain America - 2. Abigail Adams - 3. Ryan Gosling - 4. John Philip Sousa - 5. Torpedo - 6. *folklore* - 7. Wimbledon - 8. Best Buy - 9. Montgomery, Alabama - 10. Jim Thorpe

Before and After

See page 2 if you need a refresher on the rules.

1   The senior US senator from Massachusetts AND the Oracle of Omaha.

2   Drafted in 1994, this Duke alum retired from the NBA as a Clipper in 2013 AND in 1981, this show accrued a then-record eight Emmy wins for a debut season.

3   New York's Bravest AND the millennium bug.

4   The protagonist of *The Wonder Years* AND he played the T-800 model 101.

5   According to Diageo, this beverage is the best-selling distilled-spirit brand in the world AND Robert Van Winkle along with Freddie Mercury, Brian May, and David Bowie have songwriting credits on this song.

6   *Ninety-Five Theses* author AND "Never Too Much" singer.

THE MAGIC OF TELEVISION

Julie Bowen was pregnant with twins during the filming of *Modern Family's* pilot. Boxes, pillows, blankets, furniture, and crazy angles hid it from the audience.

7   Founded in 1937 in France, this women's magazine is published in the US by Hearst Publications AND Julie Bowen plays this mom in *Modern Family*.

8   This South Africa–set action movie was originally conceived as a film based on the video game *Halo* AND the zip code of Beverly Hills.

9   Since 1986, this candy's slogan has been "Gimme a break" AND this actor is one half of the stars of *2 Broke Girls*.

10   The lead singer of Mötley Crüe AND he hosted the Oscars in 2015.

ANSWERS - 1. Elizabeth Warren Buffett - 2. Grant Hill Street Blues - 3. FDNY2K - 4. Kevin Arnold Schwarzenegger - 5. Smirnoff Ice Baby - 6. Martin Luther Vandross - 7. Marie Claire Dunphy - 8. District 90210 - 9. Kit Kat Dennings - 10. Vince Neil Patrick Harris

Worsts

1. At a 15-percent Tomatometer score, *The Circle* edges out the 16-percent rating of *The Bonfire of the Vanities* as this actor's worst film.

2. This actor's worst film is arguably *Heart Condition* (1990); just two movies earlier he starred in one of his best, which also landed him the Oscar for Best Supporting Actor.

3. Exacerbated by a world war, the pandemic that began in this year landed a "five" rating, the highest and worst on the pandemic severity index.

4. Metacritic and Rotten Tomatoes agree that the first and ninth episodes are the worst installments of this film franchise.

5. In 1899, the Spiders from this city won 20 games and lost 134 for the worst-ever season standings in MLB history.

6. A contractual obligation consisting of previously released songs, original film tracks, and score songs, this 1969 album is considered the Beatles' worst.

7. Despite being in production from 1847 until 2018, this company's eponymous wafer appeared on dozens of "Worst Halloween Candy" lists.

8. With a 5.8 rating, this franchise placed dead last on the *Consumer Reports* poll of best-tasting fast food burgers.

> **THAT'S A RAZ!**
>
> In 2021, Glenn Close received an Oscar nomination and a Razzie nomination for the same role in *Hillbilly Elegy*. The Golden Raspberry Award, or Razzie, is awarded annually to terrible films, performances, and directors. Sandra Bullock famously won an Oscar in 2010 while also receiving two Razzie noms.

9. With 402 wins, 310 draws, and 388 losses, this Liverpool club holds the worst record of the six teams that have never been relegated from the English Premier League.

10. This tallest mountain in the northeastern United States has been proclaimed the "Home of the World's Worst Weather."

ANSWERS – 1. Tom Hanks – 2. Denzel Washington – 3. 1918 – 4. *Star Wars* – 5. Cleveland – 6. *Yellow Submarine* – 7. Necco Wafers – 8. McDonald's – 9. Everton – 10. Mount Washington, New Hampshire

Random Stuff You Might Know

1 This *A*-word describes a well-known, named pattern of stars that are not formally classified as a constellation.

2 The 13th-century BCE stele of Pharaoh Merneptah has in hieroglyphics the first written mention of this ancient tribe, today the name of a nation.

EASTER EGGS ARE FUN!

Did you know that Answer #1 was described earlier in this very book? So, if you're skipping around, oops!

3 The 2008 novel *One Fifth Avenue* by this *Sex and the City* author depicts events in the building of the same name.

4 Kampala is the capital of this nation.

5 Before leading Rilo Kiley, indie rocker Jenny Lewis starred opposite Fred Savage in this 1989 Nintendo product placement movie.

6 Used in sushi restaurants, this word literally translates to "I trust you."

7 Reflecting its newfound status as capital of a new republic, the city of Angora was renamed this in 1930.

8 Located east of Madagascar, this overseas department of France is the outermost area of the European Union and the eurozone.

9 *Ancistroides nigrita* is the formal name of this insect, also known as the chocolate demon.

10 Between January 1, 1950, and December 31, 2000, 43 men held the title of boxing's World Heavyweight Champion. One point each for up to 15 of them.

Change a Letter, Change Everything

This is a fun wordplay round, wherein a clue is altered to reveal an unexpected answer solved by changing a single letter in what would otherwise be a rote question. Here's an example: Jagger and Richards band named after tumbling English teatime baked goods. Answer: Rolling Scones. (STONES ➡ SCONES)

1 Holden Caulfield explores indigo and mauve in this classic J. D. Salinger novel.

> **FUN FACT**
>
> Holden Caulfield is insufferable.

2 This 1992 sequel features a nocturnal crime-fighting Chairman of the Chinese Communist Party.

3 One Direction's original members included Harry Styles, Niall Horan, Louis Tomlinson, Zayn Malik, and this sand-silt-clay soil.

4 This common Japanese car is manufactured by a *Klute* actress.

5 This Apple CEO's family hailed from Ireland's "rebel county."

6 This *Gossip Girl* star will bring you to a complete stop.

7 Hear the disapproving snort of this portrayer of Ron Weasley.

8 Ray-Ban sunglasses were created by the company ____, which was formed by a German immigrant and an ovine juvenile.

9 This mildest form of Japanese fermented soybean paste never hits the mark.

10 This "Particle Man" band is made up of a duo of Cuban American Red Sox hurlers.

ANSWERS - 1. Catcher in the Dye (Rye ➡ Dye) - 2. BatMao Returns (Batman ➡ BatMao) - 3. Loam Payne (Liam ➡ Loam) - 4. Fonda Civic (Honda ➡ Fonda) - 5. Tim Cork (Cook ➡ Cork) - 6. Brake Lively (Blake ➡ Brake) - 7. Rupert Grunt (Grint ➡ Grunt) - 8. Bausch + Lamb (Lomb ➡ Lamb) - 9. White Miss (Miso ➡ Miss) - 10. They Might Be Tiants (Giants ➡ Tiants)

309

In Other Words

1 This 1971 Rolling Stones album might be called *Tacky Digits*.

2 The tagline for this 1979 film might otherwise be "the cosmos renders inaudible your shriek."

3 Hannah Baker leaves behind a "baker's dozen grounds of intent" in this 2017 Netflix series.

4 Featured on the *Birds of Prey* soundtrack, this Megan Thee Stallion and Normani hit could have been called "Metastable Allotropes of Carbon."

5 When using *Lumbricus terrestris* as bait, please don't use X-Man Kurt Wagner.

6 This screen legend's first and last names mean "my God is an oath" and "cutter of cloth," not "star of *Cleopatra*."

7 Christina Hendricks starred in this NBC series about "adequate young women."

8 "Save Your Tears" because it shouldn't be a "Problem" to know that this singer's first and last names mean "Big Persian Compatriot."

9 In 1997, for the price of a $7,995 ticket (about $12,000 in today's dollars) you could travel at 60,000 feet on this "agreement."

10 Oliver Nelson took you on an aural journey through "Purloined Junctures" in this jazz classic.

WHAT'S IN A LETTER?

The British and French governments, the cosponsors for the creation of Answer #9, fought at length over whether there should be an *e* at the end of its name. The French really wanted it, and the British did not. Then an enterprising diplomat said—to paraphrase—"the added *e* will stand for 'excellence.'" So yeah, the French won, because that's a crappy work-around.

ANSWERS - 1. *Sticky Fingers* - 2. *Alien* - 3. *13 Reasons Why* - 4. "Diamonds" - 5. Nightcrawler - 6. Elizabeth Taylor - 7. *Good Girls* - 8. Ariana Grande - 9. Concorde - 10. "Stolen Moments"

Everything's for Sale

1 In the 1854 Gadsden Purchase, the US acquired territory from Mexico, including this now-second-most-populous city in Arizona.

2 In 2000 Netflix offered itself for sale to this company; the offer was rebuffed.

3 Big Machine Records—and with it, Taylor Swift's master recordings— was acquired in 2019 by the Carlyle Group and Ithaca Holdings, then run by this manager and executive.

4 "We Sold Our Soul for Rock 'n' Roll" claimed this metal band in a 1975 compilation album.

5 According to popular myth, Harry Frazee sold this man's contract to finance the Broadway musical *No, No, Nanette*.

6 This automobile brand sold 63,110 units in its inaugural 1958 model year, the second-most successful launch for a new car at the time.

> **PRO TIP**
>
> Although positioned as successful here, Answer #6 is often synonymous with "failure."

7 In 2011, the minor league Dayton Dragons broke the 814-game sellout-streak record for professional sports set between 1977 and 1995 by this pioneering NBA team.

8 In 2016, 12-packs of the reissue of this "supernatural" Hi-C beverage sold for more than $100 on eBay.

9 Moving an uncanny 8.1 million copies, the 1991 #1 issue of this superhero team's comic is the best-selling single issue of a comic book of all time.

10 With 64 RIAA certifications, she was the best-selling music artist of the 2000s.

ANSWERS - 1. Tucson – 2. Blockbuster Video – 3. Scooter Braun – 4. Black Sabbath - 5. Babe Ruth – 6. Edsel - 7. Portland Trail Blazers - 8. Ecto Cooler - 9. X-Men - 10. Beyoncé

Firsts and Lasts

For every beginning, there's also an ending.

1 "Last night I dreamt I went to Manderley again" begins this novel.

2 This king of film narration concludes a 1995 thriller with the line, "Ernest Hemingway once wrote, 'The world is a fine place and worth fighting for.' I agree with the second part."

3 The first line of an 1851 work implored for the reader to "Call me" this first son of Abraham.

4 "I'd never given much thought to how I could die, but dying in the place of someone I love seems like a pretty good way to go" opens this 2008 film adaptation of a wildly successful novel.

5 The Shakespearean final line "For never was a story of more woe than this of Juliet and her Romeo" is delivered by the prince of this city.

SHAKESPEAREAN GEOGRAPHY

Shakespeare set his plays in a variety of locales, but luckily there's only a few of them to remember in pub trivia. Knowing where your Billy Shakes is set can dramatically up your chances of nailing what would otherwise be a super-difficult question. Isn't that right, Timon of Salt Lake City?

6 "Okonkwo was well known throughout the nine villages and even beyond" starts this 1958 story set in Nigeria.

7 According to the last line of a film of the same name, this famous MacGuffin is "the stuff that dreams are made of."

8 "Shit!" exclaims Brian, slamming the wheel of a 1995 Mitsubishi Eclipse, thus beginning this multibillion-dollar film franchise.

9 "It was a bright cold day in April, and the clocks were striking thirteen" opens this novel.

10 According to the final line, this 1818 novel's monster "was soon borne away by the waves and lost in darkness and distance."

ANSWERS - 1. *Rebecca* **- 2.** Morgan Freeman **- 3.** Ishmael **- 4.** *Twilight* **- 5.** Verona **- 6.** *Things Fall Apart* **- 7.** *The Maltese Falcon* **- 8.** *The Fast and the Furious* **- 9.** *1984* **- 10.** *Frankenstein*

A HOW-TO GUIDE:
Put Together Your Own Trivia Night for Fun and Profit

 ere's what a well-rounded quiz night looks like in brief: four to six rounds of trivia, widely varied in subject matter, with incentives offered throughout the evening, culminating in the awarding of a grand prize, lasting approximately two hours in total. Got it? Good. Now let's take a look at how to make it happen.

Although this book presents four-round trivia contests, feel free to put together up to six rounds with more audiovisual variety in the live setting. Try adding elements like audio rounds and visual rounds with curated playlists and photo handouts, respectively. Writing a full six-round pub quiz might sound daunting, but it's absolutely worth it. For one thing, it's apt to last around two hours, which is the perfect length: not too short (people will get their money's worth) and not too long (drinking contestants won't fall out of their chairs). For another, you'll be briskly presenting each round with ample breaks in between to allow customers time to order from servers and bartenders, socialize, and generally have a good night out, a respite from their otherwise dour lives.

A Layout of the Night

Here's how to run this thing, creating an evening that moves swiftly along, keeps people in their seats to consume product, and gives enough time to shoot the breeze. After all, trivia nights should be fun for the participants and profitable for the establishment. A slow pace raises the prospect of losing customers. Run too quickly and people won't order that critical third or fourth drink! In this order:

• Introduce the evening.

• Hand out or otherwise present Round 1: Visual Round.

- State the rules and announce the prizes while teams are working on Round 1.

- Announce the subsequent rounds of the night.

- Collect and score Round 1.

- Read the answers, announce the scores, and award a prize for Best Team Name (optional).

- Repeat this for each subsequent round, timing your breaks between rounds and keeping the presentation of each round compact. To recap: Read questions, take a breather, announce scores, and get back into the content. Punctuate the night with incentives and ensure that everyone knows "we're giving away shots for the best score of the last round, so you're still in it!" and all that jazz.

Before we get into the mechanics of presenting the entire night, we first need questions. Luckily for you, this book is filled with thousands of them, organized into hundreds of fully realized trivia rounds to pick and choose from. If you just want to hop right in and start presenting with full quiz packages that I've already written for you, skip ahead to the section on how to present the night. If you're interested in writing your own questions and exploring the sophisticated, much-studied philosophy therein, continue.

How to Balance Round Subjects

Want to ensure a challenging yet fun—and ultimately fulfilling—trivia night? Of course you do. Well, lead changes are your way to do it. So how to foster lead changes? By alternately screwing people over. In other words, balance the night, round by round, mitigating the likelihood of all six rounds falling within one six-person team's theoretical wheelhouse. Simply put, if one round is about X, write the next five rounds about Y, Z, A, B, and C. For instance:

Round 1 is Visual; have fun with some photo ID'ing

Round 2 is a Subject that contrasts with the subject of Round 1.

Round 3 is Before and After, in which a team's diversity of knowledge comes into play and a wide variety of subjects can be represented.

Round 4 is Audio; it should contrast with the subjects represented in Rounds 1 and 2.

Round 5 is a Subject that contrasts with Rounds 1, 2, and 4.

Round 6 is Random Stuff, another widely varied grab-bag round encouraging diversity in team makeup. (An addendum to Round 6 is the final question of the night, a list question, which should contrast with the subjects of Rounds 1, 2, 4, and 5.)

A theoretical layout might look like this:

Round 1—Visual: City Skylines. This will likely appeal to trivia hardcores but might elicit poor scores from more pop-oriented teams.

Round 2—Subject: Recipes. Those who dismayed at City Skylines might enjoy this fun round.

Round 3—Before and After. Truly a test of a given team's diversity of knowledge.

Round 4 —Audio: Greatest Hits of 2017. Rounds 1 and 2 probably skew older, so appeal to the twentysomethings here.

Round 5—Subject: Girl TV (*Girls*, *Gilmore Girls*, and *Gossip Girl*). Appeal to the millennials.

Round 6—Random Stuff. A little bit of science, some pop culture, a sports question, history, geography, everything—just cover your bases until Question 10: The List Question. The final question of the final round (i.e., the final question of the night) should be a multi-answer list question countering the subjects represented in City Skylines, Recipes, Before and After, 2017 Hits, and Girl TV. Baseball or Oscar Winners, for example, would do nicely.

Here's another evenly matched quiz:

Round 1—Visual: Netflix Shows

Round 2—Subject: Monarchs of England

Round 3—Before and After

Round 4—Audio: Disney Channel Alumni Songs

Round 5—Subject: NCAA March Madness

Round 6—Random Stuff (list question on South American Capitals)

Here it is in practice from actual pub trivia rounds at The Waylon on West 50th Street and 10th Avenue in New York City (shameless plug). These are cumulative scores, and the leading team after each round is highlighted:

	ROUND 1	ROUND 2	ROUND 3	ROUND 4	ROUND 5	ROUND 6
Let's Get Quizzical	12	14	25	40	48	65
SQUIRREL!	9	17	26	40	50	61
Baby O'Riley	9	18	28	40	49	59
HB+HK	9	19	25	44	50	57
The Gaf-Letes	5	15	21	35	41	50
It Quiz What It Quiz	10	13	21	36	41	51
Triv and Let Die	8	14	24	30	38	46
Monsterpiece Theatre	12	13	19	31	37	45
Picklebacks	3	11	17	29	37	45
Under the Influence	8	12	15	29	35	38

In the end, a team that only led once throughout the night ended up winning on the strength of their last-round performance. That makes it more fun!

Here's another night with similar results from the rounds of Foods, Disease, Before and After, Numbered Bands, I Love the '80s, and Random Stuff:

	ROUND 1	ROUND 2	ROUND 3	ROUND 4	ROUND 5	ROUND 6
Neil Peart Drum Solo	6	13	20	36	43	58
Zuul All-Stars	4	10	20	29	39	58
Big Dicta Energy	5	12	18	28	37	55
Her?	4	14	23	28	36	55
Sad Salad	7	14	20	32	40	53
Missed Connections	9	17	23	33	39	50
One Time at Hogwarts	6	14	21	29	35	46
I Got 99 Problems	7	10	16	24	30	39
Oh? Worm?	8	15	20	26	31	38
Lambeau Legends	4	11	13	16	23	26

Missed Connections led the first half, Neil Peart Drum Solo gained momentum, and Zuul All-Stars had a surprise come-from-behind to tie for first. A very equitable result. Late-game heroics shot some teams to glory; others hoisted themselves upon their own petards.

> **FUN FACT**
>
> From William Shakespeare's *Hamlet* and meaning "foiled by one's own malicious plan," "hoist with his own petard" translates to "thrown into the air [hoist] by his own exploding bomb [petard]." Furthermore, the phrase only occurs in one of the three folios of Shakespeare's time, so scholars are divided on whether it's actually Shakespeare's words or those of a folio editor. Petards themselves were akin to a late-medieval-shaped charge—a brass or iron bell, filled with gunpowder and attached to an enemy's fortification. It's also derived from the Middle French for "to fart," so it might have been a punchline in Shakespeare's performance.

For a tiebreaker, institute *Price Is Right* rules: Closest answer without going over wins. Call up only one member from each team and ask them something like, "With Overture, Intermission, Entr'acte, and Exit Music, how long in minutes is *Gone with the Wind*?" or "How long in feet is the center span of the Golden Gate Bridge?"

Then you can award the grand prize. If they both go over, you can do it again or just award whoever is closest or flip a coin or whatever. I'm not going to be there, and it's your game anyway. You're the host. (BTW, the answers are 238 minutes and 4,200 feet, respectively.)

How to Write Each Round

When writing a Visual, Subject, or Audio round, adhere to the Rule of Eight. A team of five to six solid players should ideally get around 8 out of the 10 questions correct. One question should elicit a debate among the team. One question should have them slapping their foreheads when the answer is revealed. And one question should be a "who on Earth knows that one?" These last two questions separate the gifted from the lucky: One to two extra points per round reveal which team has put together a truly diverse group and which teams are merely trivia tourists.

Round 1: *Visual*

For the opener, I usually have up to 12 pictures printed as a handout with fill-in-the-blank lines for answers.

Rounds 2 and 5: *Subjects*

Pick subjects that will reach a different realm of expertise from those of Rounds 1 and 4. Remember that Rule of Eight.

Round 3: *Before and After*

Round 3 is always fun to write. This is your opportunity to show your cleverness and have everyone marvel at how smart you think you are. Before and After, simply put, is two questions separated by the word *and* that form one compound answer, with no partial credit allowed. Here's an example: "The president of the United States during World War I AND the singers of the 1990 hit song 'Hold On.'"

The answer, of course, is Woodrow Wilson Phillips. Woodrow Wilson was the guy in charge; Wilson Phillips sang the best song of 1990. Got it? Good.

That you can't receive any partial credit is critical to this round. It proves the mettle of each team, tests their ability to work off of one another, and ultimately rewards talent—yet still doesn't make anyone feel totally inadequate when the answers are revealed, and they find they got one half right and just missed the second half.

A couple of pointers:

- To write a Before and After round, reverse engineer it. Write the answer first, then create the question around your answer.

- Make sure your spelling is consistent. Inconsistent spellings will throw people off. "Smart Aleck" and "Alec Baldwin" don't really work together. Phonetically, yes, but not for the purposes of this game.

- Try to refrain from smashing words together. "Phuketamine" (Phuket + ketamine) is funny, but if every other answer contained separate words and this one was a portmanteau, it's unfair to most teams.

- If there's an abbreviation—like "N B C-Section"—make sure to tell everyone that there's an acronym in there so they know they're dealing with a letter or group of letters and not a full word. Be firm and clear in your explanation and don't take any guff from your contestants!

Try a couple on your own or, better yet, take a look at the hundreds of them in the rest of this book. They are fully yours to pilfer and pass off as your own.

Round 4: *Audio*

The Audio round is positioned in the middle of the night to both add variety to what otherwise is an entirely spoken evening and (hopefully) foster a dramatic change in the scores. It essentially serves as halftime. To prepare the Audio round, think of something that could tie 10 songs together.

A wide variety of music within one round (or a round specifically targeting an era or genre) allows you to either elevate teams who've tanked prior rounds or crush the dreams of the leaders. Ideally, at the end of the Audio round, an exciting lead change has occurred in which those nailing the first rounds fell to their musical inadequacies while those who felt left out found a round that really resonated and scored accordingly.

> **AUDIO ROUND IDEAS**
>
> Songs with "Blue" in the Title
> Greatest Hits of 1967
> Artist's Top-Charting Hits
> Names in the Title
> Sitcom Theme Songs
> British Bands

By awarding one point for the band or artist and one point for the song title—20 points total—you can create the opportunity for big changes in the scores. (It also helps you to avoid ties.)

Here's an example:

Audio: Drinking Songs

1. Rihanna: "Cheers (Drink to That)"
2. Beyoncé: "Drunk in Love"
3. Sublime: "40oz. to Freedom"
4. John Lee Hooker: "One Bourbon, One Scotch, One Beer"
5. LMFAO featuring Lil Jon: "Shots"
6. Hank Williams Jr. featuring Hank Williams: "There's a Tear in My Beer"

7. Jimmy Buffett: "Margaritaville"

8. Garth Brooks: "Friends in Low Places"

9. Beastie Boys: "Brass Monkey"

10. The Champs: "Tequila"

There's a lot of territory covered here: modern pop and R&B, old country, 1970s singer-songwriter, 1980s hip-hop, oldies, and a terrible, terrible song liked by the worst kind of bro. (It's the Sublime song. That's the terrible one.)

Or, try this on for size:

Audio: Greatest Hits of 2015

1. Carly Rae Jepsen: "I Really Like You"

2. Hailee Steinfeld: "Love Myself"

3. Adele: "Hello"

4. Fetty Wap: "Trap Queen"

5. Zac Brown Band: "Homegrown"

6. Demi Lovato: "Cool for the Summer"

7. Drake: "Hotline Bling"

8. Kelsea Ballerini: "Love Me Like You Mean It"

9. Wiz Khalifa: "See You Again"

10. Omi: "Cheerleader"

Would you know any of those songs? No? Good. This round wasn't meant for you. It was meant specifically to work against you and give someone else a chance to shine. Don't take it personally.

Round 6: *Random Stuff*

With varied rounds of challenging yet accessible content now finished, we come into the last round of the night, the almighty Random Stuff. That's code for "Things the Author of This Quiz Knows and Thinks

> **PRO TIP**
>
> To execute an Audio round, use Spotify or YouTube, or download your songs of choice and set them in your player, to present about 11–12 seconds of the song. That's just enough of a taste to almost get it if you don't know it immediately.

You Oughtta Know but Is Confident That You Probably Won't." In an ideal world, you'll go into the final round with your best teams clustered within only a few points of one another, maybe even with a tie for the lead. And just as each round should upset expectations and play to varied expertise, this round will do so on a question-by-question basis, culminating with the final question serving almost as a full round unto itself. Exciting!

So that's about it. A well-rounded, diverse set of questions and clues that a well-rounded, diverse group of friends could answer in a well-rounded, diverse manner.

Notes on Incentives

Not everyone is going to be good at trivia, but you want everyone to be entertained and maintain a competitive edge. Thus, offering incentives and participation awards throughout the event keeps people engaged. Choose what works for you, but here's what works for me: liquor. More specifically:

• Beginning of night: Round of shots for best team name.

• Middle of night: Round of shots for best score of the audio round.

• Consolation prize: Round of shots for the best score of the final round.

• End of night: $50 bar gift certificate for overall winner.

If you're a bar's Official Pub Trivia Host and choose to award a gift certificate, make sure that the winners cannot use it the night of the event. Get them to come back. Drive more business to the establishment. If you're a Regular Civilian and hosting for fun or a more casual event, bragging rights is still a pretty good prize!

Notes on Announcing and Enunciating

Sometimes the written question feels awkward when spoken aloud. Feel free to rearrange the clue in a way that sounds and feels more comfortable for you and your participants. Also, you likely noticed that the word *this* appears in many of my questions. That's the word you want to emphasize. (Sorry, THIS is the word you want to emphasize.) *This* serves as the indicator that the actual question follows. For instance: "Fluff fluff preamble setting the stage background info maybe a red herring THIS sci-fi sequel." That way everyone knows what the question is looking for in an answer.

For instance: "Although it finally went extinct in 1627, the wild aurochs was domesticated millennia earlier and became THIS farm animal."

One of the most annoying habits of a novice host is when announcing the answers after tabulating the score, they read the question in full and then say, "The answer to that was X." Don't do that. It's bush league. Instead, make things smoother by incorporating the answer into your re-presentation of the question. For the above question, re-present it like this: "The wild aurochs went extinct in 1627, but millennia earlier it was domesticated into today's *modern cow*."

Notes on Equipment

If you're hosting at home with friends and family, there's good news: You're done! All you basically need to do to put together a competitive quiz night is gather up some paper, write 1 through 10 on each page, and get a laptop, tablet, or smartphone to play some music for the audio round. Have fun. You can stop reading now.

If you're hosting at a bar or establishment, a couple more items are needed. I'll show how I set up and you can take it from there:

- **Mixer:** A small mixer with one to four channels should do it, so long as you have a place to plug in a microphone and an audio source for background music and audio rounds and it has an output to plug into a PA or the house speakers. Newer systems might be completely wireless, so all you'll need is a wireless mic and Bluetooth or WiFi to connect all your devices.

- **Microphone:** Although I prefer a Shure SM58, nearly any microphone will do for a PA or house system. Know what? Just get an SM58 and call it a day.

- **Music Source:** I use a laptop, but you can plug in anything that has a nice playlist of upbeat music and a place to keep a separate playlist for your audio round questions. It's important to have a music source with an easy way to change the volume because you want to lower the volume of the background music, ask the question, repeat the question, and raise the volume of the background music. This helps people talk more freely without fear of other teams overhearing and ripping off an answer.

  Bonus: When using a laptop, you can score each team on an Excel or OpenOffice worksheet. That way you can sort the score sheet by who's winning. Makes it wayyy easier to announce when you have a lot of teams, as I often do.

- **Printouts:** Create a bespoke printout, numbered 1 through 10, with the name of the bar, a logo, your social handles and hashtags, or whatever else you want. Most important, make it special, make it memorable, make it Instagram friendly, and make it your own.

Go Forth and Prosper

There you have it. You're now fully equipped to put together a pub quiz for home or business and ask some fun questions. Start getting curious, because the most random thing you encounter could later on become a really good clue to stump your friends, and maybe make you a few bucks on the side.

Above all: Have fun. Yes, that's a cliché, but this is the business of fun and entertainment. If you bring the energy, the unique content, the social media–ready branding, and a broad, inclusive attitude, you'll surely build a great product that will make your little trivia night the highlight of so many people's week. And always remember: If someone says, "These questions are too hard," challenge them to broaden their horizons. I hope this volume has done the same for you—made you think, slap your head, and say, "Why don't I know that?" Or better yet, "I have no excuse to not know that!" Now go on and get out there and blow some minds. Or at least make a couple hundred bucks.

PHOTO CREDITS

ACKNOWLEDGMENTS

I would like to acknowledge the staff and owners of the following bars and pubs, including but not limited to: Conker Hill (RIP), Van Diemen's (RIP), The Craic, The Winslow, Hibernia HK, Biddy's Pub, Woodrow's, Gaf East, and most especially, The Waylon, and above all, one bar to rule them all, Gaf West. Without the support of these establishments, I'd never have been able to excel on that game show, and without that game show, I'd never have had the opportunity to write this book. So many late nights spent, pint in hand, laptop on bar, being "that guy with his freaking laptop at the bar," writing trivia, quizzing the regulars on a round in progress, and ultimately coming back later in the week and shouting the resulting work at swelling throngs of seven or more people.

I'd also like to thank the team at *Jeopardy!* for giving me shows that luckily aligned with my interests so that I could win enough to get the mediocre notoriety necessary to publish this humble tome.

Finally, I couldn't finish this without the support of Maria, Mochi, and Miso. Some of them weren't here when I started this, but they damn well helped me finish it.

Oh. And I guess I should thank my parents, Rick and Peggy. They've always been there for me, not harassing me about grades or jobs or success or failure or pretty much anything. Just whether or not I am happy. That's some good parenting there, Richard and Margaret. Also, I have two brothers. Brendan and Cade contributed nothing at all to this book.

ABOUT THE AUTHOR

Austin Rogers is a 12-time *Jeopardy!* champion, pub quiz host, corporate trivia shill, failed singer-songwriter, terrible stand-up comedian, and Twitter antagonist. He currently resides in New York City's El Barrio and has a bicycle named Treaddie Mercury. You can visit Austin most weekends at Gaf West at 401 West 48th Street just off of 9th Avenue wherein he will take a selfie with you and then charge you for your beverages.